LISTENING *to the* LAW

LISTENING *to the* LAW

Reflections on the Court and Constitution

AMY CONEY BARRETT

SENTINEL

SENTINEL
An imprint of Penguin Random House LLC
1745 Broadway, New York, NY 10019
penguinrandomhouse.com

Photos, unless otherwise credited, are from the collection of the author.

BOOK DESIGN BY TANYA MAIBORODA

LIBRARY OF CONGRESS CATALOGING-IN-PUBLICATION DATA
Names: Barrett, Amy Coney, 1972– author
Title: Listening to the law : reflections on the court and constitution / Amy Coney Barrett.
Description: New York : Sentinel, 2025. | Includes bibliographical references and index.
Identifiers: LCCN 2025019413 (print) | LCCN 2025019414 (ebook) |
ISBN 9780593421864 hardcover | ISBN 9780593421871 ebook
Subjects: LCSH: Barrett, Amy Coney, 1972—Biography |
Women judges—United States—Biography | United States. Supreme Court—Officials and employees—Biography | United States. Supreme Court—Decision making |
Judicial process—United States | Constitutional law—United States
Classification: LCC KF8745.B39 A3 2025 (print) | LCC KF8745.B39 (ebook) |
DDC 347.73/2634 [B]—dc23/eng/20250421
LC record available at https://lccn.loc.gov/2025019413
LC ebook record available at https://lccn.loc.gov/2025019414

Printed in the United States of America
1st Printing

The authorized representative in the EU for product safety and compliance is Penguin Random House Ireland, Morrison Chambers, 32 Nassau Street, Dublin D02 YH68, Ireland, https://eu-contact.penguin.ie.

To Jesse

Contents

PART TWO
The Constitution and the American Experience

PART THREE
Thinking About the Law

AUTHOR'S NOTE

FOR THE sake of their privacy, I don't use the names of my family members in the stories I tell. The exception is Jesse, my husband, who (thankfully) can't escape being attached to me.

Because the Court's deliberative process is confidential, I don't reveal internal conversations with other justices.

I describe cases in this book, but—unless I publicly dissented or the case has been overruled—I don't express a view about their soundness. Nor, of course, do I discuss political disputes or say how I might decide issues that haven't come before me. The rules of ethics generally prohibit judges from offering opinions outside the judicial process.

Finally, while I have produced much academic writing over the course of my career, this book does not fall in that category. I am writing in the first person, describing my own approach to the law at an accessible level. While I alert you to some of the competing arguments, I don't get into the weeds of scholarly debates. If you're interested in going deeper, however, I hope this will book will inspire you to learn more.

INTRODUCTION

Since I joined the Court, it has become clear to me that many Americans are eager to know more about what a justice does and how the Court works. I receive a steady stream of questions from a wide range of people—lawyers and nonlawyers, children and adults, even visitors from foreign countries. Some questions are personal: What was the confirmation process like? How have you adjusted to the Court? What is your job like for your family? (I have also received charming letters from young children asking things like what is my favorite color and do I like my new job—answers are probably blue and mostly yes.) Others relate to the more personal side of work: What was it like to clerk for Justice Scalia? Do the justices get along? What does your normal day look like? And still others are specifically about my work at the Court: How does the Court get its cases? How does it decide them? How do you approach the job?

With questions like these in mind, I set out to write a book about the Court, seen through the lens of my own experience. But as I began writing, I realized that I wanted to broaden the frame. Because the Court is steeped in tradition, its story can't be isolated to the present moment. Almost everything that justices do today—from how we decide cases to where we meet for lunch—builds on what justices have done in the past. Nor can the Court's story be separated from the Constitution, which is both its birth certificate and life's work. The Constitution creates the Court, names it, and defines the scope of its power; resolving constitutional disputes has been the Court's critical role for more than two centuries. So in the end, I chose to weave together three themes: the work of the Court and its justices, the Constitution and its impact, and my own approach to judging. Along the way, I'll introduce you to some of the people, past and present, who have shaped what I do. If I leave you with a better understanding of the Court's role, how the Constitution shapes American life, and how I think about my job, I will have achieved my goal.

While my adult jobs—practicing lawyer, law professor, and judge—have all involved the law, this book reflects my firm belief that law is not reserved for those with legal training. I'm lucky to have a multitude of friends and family who are not lawyers, some of whom read draft chapters to let me know when my descriptions got too technical. With the benefit of their help, I hope that I've made this book accessible to anyone interested in the Court, lawyers and nonlawyers alike. The business of the Court affects every American, and the Constitution belongs to all of us. Though the Court occupies a central place in American government, it is still a somewhat opaque institution. The process of judging, which happens behind closed doors, can seem like a mystery. It shouldn't.

To give you a sense of what lies ahead, this is how I've organized the book. After sharing about my own life in the law, I proceed in three parts:

Part 1, "The Court and Its Work," relates how I think about my job, how I go about deciding cases, and how the Supreme Court fits into the bigger picture of our government.

Part 2, "The Constitution and the American Experience," turns to our founding document. Knowing what the Constitution says is essential to understanding what the Court does. At the same time, the Constitution is more than words on a page—it came to life at a particular historical moment and has been shaped by many Americans in the years since. This part grounds the Constitution's story in the experience of its flesh-and-blood creators and explains how it enables Americans to live together today.

Part 3, "Thinking About the Law," describes my approach to interpreting the law. The Constitution is more than two centuries old, and federal statutes are often long and complex. On top of that, the Court must apply these laws to situations that would surprise their drafters. Handling these problems in a manner that is both consistent and faithful to the law requires a plan. I tell you about mine.

Listening
to the
Law

Chapter 1

MY LIFE IN THE LAW

My great-grandmother's house.

ON MY desk at home, I keep a picture of my great-grandmother's small house. I didn't know my great-grandmother; she died five years before I was born. Nor did I ever visit the house while family lived in it. I saw it for the first time almost ten years ago, when my siblings and I rented a party bus to take my parents on a "This Is Your Life" tour of New Orleans for my father's seventieth birthday. As lifelong New Orleanians, my parents have a long list of places with special memories, including this house on Green Street, where my mother spent many Sunday afternoons. On a lark, we knocked on the door to see if the owners would let us peek inside. They did.

The thing that struck me most was its size: tiny. The house was a single-story with a small living room, compact kitchen, and three bedrooms. The space seemed suitable for a small family. My great-grandmother, however, was a widow with thirteen children. (In a moment that must have been heart-wrenching, she discovered her pregnancy with the thirteenth after her husband's funeral.) She purchased the house with the proceeds of her husband's life insurance policy, knowing that no one would rent to a woman living alone with such a large family. The children didn't all move in with her: one had tragically died, and the oldest few were living independently. Still, the house was bursting at the seams. While I was surveying the tight space, my mother told me that my great-grandmother had also taken in three relatives who needed lodging. It was the Great Depression, so everyone was struggling. And as if she didn't have enough mouths to feed, she welcomed the many homeless men traveling through the neighborhood with food on the back porch. (She allowed them to sleep under her raised house until one fell asleep with a cigarette in his mouth and started a fire. After that, it was dinner only.) Little wonder that my great-grandmother has legendary status in our family.

Though my great-grandmother's generosity is inspiring, it's not why I keep the picture. Standing inside her small house, I couldn't believe how much she had fit into her life. At the time we made this visit, I was feeling more than a little sorry for myself. My husband, Jesse, and I were balancing two careers (I as a law professor, he as a federal prosecutor) and seven young children. On the one hand, we had every reason to be happy—we loved each other, our children, and (most of the time) our jobs. On the other hand, life had also thrown us some curveballs—like our youngest son's diagnosis of Down syndrome, which added new medical appointments and educational challenges to our already full schedule. I was feeling overwhelmed and wondering whether we could pull it all off. This window into my great-grandmother's life strengthened my resolve. Somehow, she always managed to find the resources, space, and time. With much less than I have, she took on much more. Looking at the photo reminds me of a woman who stretched herself beyond all reasonable capacity. I'm not sure that I'll be able to manage my life with the same grace that she had. But she motivates me to keep trying.

I DIDN'T GROW up wanting to be a lawyer. Since I loved to read, I dreamed mostly about being an author or an English teacher. That was true through college, where I majored in English and spent most of my time reading literature and writing essays about it. Inspired by my college mentors, I considered pursuing a PhD in English, followed by a career as an English professor. But when it came time to apply, I hesitated. I loved literature but felt pulled by law. It too relied on words, but to a very different end. Law governs the relationship of the government to its citizens and its citizens to one another. It matters in everything from the sale of property to a criminal trial to the structure of government. No matter the context, law has real-world consequences. I wanted to know how it worked and to help people navigate it. (I also thought it might be easier to get a job as a lawyer than as an English professor.) In 1994, I walked into my first class at Notre Dame Law School.

I loved studying the law. Granted, reading cases was not as captivating as reading Shakespeare—but they held my attention all the same. I liked pulling out their logic to see whether it held up. Both in and out of class, I enjoyed debating issues like how the Constitution should be interpreted and whether it was just. And though I had the same nerves as every other first-year law student staring down final exams, I did well, which increased my confidence. While home on a holiday break, I ran into a high school teacher who asked how law school was going; I recall gushing that I had found the perfect fit. Saying it out loud drove home how true it was. From the first day of class, I never doubted my choice to become a lawyer.

I was unsure what kind of law I wanted to practice, but I knew where I wanted to do it: New Orleans, where I grew up and where my tight-knit extended family still lived. I thought I'd start at a law firm and perhaps shift later to teaching or public interest work. I was not, however, focused single-mindedly on my career—I wanted the path I chose to be compatible with raising the children I hoped to have. I loved growing up in a large family and wanted to have one myself. When I considered my future, I thought mostly about how to pull off being a working mother with a full house. Becoming a judge was not my ambition.

I left Notre Dame in May 1997 with a diploma and friendships I still treasure. And taking what I saw as a detour on my way to New Orleans, I headed to Washington to spend two years as a law clerk, a job that functions as a highly prized apprenticeship for a recent law school graduate. (I'll tell you more about the work of law clerks later in the book.) I worked first for Judge Laurence H. Silberman on the United States Court of Appeals for the District of Columbia Circuit and then for Justice Antonin Scalia on the Supreme Court of the United States. Both clerkships influenced me greatly—in fact, they changed the course of my career.

I had never met anyone like Judge Silberman. In addition to stints in private practice, he had served as the ambassador to Yugoslavia, deputy attorney general, solicitor of labor, and undersecretary of labor. His interests were as varied as his experience. We clerks (there were three of us) had to be ready to field questions not only on our cases, but also on foreign affairs, domestic politics, twentieth-century world history, and even his hobby of boating. We went to lunch several times a week, often at the Department of Labor cafeteria (which the judge loved for nostalgia's sake), where he regaled us with stories about his service in the Nixon and Ford administrations and his years at Dartmouth and Harvard.

Time with the judge was good for me in many ways, but particularly because it pried me out of my office. Since I can remember, I have had a somewhat obsessive focus on efficiency, devoting every minute to reducing my to-do list. (That has not escaped the notice of my friends: I am often teased for my fast walk, which minimizes time spent in transit.) I dislike yielding time to lunch, and left to my own devices that year, I would have stayed buried all day in briefs, books, and draft opinions. Judge Silberman would have none of it. He carried more than triple my workload at the court and performed it with ease, whether peppering advocates with questions at oral argument, spinning the straw of our draft opinions into gold, or scrapping our drafts entirely to write his own. Still, he made time for relationships. I remember much more about our lunches than the cases I worked on that year, and I emerged from my clerkship with a lifelong mentor. His example has affected the way I conduct my professional life—he taught me that relationships are part of work, not a distraction from it.

The following year, I got to see Justice Scalia's approach in action when I served as his law clerk, a job that entailed helping him to prepare for oral arguments, researching legal issues, and preparing draft opinions. Because Justice Scalia didn't need much assistance in any of these tasks, the clerks were only marginally useful to him—but our time with him was invaluable to us.

We clerks had the opportunity to see the private side of a public figure. By the time I began working for him in 1998, Justice Scalia was a well-established intellectual force both on and off the Court. His opinions made it into law school textbooks because they were not only incisive, but witty too, and his public speeches drew large crowds of lawyers and nonlawyers alike. To say that I was intimidated when I interviewed for the job is a massive understatement. (Truth be told, I never got over that intimidation during all the years I knew him—he was just that smart and self-possessed.)

It was a different story with the justice in private. We heard him belt opera tunes from his office (he had an excellent voice), joined him at his favorite Italian dive for anchovy pizza (he made us all try it at least once), and were entertained by stories from his hunting trips (his favorite pastime). We once got our hands on a picture of him dressed in camouflage, proudly holding a wild turkey, and had a computer mousepad made with it. We snuck it onto his desk, slightly concerned that we had overstepped, but when he found it a few hours later, we could hear his laughter down the hall. Justice Scalia mixed intensity with humor and a fiery personality with kindness. And while he was serious about his work, it never displaced his more fundamental commitments to his family and faith.

With Justice Scalia as a law clerk. (Photo by Franz Jantzen, Collection of the Supreme Court of the United States.)

I once attended an event related to the release of one of his books, and he spoke to the crowd with his characteristic vigor and humor. When I talked to him privately afterward, however, his demeanor was entirely different. He was somber, his voice marked by grief. Confiding that his son-in-law had just died, he asked me to pray for his newly widowed daughter and her children. I assured him of my prayers and walked away with renewed admiration for the fully human person who was Antonin Scalia. He was so much more than a boisterous, brilliant public figure. Throughout my career, both his personal and professional life have inspired me.

When my clerkship ended, I spent a few years practicing law in Washington, D.C. I married Jesse Barrett, a fellow Notre Dame graduate, in 1999. We seriously considered moving to New Orleans—I'm not sure that I've ever fully shaken the desire to live in my hometown. Instead, we returned to our alma mater, in South Bend, Indiana. I served on the faculty for fifteen years, Jesse practiced law, and we had the big family that we both wanted.

Jesse and me at his graduation from Notre Dame Law School.

Jesse and I have seven children, which required us then, and requires us now, to strive for efficiency (think fast walking) and balance. To make our family of nine work, we integrated our personal life and our work life. We lived close to campus, and our children loved to visit me at my office. I kept a basket of toys for them there, and they were very comfortable roaming the halls of the law school, where the annual Halloween trick-or-treating was one of their favorite events. (In all seriousness, giving up that event was one of their biggest complaints about moving.) I frequently visited their classrooms for parties and Christmas pageants, and they occasionally visited mine for less engaging attractions like lectures in constitutional law. I wrote law review articles at home, and they used the backs of my printouts as scratch paper for drawing. Law students came to our house for dinner, and my children came for lunch at the law school café.

Meanwhile, our children also had a window into Jesse's work. When he was a federal prosecutor, they attended some of his trials, and they peppered him with questions about his cases at the dinner table. (His criminal prosecutions were much more interesting to them than the substance of my law school lectures.) Our younger children went through a phase of writing out pretend "indictments" of one another, charging imaginary crimes or violations of our family rules. I have saved some of those for the family scrapbooks. When Jesse left the government for private practice, they missed the excitement of criminal law. On the upside, they fought for the chance to spend days off from school at his new office, which—unlike mine—had a kitchen stocked with snacks and soda.

In other words, daily life was not divided into "law" and "parenting." It was all happening at once—which was healthy, because it kept law in perspective for me. Law is but one piece of what it takes to make a healthy society, and it (like everything else in life) exists in the midst of relationships.

Our life was good, but like anyone's, it was not perfect. Children had personal struggles and hard diagnoses; there were challenging pregnancies and adoption adjustments; and friends and relatives struggled with illness. Like everyone, we hit rough patches at work. Overall, though, we considered ourselves fortunate and never imagined that the pattern of our life would change.

But in 2017, things took a turn that I had not anticipated: I became a federal judge. The opportunity was unexpected but appealing. I was drawn to the idea of public service and having a more direct influence on the law; Jesse was completely supportive. President Donald J. Trump nominated me and the Senate confirmed me to a seat on the United States Court of Appeals for the Seventh Circuit, which is based in Chicago and hears cases from Illinois,

Indiana, and Wisconsin. I substituted tenure at a university for a lifetime appointment on the bench—both secure jobs—and thought this transition from teaching cases to deciding them would be my last career change.

The new job required adjustments to our schedule, but not a move. I drove to nearby Chicago to hear arguments, but my primary chambers were in South Bend, just a few minutes from our home. Like my campus office, my chambers became a popular destination for the kids. My offices happened to have an attached courtroom—not a typical feature in the chambers of an appellate judge. The younger children conducted pretend trials from the bench and played with the foosball table that I put in the courtroom for my clerks. The older girls, in high school by then, brought their mock trial teams to the courtroom, which was a good place for me to be a guest coach offering a crash course on the rules of evidence. Life continued to hum along.

Judge Silberman administering the oath at my Seventh Circuit investiture ceremony. (© 2018 Julian Velasco.)

I really loved my job on the Seventh Circuit and settled into the rhythm of hearing arguments and writing opinions. But after a few years, life took another turn: the White House counsel, who runs the judicial selection process for the president, invited me on behalf of President Trump to interview for a seat on the United States Supreme Court. Though I was deeply honored, I thought hard about whether to go forward. I knew that if I was chosen, both the confirmation process and the work of serving on the Court would require sacrifices, particularly from my family. Unlike my job on the Seventh Circuit, this one would require a move to Washington, D.C. We had a good life, wonderful friends, and close family in South Bend. We were attached to our old Prairie-style home, which was a short walk to campus for tailgates during football season—a fall family highlight. The move would mean changes for Jesse's career and new schools for the children. We knew that public criticism was sure to come. And if I was nominated and confirmed, there would be a long-term loss of privacy for all of us. Public service was appealing, but the changes to our personal life were not.

In fact, I felt a pit in my stomach when I considered what might lie ahead. I had been considered for a seat on the Court two years earlier, when Justice Anthony Kennedy retired. Being a finalist had thrust me into the spotlight, which (to put it mildly) was not enjoyable. There had been an avalanche of news stories and social media posts—true and untrue, kind and cruel. It was difficult to have my life so publicly picked apart. There had also been a loss of physical privacy. Multiple camera crews parked outside our house and followed me by car when I pulled out of the driveway. I had one experience, funny only in retrospect, of realizing that I had been followed to church on a Sunday morning. I spent the whole Mass, not in prayer, but plotting an escape—a plan that culminated in my sneaking out a side door, scaling a fence in high heels, and—to the surprise of the associate pastor sitting on the rectory porch—dropping into the priests' vegetable garden. (He was a happy co-conspirator; he took my keys and retrieved my car from the parking lot, allowing me to avoid the cameras

The Barrett family outside our South Bend home just before we moved to Washington. (Photo by Anastassia Tess Cassady.)

after all.) The scrutiny had affected my family too—given the number of strangers who had started walking past and driving by our house, Jesse and I were reluctant to let our kids play in the yard. It was not an experience I was eager to repeat.

Jesse and I had a very brief time to make one of the biggest decisions in our marriage. His position was full support on one condition: if we did it, we had to "burn the boats." The phrase comes from a military strategy used by Alexander the Great, who, after landing on the shores of enemy territory, ordered his men to burn the ships they had come in. With the option of exit gone, there was no choice but to forge ahead, no matter the challenge. Likewise for us. There would be difficulties in store, some we could anticipate and others we couldn't. Jesse wisely thought that it would be unsustainable to face the difficulties—whether in the confirmation process or beyond—if we gave ourselves the option to look back, wishing that we could unwind what we had done. There would be no second-guessing and no turning back to our comfortable life in South Bend.

So despite what might seem like a self-evident decision from the outside, saying yes to the interview, and then to the nomination, was not an easy call. I had just watched Brett Kavanaugh, whom I knew and respected, undergo a brutal confirmation process, and I was afraid of what I might face. I was reluctant to give up the good life we had for one that might prove to be less happy. Yet it seemed cowardly to bow out because we didn't want to make the sacrifice. As I later told the Senate Judiciary Committee, I believe deeply in the rule of law and the Supreme Court's role in preserving it; I also think that Americans of all backgrounds deserve an independent Supreme Court that interprets our Constitution and laws as they are written.[1] It seemed strange to hold those views and be unwilling to serve, given that any nominee would face the same hardships. I accepted the interview and flew to Washington, D.C., to meet with President Trump. He announced my nomination on September 26, 2020, and the Senate confirmed me a month later. I have served as an associate justice since.

Life continues in some ways as it did before, with a mix of kids and cases. My alarm goes off at five in the morning, and I (usually) get up right afterward. Our kids get up at six thirty during the school year, so I start early if I want to accomplish anything on my own to-do list. We have one college graduate and two children in college, but the younger four are still at home—and once they're up, I switch gears to making sure they have lunches, homework, sports equipment, and a handle on the after-school schedule. The older three in the group are mostly self-sufficient and are out the door quickly. Our youngest, who has Down syndrome, is a different story. His school day starts later, so he joins the kitchen chaos after it is well underway. When his siblings leave, he has a window of time as an only child. He and I get ready together; I pack my briefcase while he packs his backpack. All the while, music plays at his request. Thanks to his playlist, I later walk the halls of the Court with his top tunes on repeat in

President Donald J. Trump announces Judge Amy Coney Barrett as his nominee for Associate Justice of the Supreme Court of the United States in the Rose Garden of the White House on Saturday, September 26, 2020. She was joined by her husband, Jesse Barrett, and their children. (Official White House Photo by Shealah Craighead.)

my head—an eclectic mix ranging from the soundtrack of Disney's *Encanto* to "Cha Cha Slide."

Normally, our morning routine runs smoothly because Jesse and I run it together. Stakes are higher now, though, given my job. One tense morning sticks out. Jesse was out of town for a weekend with one of our daughters on a college visit in October 2021 and his Sunday return flight was canceled. For the very first time, he missed trick-or-treating with the kids, which was disappointing. The consequences for Monday morning, however, were downright stressful. The Court was hearing argument in a high-profile case, and our youngest child had a school holiday. Jesse had planned to be home with him, so I was now left without coverage. Had I still been a law professor, I could have rescheduled class; had I still been on the Seventh Circuit, I could have arranged to participate remotely. But remote participation is rare at the Supreme Court, and the press usually asks for an explanation when it happens—which they were sure to do here given the profile of the case. I didn't think that my childcare emergency needed to be national news and was desperate to find backup. Fortunately, I worked something out at the last minute, got to the Court on time, and Jesse made it home later that day.

All to say that, like most parents, I sometimes feel like I've done a day's worth of work before I get my children, much less myself, out the door. That was also true for me as a law professor and as a court of appeals judge. The difference now is that my two worlds—home and work—stand in greater contrast.

In some respects, my job is the same as it was on the court of appeals: I read briefs, consider the arguments, and offer my best judgment about what the law requires. But in other respects, the job is very different. The Supreme Court's decisions affect the whole country rather than a portion of the Midwest. Because some of our cases involve issues about which people care passionately, the Court receives intense scrutiny, which presents its own challenges. And because the position requires the capacity to ignore public opinion, including harsh criticism, I've had to acquire a thick skin.

I would be lying if I said that the last several years have been easy. The confirmation process was hard, and it has been difficult to have practically every aspect of my life be made public. Now that I'm on the Court, I've had to adjust to being a public figure, accompanied even to the grocery store by a security detail. I am happiest with old friends who knew me before I became "Justice Barrett," and I am wistful when we're back in South Bend. More than once, I've had to remind myself that we burned the boats.

My family has also had to adjust. Jesse could not pursue various career opportunities due to potential conflicts with my job. One of our sons learned to drive, with me in the passenger seat, while a security vehicle followed him. (I actually had to tell him, "No, you can't try to outrun the security detail.") And for better or worse, each child has notoriety as my son or daughter. (Though sometimes they manage to fly below the radar: one daughter sheepishly confessed that when a coworker ranted about "that Amy Coney Barrett woman," she didn't tell him that I was her mother. I assured her that she had done the right thing.) There were also protests outside our home after the *Dobbs* case, which overruled *Roe v. Wade*'s holding that the Constitution protects a right to an abortion. People often ask whether the protests were hard for our children. They were certainly unnerving at first, and I continue to feel terrible about the disruption they caused our neighbors. But our children quickly got used to protests (words I never thought I'd say), and it proved to be an occasion for valuable family conversations.

President Donald J. Trump and Jesse Barrett look on as Supreme Court Associate Justice Clarence Thomas swears in Judge Amy Coney Barrett as Supreme Court Associate Justice Monday, October 26, 2020, on the South Lawn of the White House. (Official White House Photo by Andrea Hanks.)

Though there have been challenges, none of us has regrets—we're happily and firmly rooted in our new life. That goes for me too, and not just because Jesse and I resolved not to look back. I have been given the opportunity to serve the institution that has been charged with guarding the rule of law since it opened for business in 1790. As modern-day Americans, we might take the rule of law for granted, since it is the only reality we have ever known. But it isn't a given. It's a gift that each generation of Americans inherits to protect, and I am honored to play a small part in that process.

Part One

The Court and Its Work

Chapter 2

THE COMMISSION AND THE OATH

ALTHOUGH I became an associate justice in October 2020, COVID delayed my formal investiture ceremony for almost a year. At this event, held in the courtroom, a representative of the executive branch delivers the commission—which is the document formally appointing the justice. The brief, scripted ceremony is steeped in tradition. The new justice sits in front of the bench in a chair once used by Chief Justice John Marshall, who was appointed by President John Adams; the other justices are in their usual seats behind the bench.

It is difficult to describe what I felt in that moment. During my first term, I had listened to cases remotely, in the isolation of my office. I hadn't worn a robe all year, much less joined my colleagues on the bench. Now, in the grandeur of the courtroom, my connection to the other justices was palpable. Looking up at my colleagues, I was acutely aware that I don't work alone, but shoulder to shoulder with eight other people. And sitting in that centuries-old chair, I viscerally felt that while the Court's work was new to me, I was picking up where others have left off. Names of prior justices raced through my mind, some from the nineteenth century, like Joseph Story and John Marshall Harlan, and others from the twentieth century, like Sandra Day O'Connor, the first woman on the Court, and Antonin Scalia, my own mentor. Humbling company, to say the least. Yet it was moving to know that whatever my own contributions to the Court may be, my commission and commitment are the same as those of every other justice, past and present.

With family and friends watching, the clerk of court read from the commission, which—underscoring the Court's continuity—uses language dating to the very first chief justice, John Jay:

> Know Ye; That reposing special trust and confidence in the Wisdom, Uprightness, and Learning of Amy Coney Barrett of Indiana, I have nominated and, by and with the advice and consent of the Senate, do appoint her Associate Justice of the Supreme Court of the United States and do authorize and empower her to execute and fulfill the duties of that Office according to the Constitution and Laws of the said United States and to Have and to Hold the said Office, with all the powers, privileges, and emoluments to the same of right appertaining unto her, the said Amy Coney Barrett, during her good behavior.

President Joe Biden's deputy attorney general then delivered the commission signed by President Trump—because of the delay occasioned by the pandemic, the administration had changed between the time of confirmation and investiture. This disconnect, while atypical, nicely demonstrates the judicial branch's independence from the political ebb and flow of the White House. Once a judge is on the bench, she is a United States judge, not a Democrat or Republican official beholden to a particular administration or party.

Chief Justice John Roberts, Jr., who heads both the Supreme Court and the judicial branch, administered the oath. (Because I had been sworn in the prior year, I was renewing the vow rather than making it for the first time.) While raising my right hand, I pressed my left hand on the Bible that I've used since the second grade and swore that "I will administer justice without respect to persons, and do equal right to the poor and to

Standing at the top of the Court's steps with Chief Justice Roberts after my investiture ceremony. (Photo by Franz Jantzen, Collection of the Supreme Court of the United States.)

the rich, and that I will faithfully and impartially discharge and perform all the duties incumbent upon me as Associate Justice of the Supreme Court of the United States."[1]

That's it: the commission and the oath. Every justice takes the bench in exactly the same way, with neither toasts and speeches, nor pomp and circumstance. The austerity of the ceremony distills the job to its essence. The Court is a historic institution in which each justice temporarily occupies a seat. And as if to drive that home, my job has a number: I'm the 103rd associate justice, standing in a line that stretches into the past and will continue into the future. In this role, I have been appointed to fulfill certain duties, and I have sworn to perform them faithfully and impartially. I am constantly aware of this responsibility—though in explaining it to others, I've realized that its scope isn't necessarily intuitive.

A FEW MONTHS before my investiture, I spent an afternoon with a favorite aunt. We're close, despite fundamentally different opinions on a variety of topics. (In fact, she'll openly say that while she loves me, she would have preferred my seat to be filled by the nominee of a Democratic president.) My aunt isn't a lawyer, but she began following the Supreme Court after I joined it. Sitting on her living room couch, she expressed disappointment that opinions (including mine) were often driven by what she called "legalities." "Amy, I thought the Court was supposed to be about doing justice," she lamented.

I get where she was coming from. "Doing justice" doesn't call to mind a judge parsing statutory language; it sounds more like King Solomon, who famously mediated the dispute between two women claiming the same baby. In a brilliant (if high risk) strategy, Solomon proposed to divide the baby in half, betting that the true mother would relinquish the child rather than see him die.[2] Fortunately, Solomon was right. And because he achieved the just result, the Old Testament memorializes this story to illustrate Solomon's wisdom. In fact, Solomon is also honored on a frieze in the courtroom of the Supreme Court, where he appears as one of the "great lawgivers of history."

It's notable to me that Solomon's wisdom came from within. He didn't resolve the case by turning to sources like laws passed by a legislature or precedents set by other judges. Nor was there any limit to the kind of solution he could impose—after all, his proposed remedy was to literally split the baby. Solomon's authority was bounded by nothing more than his own judgment. But that wasn't cause for concern, because the man and wise rule were one and the same.

If you'd asked me before law school, I may well have identified Solomon as the ideal judge. And in a certain respect, he is—it's appealing to entrust a dispute to someone who resolves it with reference solely to principles of justice. Solomon, however, stands out for a reason: his wisdom was flawless. Those who framed and ratified the Constitution didn't expect the same to be true of federal judges. Here's what James Madison had to say:

> If men were angels, no government would be necessary. If angels were to govern men, neither external nor internal controls on government would be necessary. In framing a government which is to be administered by men over men, the great difficulty lies in this: you must first enable the government to control the governed; and in the next place oblige it to control itself.[3]

My family will quickly assure you that federal judges are not angels. By constitutional design, we don't function like Solomon or some of his companions on the courtroom frieze—a group that includes Hammurabi, Moses, Confucius, and King Louis IX. For each of these men, doing justice was a matter of innate wisdom or divine inspiration. The law and the lawgiver were intertwined.

It doesn't work that way in our democratic republic. As Thomas Paine put it, "[I]n America *the law is king*."[4] We judges don't dispense justice solely as we see it; instead, we're constrained by law adopted through the democratic process. We exercise authority that the people have given us and resolve disputes according to the ground rules that the people have prescribed. It's a unique role created and defined by the Constitution.

The nomination and confirmation of federal judges, including Supreme Court justices, should be seen through this lens. If a judge functions like Solomon, everything turns on the set of beliefs that she brings to the bench. Does she believe that the death penalty is unjust? That abortion is immoral? That affirmative action is a social good? If a judge resolves disputes according to her own sense of right and wrong, then those choosing the judge better be sure that they like her beliefs.

But in our system, a judge must abide by the rules set by the American people, both in the Constitution and legislation. Thus, the most important question for a nominee is whether she will honor her commitment to do so. Though the confirmation process sometimes suggests otherwise, it shouldn't matter what the nominee thinks about the death penalty, abortion, affirmative action, or any other politically charged topic. What matters is whether she will respect the people's resolution of such issues.

Frankly, that takes self-discipline. A judge may be rightfully outraged by the crimes committed by a violent defendant. But the Constitution entitles a defendant to certain procedural protections, and if the defendant didn't receive them, the judge is obligated to rule in his favor—even if she thinks the result unjust to the victims. Or a judge may be passionately opposed to capital punishment. But many states, as well as the federal government, still authorize the death penalty. If a defendant's challenge to his death sentence lacks legal merit, the judge must set her personal beliefs aside and allow the execution to go forward.

The judicial oath demands no less. The Constitution requires that all federal and state officials, including judges, "be bound by Oath or Affirmation, to support this Constitution."[5] To enforce this requirement, Congress mandates that all federal officials swear to "bear true faith and allegiance" to the Constitution and to "well and faithfully discharge the duties of the office."[6] Federal judges take an additional oath, swearing to "administer justice without respect to persons" and to "faithfully and impartially discharge" their duties under the Constitution.[7] Each of these oaths is a promise to leave personal preferences and biases at the courthouse door. The guiding principle in every case is what the law requires, not what aligns with the judge's own concept of justice.

The robing of a new judge, which is part of the investiture ceremony in many courts, is a poignant symbol of this commitment to the rule of law. During my Seventh Circuit investiture, I sat in the courtroom, wearing a navy dress, while my new colleagues sat on the bench behind me, wearing black robes. At the end of the ceremony, my parents clothed me in the black robe that was their gift to me that day, signaling the transition to my new role. In preparing for that moment, I discovered that the tradition of federal judges wearing black robes was begun by Chief Justice John Marshall in the early years of the republic. Before Marshall, justices wore colorful robes: some mimicked the scarlet and ermine robes worn by British judges; others wore the academic gowns of the universities at which they had been educated. But on the day that he took the oath as chief justice, Marshall did something different: he wore a simple black robe. His biographer Jean Edward Smith says that Marshall chose it to symbolize the humility that he thought should characterize the judicial role.[8] The other justices soon followed suit,

My parents robing me at my Seventh Circuit investiture ceremony. (© 2018 Julian Velasco.)

as have all federal judges in the centuries since. We do it not because of any rule, but because of the long-standing tradition that each judge honors.

I like thinking of the black robe as a symbol of humility. But the choice of all federal judges to wear it has transformed the black robe into something more: our identical, nondescript robes underscore that we speak for the rule of law, which is impersonal, rather than the will of the individual. This isn't to say that interpreting the law is a mechanical exercise or that judges agree in every case. Yet if we do our job well, our differences stem from good-faith disagreements about what the law requires rather than a clash of individual policy preferences.

It is fitting, then, for a federal judge to begin an investiture ceremony in distinct dress but to end it in a robe that represents a common commitment to the laws of the United States. Every federal judge is unique, coming to the job with her own character, experiences, and beliefs. Like Americans more generally, judges hold diverse views about the values by which a just society should live. Yet under the Constitution, the choice between these competing views is made by citizens in the democratic process, not by judges settling disputes. On the bench, we must suppress our individual beliefs in deference to those that have prevailed in the enacted law. Our job is to protect the choices that citizens have made, even when we disagree with them.

Such disagreement is inevitable, because no honest judge can escape the collision between her beliefs and the enacted law. Most of the time, judges wrestle with the difficulty in private, but sometimes, they give us a glimpse of it. Justice Scalia and Justice Anthony Kennedy were both open about their internal conflict in *Texas v. Johnson*, a case in which they joined the majority of the Supreme Court to hold that the Free Speech Clause of the First Amendment protected Gregory Lee Johnson's right to protest by burning the American flag.[9] As patriots, Scalia and Kennedy were deeply offended by flag desecration. Scalia later told a law school audience, "I hate the result [in *Texas v. Johnson*]," and "I would send that guy to jail so fast if I were king."[10] Justice Kennedy wrote a concurrence in the case describing the dilemma:

> The hard fact is that sometimes we must make decisions we do not like. We make them because they are right, right in the sense that the law and the Constitution, as we see them, compel the result. . . .
>
> I do not believe the Constitution gives us the right to rule as the dissenting Members of the Court urge, however painful this judgment is to announce.[11]

Justice Sonia Sotomayor expressed a similar sentiment in *Terry v. United States*, which was decided a few months after I joined the Court.[12] In 2010, Congress passed a statute shortening the sentences imposed on crack offenders (who are predominately black) to bring them in line with those imposed on cocaine offenders (who are predominately white). Tarahrick Terry, who had been convicted of a crack offense two years earlier, sought the benefit of that law. The Court unanimously held that Terry was not entitled to resentencing, because while Congress had made the change retroactive for some crack offenses, it had not done so for Terry's offense.[13] Writing separately, Justice Sotomayor emphasized the unfairness of denying Terry an opportunity to seek a sentence consistent with Congress's recognition that the prior law was unduly severe. But correcting that injustice, she explained, was a job assigned to the political branches.[14]

For me, death penalty cases drive home the collision between the law and my personal beliefs. Long before I was a judge—before I was even a member of the bar—I co-authored an academic article expressing a moral objection to capital punishment.[15] Because prisoners sentenced to death almost always challenge their sentences on appeal, the tension between my beliefs and the law is not one that I could avoid as a young law clerk, much less now as a judge. Soon after my appointment, the Court considered a death sentence imposed on Dzhokhar Tsarnaev, one of the Boston

Marathon bombers. The court of appeals had vacated Tsarnaev's sentence, and the United States argued that it had done so in error. I thought that the United States was right, and I joined the Court's holding that Tsarnaev's death sentence was valid.[16]

That was not the only course open to me. Given my view of capital punishment, I could have looked for ways to slant the law in favor of defendants facing the death penalty. There were, after all, plausible arguments going Tsarnaev's way—the court of appeals agreed with him, as did three of my colleagues in dissent. Had I voted in favor of Tsarnaev, no one would have known that I did it because I objected to the death penalty rather than because I concluded that Tsarnaev had the better of the argument.

But that would have been a dereliction of duty. The people who adopted the Constitution didn't share my view of the death penalty, and neither do all my fellow citizens today. Quite the contrary: twenty-seven states authorize capital punishment, as does the federal government.[17] If I distort the law to make it difficult for them to impose the death penalty, I interfere with the voters' right to self-government. My office doesn't entitle me to align the legal system with my moral or policy views. Swearing to apply the law faithfully means deciding each case based on my best judgment about what the law *is*. If I decide a case based on my judgment about what the law *should be*, I'm cheating. I found the vote distasteful to cast, and I wish our system worked differently. Yet I had no doubt that voting to affirm the sentence was the right thing for me to do. Had I concluded that casting such a vote was immoral or that I couldn't fairly judge the case, the right thing to do would have been to recuse—not to cheat.

It may sound counterintuitive, as it did to my aunt, but making judgments about what the law requires isn't always the same thing as deciding what is just. In the Boston Marathon bombing case, the Court held that there was no legal impediment to executing Tsarnaev, not that executing him was moral. In *Terry v. United States*, the Court held that the law did not permit resentencing, not that Terry's original sentence was fair. And in the flag-burning case, the Court held that the First Amendment protected that act of protest, not that flag burning is virtuous. In a system where judges are not Solomons, their role is limited. They are referees, not kings, because they decide whether people have played by the rules rather than what the rules should be. As much as some people might admire Solomon, he wouldn't make it through a confirmation hearing if he proposed to decide cases in accordance with his own conscience. That's as it should be under our Constitution.

Some suggest that people of faith have a particularly difficult time following the law rather than their moral views. (I faced that criticism as a Catholic, most sharply when the Senate Judiciary Committee conducted a hearing to consider my nomination to the Seventh Circuit.) I'm not sure why. Fortunately for the health of our country, people of faith are not the only Americans with firm convictions about right and wrong. Nonreligious judges also have deeply held moral commitments, which means that they too face conflicts between those commitments and the demands of the law. A secular humanist who passionately believes that access to abortion is a moral imperative must set aside her views, no less than the judge whose faith informs a moral objection to abortion. *Whatever* the source of the conviction, it cannot affect the outcome of the case.

It bears repeating that judges are not angels. As fallible humans, we are susceptible to the temptation of allowing our biases to creep in. It is important, then, for the president and Senate to select judges who understand the limits of their role and have the humility to respect those limits. Once confirmed, judges must be alert to the temptation to advance justice as they see it. That requires self-awareness about one's preferred result, especially in difficult cases—Justices Scalia, Kennedy, and Sotomayor were frank about the divergence between what they preferred and what the law required. A judge who never sees such divergence should do some soul-searching, because as Justice Scalia rightly observed, "The judge who always likes the results he reaches is a bad judge."[18]

Deciding cases with an eye to their preferred results is not the only temptation judges face. That's a form of inside pressure: a judge fighting against the pull of her own beliefs. But there is also outside pressure, especially in cases that generate intense national interest. When a court has a high-profile case, legal commentators quickly disseminate their views. Law professors debate on legal blogs and podcasts, columnists write op-eds in major newspapers, and politicians proclaim their views everywhere from the floor of Congress to the steps of the Supreme Court. Long before a vote is cast, it is often evident who will praise and who will criticize a judge's vote, and on what grounds. That creates a risk that judges will allow their votes to be influenced by a desire to curry favor with or avoid criticism from certain outside voices—particularly those with the power to enhance or destroy reputations.

Relationships matter too, because judges may care as much or more about the opinions of people or groups to whom they have more personal ties. They may have been involved with policy groups before joining the bench; they may have friendships from time spent working in Democratic or Republican administrations. And all judges have social groups like friends, neighbors, and family, many of whom may care deeply about cases on the docket. Who doesn't want the approval of friends? A decision that disappoints those with whom a judge has personal ties may strain or even end relationships that matter to her.

In short, there are multiple sources of outside pressure on judges. The source of the pressure may vary from judge to judge, or even from case to case. Sometimes, the outside pressures may be mutually reinforcing—for example, a judge's social groups may share the opinions of or belong to particular elite institutions. Other times, the outside pressures may conflict—for example, a judge may be aware that the will of those with cultural megaphones (and therefore the power to unleash a tide of accolades or criticism) is pitted against the will of fellow jurisprudential travelers (whom the judge may be naturally inclined to please and loath to disappoint). By personality, a judge might care more about her standing with some groups than others—for example, she might find it harder to withstand pressure from a spouse and children than from the media. The upshot is that a judge inclined to take her cue from outside voices has many to choose from, and they may well pull in opposite directions.

To be sure, no one thinks a judge *should* decide cases based on concern for her social standing. No judge, however, should make the mistake of thinking herself impervious to the desire for admiration or fear of scorn. Few people are naturally indifferent to what others think of them. If that were the default state of human nature, parents wouldn't have to teach children to do what is right even if it makes them unpopular. Choosing truth over status requires strength of character, and achieving it requires mastering the natural impulse to be a people pleaser.

This mastery, a virtue for anyone, is a matter of duty for a judge. The oath demands a willingness to be unpopular—a judge moved by the external pressure of public opinion doesn't "administer justice without respect to persons" or "faithfully and impartially discharge" her duties under the Constitution.[19] The difficulty of following through on this commitment isn't new. Under tremendous public pressure while he was presiding over the treason trial of Aaron Burr, Chief Justice John Marshall offered these words to the crowd before announcing a sure-to-be-unpopular ruling in Burr's favor:

> No man is desirous of placing himself in a disagreeable situation. No man is desirous of becoming the peculiar subject of calumny. No man, might he let the bitter cup pass from him without self-reproach, would drain it to the bottom. But if he has no choice in the case; if there is no alternative presented to him but a dereliction of duty or the opprobrium of those who are denominated the world, he merits the contempt as well as the indignation of his country who can hesitate which to embrace.[20]

Just as it's a problem when a judge likes all the results she reaches, so too is it a problem if the judge wants *others* to like the results that she reaches.

The Constitution's guarantees of life tenure and salary protection for federal judges are designed to fortify a judge's resolve to stand firm against the tide of public opinion. Judges are tasked with upholding the Constitution against encroachments by Congress, the president, and the states. In the usual case, the political branch or state responsible for the offending policy will not appreciate being told no, and when the policy commands majority support, the electorate may share the resentment. The judge must soldier on anyway—a job made easier by the knowledge that while she may lose friends or public esteem, she will at least keep her job. As Alexander Hamilton observed in defense of the life tenure promised by Article III of the Constitution, "[N]othing will contribute so much as this to that independent spirit in the judges which must be essential to the faithful performance of so arduous a duty."[21]

History contains many examples of judges who displayed this independent spirit in the face of public anger at their on-the-job choices. Chief Justice John Marshall was burned in effigy by a mob angered by the ruling that led to Aaron Burr's acquittal.[22] Marshall also endured harsh criticism in the press and the threat of impeachment.[23] Chief Justice Earl Warren, accused of being too pro–civil rights, too pro-criminal, and too anti-religion, was protested at public events, booed by the crowd when he arrived at football games, and greeted by "Impeach Earl Warren" signs along America's highways.[24] An anticommunist organization called the John Birch Society sponsored an essay contest for college students, offering $1,000 (the equivalent of about $10,000 today) for the essay that presented the best grounds for impeaching Warren.[25] Anti-Warren sentiment took a dark turn when a radio host said that Warren should be hanged.[26]

Justice Hugo Black, a member of the Warren Court, endured a venomous response to his vote in *Brown v. Board of Education*. As a former senator for the state of Alabama and a past member of the Ku Klux Klan, Justice Black shocked his home state by joining the Court's opinion, which held that racially segregated schools are unconstitutional.[27] After his vote, Justice Black was ostracized by his fellow Alabamans, who called him a "renegade" and "Judas Iscariot."[28] The Secret Service gave him a bulletproof vest to wear when walking the streets of Birmingham. His law school classmates did not invite him to their class reunion. The state legislature passed a resolution recommending that Black not be buried in the state, and for several years afterward, the legislature passed resolutions condemning him.[29] On top of this, the justice's son, Hugo Black, Jr., who still lived in Alabama at the time, experienced so much harassment that he eventually gave up his law practice and moved to Florida.[30] After a while, Justice Black decided to stop returning to Alabama altogether, though the decision caused him great sadness.[31]

The lower court judges who enforced the Supreme Court's desegregation decisions paid a high price too. Judge Elbert Tuttle, an appellate judge on the New Orleans–based Fifth Circuit, received obscene phone calls at his personal residence at all hours of the day and night. (Much to the frustration of callers, Tuttle's wife would unfailingly respond with southern charm: "Thank you *so* much for calling. We *do* appreciate it.")[32] After the Montgomery bus boycotts, Judges Frank Johnson and Richard Rives, both of whom were federal judges in Alabama, were similarly in the public eye when they issued a decision invalidating Alabama's segregated public transportation system.[33] They received hate mail and death threats, and Judge Rives was excluded from his church and lunch club. Then it got worse. Opponents vandalized the grave of Judge Rives's son and bombed the home of Judge Johnson's mother.[34]

These are just a few of many well-known examples. The violence endured by Judges Johnson and Rives is thankfully rare; neither violence nor the threat of violence should be the price of public service. Nonetheless, I suspect that many judges have faced harsh criticism in some form from those who dislike their decisions. I've had my share, including death threats, lewd packages, protests at my home, and a few ugly public encounters. (Justice Brett Kavanaugh has faced worse—an armed man showed up at his home with plans to assassinate him.) I can take it; these last years of being in the public eye have toughened me up. But being the target of protest has changed my daily life, from the now-constant presence of security to now-guarded social interactions.

Chief Justice Warren had the right attitude about public backlash. When a friend asked him how he felt about it all, Warren simply replied that "everyone who has a difficult position in the public service must condition himself to the theory of Mark Twain that a few fleas are good for any dog."[35] As Twain said, that keeps him from worrying so much about being a dog. Opposition generally accompanies jobs that require the making of tough decisions, which is particularly true for those accountable to the public trust. A government official who encounters no significant disagreement in performing her duties probably doesn't have significant responsibilities. If nothing else, some opposition is a good reminder of the weight of the job. Besides, adulation fuels pride, which itself can cloud behavior both on and off the bench. It's not a bad thing for anyone, including a judge, to be taken down a notch. And in a society devoted to free speech, criticisms of public officials go with the territory.

CYNICS MAY THINK that judicial decisions are inevitably tainted, whether by the judge's own preferences or the preferences pressed upon her by others. It would be unrealistic to maintain that such biases never creep in; sometimes, they surely do. But the judges I know—even those with whom I sometimes disagree—try to do their best by the law. Anyway, it strikes me as a fool's errand to make decisions with an eye toward public approval, because in our large, diverse country, every hotly contested decision will draw praise from some and criticism from others. A judge who cannot steel herself against fear of criticism and desire for praise will not only be bad at the job, but also miserable in it. My father was fond of telling my siblings and me, "Control your emotions, or they will control you." That is sage advice in many situations, including this one. I can't banish my emotions, but I can do my best to keep them out of the driver's seat.

Chapter 3

WORKING TOGETHER

When asked whether we get along at the Court, I often tell the story of my first day on the job. My stress level was off the charts. I had just finished the intense confirmation process, which included meeting with senators, filling out what seemed like endless forms, preparing for a hearing before the Senate Judiciary Committee, and the hearing itself. During those weeks, I had received an abundance of kindness and support, but I had also faced hostility. Now, having been through the wringer, I had no time to catch my breath. I was about to start a difficult, high-profile job. I didn't yet have law clerks, judicial assistants, or even office supplies. I had to get ready for my first round of oral arguments, which were just days away. I had to find a place to live. And after weeks of separation from my family during the confirmation process, I was facing months more. Jesse and I had decided not to move our family until after the school year, so from November to June, I split my time between Washington and South Bend. For a host of reasons, then, the morning of Tuesday, October 27, was not my best emotional moment.

To top it off, I wasn't sure what kind of reception I would receive from my new colleagues. In most jobs, an employee entering a building on the first day knows that the institution wanted her—after all, she was hired, presumably because someone in charge thought she would be a good fit.

Not so at the Court. Nobody there had recruited me, interviewed me, or hired me. I was thrust upon my new colleagues, some of whom had never met me and none of whom had chosen me. They were still grieving the loss of their cherished and long-serving friend, Ruth Bader Ginsburg, whom I replaced. And I knew that my appointment must have been disappointing to several, who had not only lost a friend, but also gained a colleague with some jurisprudential differences. So what happened next was a welcome surprise.

I will always be grateful to my colleagues for the warmth of their welcome. I won't use names, out of sensitivity to privacy—people should not have to worry that personal gestures of kindness will be broadcast. But because we have shared this story in joint appearances, I will say that on my very first day, Justice Sotomayor sent bags of Halloween candy to my

The current Court. (Photo by Fred Schilling, Collection of the Supreme Court of the United States.)

chambers for Jesse (who was there for my swearing-in) to bring home to our children in South Bend. And hers was not the only gesture of warmth. Welcome notes waited on my desk. Upon learning that I had no assistants, one justice dispatched his staff to my chambers to answer phones and stock paper and pens. Two others shared bench memos that their law clerks had prepared for the upcoming cases. Another gave me a lead on a place to rent (which panned out, to my relief). The ensuing weeks and months brought lunch invitations, dinner invitations, and phone calls. My new colleagues were more than civil—they were kind.

So yes, we get along.

There is an indispensable human element to judging. Unlike some courtrooms, which are run by a single judge, the Supreme Court is made up of nine judges. And because we hear cases together, decisions require collaboration and sometimes compromise. We speak informally in chambers and by telephone. We talk as a group in conferences after arguments. We attempt to persuade one another by writing memoranda. We read one another's draft opinions and request changes. A justice who takes a "my way or the highway" attitude will find it impossible to write an opinion representing the majority's view. Moreover, all this happens in a small group whose members serve alongside one another for many years, so ruptured relationships are not a short-term problem. We are stuck with one another whether we like it or not.

Because the Court cannot function well without collegiality, the work drives home the importance of balancing a commitment to ideas with a commitment to respect people who don't share them. I can't help but think of what Justice Scalia had to say about this: "I attack ideas. I don't attack people. And some very good people have some very bad ideas. And if you can't separate the two, you gotta get another day job. You don't want to be a judge—at least not a judge on a multi-member panel."[1]

Those words resonate in many areas of my life, even at the family dinner table, where I've had to learn in a distinct setting how to get along in a different group of nine. As my children become adults, they're increasingly vocal about their own opinions, which don't always align with mine. We discuss ideas vigorously when they touch on topics we care about, but we try to do it respectfully and in the right spirit. I like what G. K. Chesterton said about his brother—that the two argued incessantly but never quarreled.[2] A good argument involves logic and a search for truth; a quarrel is an effort to tear down your sparring partner. I suspect that few want to see themselves in Benjamin Franklin's story about "a certain French lady, who in a little Dispute with her Sister, said, I don't know how it happens, Sister, but I meet with no body but myself that's *always* in the right."[3]

The line between arguing and quarreling is one I try to walk with any number of family members and friends. True, I could limit the tension by avoiding people whose beliefs differ from mine. But that would make my life less rich by excluding many wonderful people from it. I could also limit the tension by avoiding discussion of sensitive topics with those who are likely to disagree with me. Sometimes that's the right strategy, because there's a time and place for everything. But sparring with intellectual opponents is the way to hear the other side of the argument. An echo chamber repeats mistakes as readily as truths, so refusing to engage with those who disagree is the easy way out. Shunning others just because they disagree with you is also a recipe for a lonely and ultimately unhappy existence.

In any event, such an out is unavailable on the Supreme Court. For one thing, a justice does not choose her colleagues. Instead, a judicial appointment is like an arranged marriage with no option of divorce: it locks you into a long-term relationship with people someone else picked. Justices have no power to screen new colleagues for personality or judicial philosophy, so they can't surround themselves with the like-minded.

Nor is there any running away from disagreement. Quite the contrary. As I'll explain later in the book, *all* federal appellate courts sit in panels of judges. So in the federal system, all appellate courts are premised on the possibility of disagreement. Why else have multiple judges decide every case? If we didn't expect differing views from different judges, there would be no reason to have more than one appellate judge. It may be that "many hands make light work." But the real point is that many hands make it more likely that a court will get it right. Different judges with different viewpoints improve decision-making by increasing the odds that no one misses the winning insight in a case.

This creates a paradox of appellate judging. Sometimes diverse perspectives lead to one answer or even a compromise upon which all nine justices can agree. Other times those diverse perspectives lead to dissents and concurrences. These opinions aren't only a means of explaining our reasoning to the public. They're also part of a continuing conversation between justices trying to convince one another to see the case their way. Sometimes, that happens: I have changed my vote after being persuaded by a circulating opinion, and I'm not the only one. Sometimes, though, disagreement remains.

There is much to be said for unanimous decisions, as the public can rest assured that all nine justices saw it the same way. But consensus doesn't emerge in every case, and it's unrealistic to expect it to—most of our cases involve questions that have already divided other appellate judges in the system. Oddly enough, consensus in some cases and respectful division in others can *both* be signs of well-functioning appellate courts.

The possibility of dissent remains a centuries-old feature, not a flaw, of the Court's deliberative process. And when handled well, disagreement is a source of strength, rather than a reason for regret. History contains many examples of the value of decision-making in a diverse group. For an example outside the judiciary, consider the administration of Abraham Lincoln. Lincoln took diversity in a direction that some might find extreme: he populated his cabinet with men who had been his competitors for the Republican presidential nomination, and some were even among his harshest critics. As Doris Kearns Goodwin recounts in her book *Team of Rivals*, Lincoln relied on these relationships to carry the nation through the Civil War. Rather than hindering their ability to work together, their rivalry sharpened Lincoln's thinking and helped unite the factions within the fledgling Republican Party.[4]

Lincoln's approach was particularly striking when it came to William Seward, his secretary of state. Seward made no pretense of his view that he belonged in the presidency. Yet Lincoln invited him to talk daily, and by hearing each other out, Lincoln and Seward bridged the gap between them, ultimately becoming close friends.[5] Their relationship illustrates that people can work together despite their differences—even more, that such relationships can be fruitful.

Lincoln and Seward are not the only public servants to recognize the value of such friendships. Take the relationship between Justices Scalia and Ginsburg. On the Court, they were, as often as not, intellectual opponents. And before they became judges, it would have been easy to wonder how such polar opposites could ever find anything in common: Scalia, a Catholic man, was a leader in the conservative legal movement; Ginsburg, a Jewish woman, was a leader on the liberal side. Yet when they became colleagues (first on the Court of Appeals for the D.C. Circuit and later on the Supreme Court), they also became dear friends. Mutual respect, a shared love of opera, and traditions like their families' annual New Year's dinner knit them together despite their substantial differences of opinion about matters of law. A picture tells a thousand words: a snapshot of the two riding an elephant together in India captures the relationship perfectly.

The friendship helped them both. Scalia once called their relationship a "mutual improvement society" because they valued each other's intellectual rigor and knew that each would sharpen the other's thinking.[6] If you doubt me, take a look at Ginsburg's majority opinion and Scalia's dissent in *United States v. Virginia*,[7] in which the Court held that the Virginia Military Institute, then a males-only state military college, was constitutionally obligated to admit women.[8] Ginsburg and Scalia were both at the top of their games, and it is perfectly clear what each thought of the other's

Justices Scalia and Ginsburg riding an elephant together. (Collection of the Supreme Court of the United States.)

argument. Yet they didn't allow their conflict over this issue—or other issues like abortion, the Second Amendment, and voting rights—to destroy their affection for each other. Our divided country could learn a lot from their example.

To be sure, not every working relationship matures into friendship. But even when friendship lies out of reach, civility does not. John Adams said this about Benjamin Franklin: "That I have no friendship for Franklin I avow. That I am incapable of having any with a man of his moral sentiments I avow. As far as fate shall compel me to sit with him in public affairs, I shall treat him with decency and perfect impartiality."[9] There's no reason to treat colleagues any other way.

Debating ideas while respecting people is sometimes a tricky thing to do, especially for those who care passionately about principles with real impact on the American constitutional order. How should the Constitution be interpreted? (For example, how much does history matter?) Which rights does it protect? (The right to have a gun?) How does it allocate power among the branches of the federal government? (Can the president seize private property in wartime without congressional authorization?)

For any judge, handling such debates is about controlling both the mouth and the pen. Opportunities for rancor, both public and private, are many. In the heat of oral argument, it's tempting to speak sharply, either directly with advocates or indirectly with colleagues on the bench. The same temptation is present in private interactions, such as conference discussions or internal memoranda. Perhaps the trickiest interaction is between majority and dissenting opinions. When circulated internally, dueling opinions aim to persuade other justices, but once published, each opinion aims to persuade the public. Short term, the best lines in opinions may be quoted in the news; long term, every word is memorialized in the body of law that students learn and lawyers consult. That judicial opinions are public and permanent raises the personal and institutional stakes of conducting the argument well. Justices draw different rhetorical lines by function of personality, writing style, or passion felt. I can't say that I always like the rhetoric in others' opinions—or that I never write too harshly myself. Still, I truly believe that even the sharpest exchanges on the Court are driven by disagreement about the law rather than personal animosity.

Maintaining relationships is made easier by spending time together. To state the obvious, every member of the Court is a person, not a package of ideas. Knowing one another *as people* fosters collegiality. Toward that end, members of the Supreme Court have long observed traditions, big and small, to knit us together as persons.

The tenure of John Marshall, known in history as the "Great Chief Justice," illustrates the importance of such traditions to the work of the Court. When Marshall assumed leadership of the Court in 1801, the justices were not a cohesive unit and the Court's institutional fate was uncertain.[10] The end of the story is well-known: Marshall solidified the Court as an independent and powerful third branch of government. Law students learn that Marshall accomplished this through judicial opinions in landmark cases like *Marbury v. Madison*, which established the power of judicial review.[11] (I will say more about that case in a later chapter.) But Marshall's leadership involved more than navigating public-facing disputes with the president and recalcitrant state courts. It also required behind-the-scenes work on collegiality—and masterful work at that.

When Marshall began, the Court was full of strong personalities, as has been true through the centuries. Most of the justices were older than Marshall, and each was a notable figure in his own right. Marshall was determined to build a spirit of friendship and unity among them, but success was not inevitable. At the time, the justices did not all live in the same state, much less work in the same building. They traveled to Washington to hear cases during the Court's term, which, in those days, was brief. While there, the justices took up temporary residence in boardinghouses. They heard oral arguments in a borrowed room on the ground floor of the Capitol Building, and, lacking office space, worked where they lodged. When a case was decided, no single opinion represented the Court's view. Instead, each justice expressed the rationale for his individual vote, but no opinion explained the reasoning of a united majority.

Marshall changed the Court's culture. One of his most important innovations was to have all the justices stay at the same place when they were in Washington hearing cases. During those weeks, they had meals together, which enabled them to discuss cases and grow in friendship. This yielded benefits not only for the justices themselves, but also for the law. During Marshall's time as chief justice, the Court abandoned the practice of writing a series of individual opinions in favor of having one opinion represent the view of the Court. That was necessary to developing a system of precedent, in which one case builds on the next; without a majority opinion, later courts have no binding reasoning to follow. And Marshall went even further than instituting the majority opinion—he strongly discouraged any separate writing, concurrence or dissent.[12]

Separate writings are common today, and lawyers debate whether they help or harm the Court. It's possible that the answer depends partly on the historical moment. Presenting an entirely unified front, for instance, may have been important during Marshall's tenure, when the Court was first establishing itself as a coequal branch of government and creating an initial body of precedent. Separate writings may be more valuable now to the extent that justices are grappling with a vast, complicated body of precedent and explaining its implications to a more populous country and more complex federal judiciary.

One anecdote I particularly like about the Marshall Court's time involves the justices' shared lodging. Justice Joseph Story reported that at their nightly dinners, the justices abstained from wine "except in wet weather." Marshall, who relished a good Madeira, devised a way of circumventing the rule. He sometimes asked Story to "step to the window and see if it looks like rain." If Story reported sunshine, Marshall would reply that "our jurisdiction extends over so large a territory that the doctrine of chances makes it certain that it must be raining somewhere"—and they would enjoy a glass of wine anyway.[13]

As Marshall well knew, there is a connection between food and friendship. I appreciate, therefore, that echoes of his boardinghouse tradition still exist on the Court. After we are together for oral argument or Friday conference, the justices usually have lunch around a big table in the Justices' Dining Room. We have a hard-and-fast rule of conversation at lunch: no discussing cases. Instead, we discuss books, movies, history, sports, kids, vacations, and so on. We celebrate birthdays with a song (usually off-key) before lunch.

I was advised that it's most important to attend lunch on the day of a difficult conference vote, and I've tried to keep that in mind. While those are the days when it's most unappealing to go, they are also the days when it is easiest for the seeds of discord to take root. Collegiality isn't always an act of the heart—it is sometimes an act of the will. The dividends, though, are worth the discipline.

The spouses of the justices also have a lunch tradition. Once a quarter, they eat together at the Court in the Natalie Cornell Rehnquist Dining Room (named to honor the wife of Chief Justice William Rehnquist), informally known as the spouses' dining room. The spouses take turns planning the meal in teams, and, like the justices, they celebrate milestones in one another's lives. All the justices, even those without a spouse present, typically pop in toward the end of lunch to say hello. Spouses of retired or deceased justices remain in the "Court family" and routinely attend the gathering. For my first two years on the Court, Jesse was the only man in the group, just as John O'Connor, Sandra Day O'Connor's husband, had been many years before. After the confirmation of Justice Ketanji Brown Jackson, Jesse gained the company of her husband, Patrick Jackson.

Place setting for my New Orleans–themed welcome dinner at the Court. (Photo by Fred Schilling, Collection of the Supreme Court of the United States.)

There are welcome dinners too. By tradition, the second-most-junior justice hosts dinner for the newest justice. The dinner is small—only justices and spouses—which makes conversation easier. In a gesture of warmth, the host tries to fit the dinner to the particular interests and personality of the guest of honor. For Justice Brett Kavanaugh's welcome dinner, for example, Justice Neil Gorsuch arranged for the unofficial mascots of the Washington Nationals baseball team (Kavanaugh is an avid fan) to race through the halls of the Supreme Court. For my welcome dinner, Justice Kavanaugh planned a New Orleans–themed menu and entertainment in recognition of my hometown. Each justice received a Mardi Gras mask, and a jazz singer treated us to New Orleans favorites like "When the Saints Go Marching In" and "The Second Line." To welcome Justice Ketanji Brown Jackson, I hosted a dinner with her favorite dishes, and, having learned that she particularly loved the musical *Hamilton*, I asked a Broadway performer to sing selections for us after dinner.

I've been lucky that good relations between the justices have continued throughout my time on the Court. I don't take this collegiality for granted, for relationships on the Court have not always been smooth sailing. Justice James McReynolds, an anti-Semite, refused to speak to his Jewish colleagues, Justice Louis Brandeis and Justice Benjamin Cardozo.[14] Justice Hugo Black and Justice Robert Jackson, both Roosevelt appointees, became bitter enemies, largely because of Jackson's ambition to become chief justice and Black's willingness to hold a grudge.[15] Black also feuded with Justice Owen Roberts, to whom he had once been close. Their relationship became so poisonous that Roberts refused to participate in the traditional exchange of handshakes before oral argument, and Black prevented Chief Justice Harlan Fiske Stone from publishing a formal letter of appreciation upon Roberts's retirement.[16]

Such relationships were spectacular failures. But the tragedy lay not only in the initial breaks, but also in the failure to repair them. Any relationship—be it between spouses, friends, or colleagues—eventually leads to some failures, sometimes large and sometimes small. The story of John Adams and Thomas Jefferson is worth recounting for its illustration that reconciliation can follow rupture.

Adams and Jefferson began as friends. They met in 1775 as delegates in the Continental Congress and spent time together during diplomatic missions to Europe.[17] Their families were very close while living abroad.[18] Abigail Adams cared for Jefferson's daughter Polly, and Jefferson took Adams's son John Quincy under his wing.[19] As Abigail confided to Jefferson, there had been few people in her husband's life with whom he could associate with such "perfect freedom and unreserve." Jefferson, she wrote, was "one of the choice ones of the earth."[20]

But as political differences sharpened, their relationship became increasingly strained. Adams was a Federalist committed to a strong central government; Jefferson, on the other hand, was a Democratic Republican committed to keeping more power in the hands of the states. When they competed for the presidency in the election of 1800, both sides engaged in ad hominem attacks and smear tactics.[21] After Jefferson's victory, the two went eleven years without speaking.[22]

In 1812, Adams and Jefferson began to correspond again. With the perspective of age and experience—not to mention humility in letting go of pride and old wounds—they were able to rekindle their friendship, exchanging 158 letters over the next fourteen years. As time went on, they opened up to each other about some of the more difficult parts of their history.[23] In one letter, Jefferson mused:

> To me then it appears that there have been differences of opinion, and party differences, from the establishment of governments to the present day, and on the same question which now divides our country, that these will continue through all future times . . . that opinions, which are equally honest on both sides, should not [a]ffect personal esteem or social intercourse.[24]

Jefferson and Adams maintained their connection until, poignantly, they died on the same day: the fiftieth anniversary of the Declaration of Independence.

Perhaps it's as simple—and stark—as this. When tensions rise, as they inevitably do, it's better to end things like John Adams and Thomas Jefferson than like Alexander Hamilton and Aaron Burr: die in friendship, not in a duel. Live life like Justices Scalia and Ginsburg, who accompanied serious and vigorous public debate with warm personal friendship and mutual respect.

In my observation, it's all too easy to let temper and discord triumph over civility and calm. At bottom, success turns on our ability to conquer pride with virtue. Through my failures, I've learned that this can require a Herculean effort. It's difficult not to dwell on harsh criticism, desire praise, or envy others. That was true when I was a teenager, and it's true now. I have learned that any victories in that lifelong battle depend on humility, especially in the way I view myself relative to others. Fortunately, there are examples to emulate. Here are two stories, one old and one more recent.

The first is from the life of John Marshall, who—while indisputably confident—was also humble. He lived in Richmond, where he spent a great deal of time caring for his sickly wife. That care included taking over tasks that would have been traditionally hers, like overseeing the weekly housecleaning. He did more than supervise—visitors found him "with his sleeves rolled up and a handkerchief tied about his head, helping to scrub the floors and set the house to order."[25]

Marshall was also notorious for sloppy dress even when he wasn't cleaning. So who could blame the poor new guy in town, who saw the shabbily dressed chief justice at the market and asked to hire Marshall to carry home a newly purchased turkey? Rather than informing the new neighbor that he was the chief justice of the United States, Marshall added the turkey to his load and delivered it to his neighbor's house. When an amused bystander revealed Marshall's identity, Marshall reassured the embarrassed newcomer, saying that it was only neighborly, given that "we were going the same way."[26]

The second comes from the life of Antonin Scalia. After Justice Scalia's death, Jeffrey A. Tucker published a story relating a scene that he had witnessed in a near-empty church.[27] Justice Scalia was praying alone in a pew, when a woman covered with open sores approached him. Tucker described her as the kind of "troubled person that you meet in large cities and quickly walk away from."[28] But Justice Scalia took her hands and held her close. As Tucker puts it, "He didn't recoil. He stood there with conviction. And love."[29] After comforting her, Justice Scalia pressed money into her hands and left the church, unaware that anyone had seen him.

An encounter with a man in a market or a woman in a church may seem to have little to do with collegiality on the Supreme Court. But to my mind, these interactions are all of a piece. There is no "on/off" switch that changes the way you relate to people in different settings. All human relationships depend on kindness and humility. True, relationships on the Court sometimes operate under the stress of disagreement about issues of immense national importance. But that, to my mind, heightens the importance of collegiality. The success of a multi-member court rides on the ability to disagree respectfully. The success of a democratic society does too.

Chapter 4

DECIDING A CASE

EVERY SUMMER, we go on vacation with my parents, siblings, and their families. Jesse calls it vacation with a little "v" because it is anything but a time of quietly sipping cocktails on a beach. My parents, the Coney children, and spouses add up to sixteen adults, and, as of this writing, there are thirty-five (yes, thirty-five) grandchildren. I take that as a testament to my parents, who made having a big family so attractive that their children all value it. In any event, the week is fun but chaotic, and always involves packs of cousins running back and forth between houses. It also typically includes multiple (daily) trips to the grocery store, regular medical mishaps, and jaw-dropping amounts of laundry.

The summer that the Court decided *Dobbs v. Jackson Women's Health Organization*,[1] which overruled *Roe v. Wade*, one of my brothers-in-law arrived at "Coney Family Vacation" (as we affectionately call it) with a copy of the opinion in hand. I was surprised. He is not a lawyer, and seventy-nine pages of legal analysis—not to mention an additional ninety-one pages of concurring and dissenting opinions—is hardly a leisure read. Plus, after the stress of recent months, which had included a leaked draft, investigation of the leak, security threats, and protests, not to mention the pressure of making a momentous decision, *Dobbs* did not top the list of things I wanted to talk about on vacation. But my brother-in-law held up the thick stack of paper and said, "You always say 'read the opinion,' so that's what I'm doing."

I hugged him. I do always advise people to read the Court's opinions, but I doubt many people—including lawyers—take me up on it. A court decision is more than its bottom line (that the judgment below is affirmed or reversed) or its headline (that the Court overturned *Roe v. Wade*). It includes an opinion describing the Court's rationale, which gives every reader an opportunity to critique the decision on the merits. Chief Justice Earl Warren bemoaned in 1965 that "[i]t would do well if people read our decisions before they attacked them."[2] I agree and add that the same is true for people who praise our decisions. A headline equips someone to say whether she loves or hates the result; only the opinion enables her to say whether she agrees or disagrees with the Court's legal analysis.

Granted, some opinions—like *Dobbs*—may take time to plow through. (That said, my brother-in-law read *Roe* in addition to *Dobbs* because he

Coney family vacation in the summer of 2023, with most of the family there.

wanted the full picture, and when we talked, he showed an impressive grasp of the legal arguments. So don't give up too quickly.) If an opinion is too hard to follow, an analysis from a reliable source is a good option. If it's hard to find an analysis that is neutral, or at least transparent about its biases, try multiple sources to get a sense of the debate. The point is that an informed citizen should know not only *what* the Court did, but also *why*. Without the opinion, or at least a reliable proxy, an observer is simply not equipped to judge whether the Court's decision is sound.

Opinions are the Court's most important work product. They represent the culmination of a decision-making process that begins when briefs are filed and ends when the author gives the Court's Publications Unit "the okay to print." Some cases resolve a technical dispute of minimal general interest, and others more visibly affect American life. All receive, however, the close attention of the Court. And in contrast to the decisions of presidents and governors, state legislatures and Congress, issues before the Court are not resolved by an up or down vote driven by what the electorate wants. They are resolved by an (often painstaking) analysis of existing laws, both statutory and constitutional, and the Court's conclusion may be at odds with what a majority of the electorate supports. The judicial task of working toward the best legal answer happens largely behind closed doors, but there is no mystery to it. This chapter describes how I go about it.

Before Oral Argument

Any appellate judge does a lot of reading. For me, every case involves, at a minimum, the parties' briefs; a memo written by a law clerk; and the relevant cases, statutes, and regulations. Sometimes, I also read amicus briefs (amicus is Latin for "friend," indicating that the brief is submitted by a "friend of the court"). And where relevant, I read secondary materials like treatises and law review articles, and historical sources like *The Federalist Papers*.[3] Still, it is mostly a closed universe—the parties bear primary responsibility for presenting their arguments and designating the important sources.

I start with the briefs from the petitioner (the party who lost in the court below) and the respondent (the party who won). I also read any brief from the solicitor general, who represents the United States. The solicitor general is sometimes called "the tenth justice," because while she advocates for her client (the federal government), her advocacy is tempered to at least some degree by an interest in helping the Court get it right.[4] A lawyer for a private party, by contrast, single-mindedly pursues her client's interests. The Court so values the views of the solicitor general that she is often allotted time for oral argument even when the United States is not a party to the case.

At the outset of my preparation, I don't read the amicus briefs. Amici (plural of "amicus") may have functioned as neutral "friends of the court" in English common law courts,[5] but if that model was ever used in the United States, it didn't last long. Starting in the early 1800s, the Supreme Court permitted the states and the United States to appear as amici in suits that implicated government interests—and they obviously advocated to protect those interests.[6] By the early 1900s, the NAACP and other interest groups were filing amicus briefs.[7] The number of such briefs increased along with the Court's docket, and by the 1940s, they were filed so frequently that, as one commentator puts it, "[T]hey were beginning to be regarded by the Court as potential sources of irritation."[8] Their number has increased markedly in the decades since, especially in cases that generate public attention.[9] To give you a sense of the scale, eighty-four amicus briefs were filed in *City of Grants Pass v. Johnson*, which addressed whether the enforcement of anti-camping ordinances against the homeless violates the Cruel and Unusual Punishments Clause.[10] In high-profile cases like *Grants Pass*, submissions from amici often take up half a bookcase shelf in my office.

Any person or organization can submit an amicus brief. They come from law professors, businesses, foreign countries, advocacy organizations, members of Congress, trade associations, and the like. Supreme Court rules require amici to make certain disclosures: most important, they must state their interest in the case and reveal any person or organization who contributed funds to the brief's preparation.[11] Knowing the potential bias of the author allows the justices to put the brief's arguments in perspective. A brief funded by a business advocacy group taking the side of a corporation may be persuasive but, like any piece of advocacy, should be read with the author's self-interest in view.

I routinely read some amicus briefs, like those filed by state governments. But amicus briefs are not universally useful. Many dwell on policy arguments instead of the law, and while some are well written and well researched, others are not. Given the volume and uneven quality of amicus briefs, I don't read them all. My law clerks review them and flag the helpful ones.

Once I'm done with the significant briefs, I turn to the memo prepared by the law clerk assigned to the case. Before oral argument, the clerk's principal task is to write a memo that reviews the parties' arguments, analyzes the relevant law, and recommends an outcome. Unlike the briefs of the parties, the clerk's "bench memo" (named for its purpose of preparing a judge for the bench) is designed to be a neutral legal analysis. The bench memo is not unique to the Supreme Court; it is commonly used by judges in all courts. But it can be used differently depending on the case and the court. When I served on the Seventh Circuit, a trusted, more experienced colleague recommended that I read the bench memo *before* the briefs. The quality of the briefing varied significantly across cases, and it was sometimes difficult to discern what issue the party was appealing, much less to untangle the party's arguments. The bench memo allowed me to approach the briefs with a handle on what was at stake. During my time on the Seventh Circuit, that was good advice. At the Supreme Court, by contrast, the question presented is crystallized, and the quality of briefing is almost always superb. So I switched the order and now read the briefs first. I prefer to form my own preliminary views before I read the clerk's assessment and recommendation.

Though the memo is the clerk's own work product, she doesn't prepare it in a vacuum. In the course of working through the arguments, she has conversations with her co-clerks, as well as with the clerks working on the same case in the other eight chambers. The completed memo goes in a binder (called a "bench book") that also contains the lower court opinions, principal judicial decisions addressing the legal issues in the case, and relevant sections of the lower court record, such as key testimony or exhibits. After some back-and-forth with the assigned clerk, I sit down at a computer, do additional research if necessary, and write up my own analysis. In some cases, I'm practically certain of my view, particularly if it's an issue that I've dealt with before. In others, I have a preliminary sense, stronger in some cases than others. And there is a small subset of cases in which a first reading of the briefs leaves me evenly divided. Oral argument is most likely to move me in the latter two situations, but I'm always open to hearing what the lawyers say in the courtroom.

Oral Argument

The Court has always heard oral argument as part of the process of resolving a dispute. Its format, however, has changed over time. Between 1815 and 1835, during the tenure of Chief Justice John Marshall, the Court sat from January or February to March and heard oral argument from 11:00 a.m. to 4:00 p.m. with no lunch break.[12] The oral argument of the early Court differed in several ways from the oral argument of today. No time limits were imposed on lawyers arguing before the Court, so arguments frequently lasted for days, even weeks.[13] That was not necessarily frowned on by the justices, who were, after all, in control of the format. Nonetheless, there were occasional complaints. Justice James Iredell (who was appointed by George Washington) lamented that the Court was "incessantly employed," notably by one weeks-long argument in which a lawyer spoke for three days.[14] Justice Joseph Story (who was appointed by James Madison) described arguments "[a]s excessively prolix and tedious."[15]

Prolix or not, oral argument dominated the work of the early Court. For one thing, advocates didn't file briefs in those days, so oral argument did double duty. For another, many spectators deemed the early nineteenth century the golden age of American oral advocacy. Legendary orators, including William Pinkney, Daniel Webster, and Henry Clay, filled their presentations with references to legal treatises, *The Federalist Papers*, the Bible, and Roman and Greek mythology. (Perhaps the literary references made up for the lack of case law from the brand-new Court.) These arguments were considered the best theatrical performances in Washington, and the performers did not disappoint. There are stories of Henry Clay helping himself to Justice Bushrod Washington's tobacco during oral argument;[16] of the justices pausing oral arguments to give a lawyer time to sober up;[17] and of lawyers, especially William Pinkney, pandering to the ladies in the audience.[18] Imagine a modern lawyer showing up to oral argument drunk or approaching the justices' bench to help himself to a cup of coffee. Safe to say, these aspects of oral argument at the early Court are relics of the past.

As decades went by, the Court's workload expanded.[19] To promote efficiency, the Court adopted a rule in 1849 that had two important components. First, no counsel was permitted to speak for more than two hours without special leave. Second, counsel was required to submit a printed brief in advance of oral argument.[20] Perhaps as a result, the nature of oral argument changed. The justices began to view advocates as resources rather than orators, and questioning by the justices picked up steam. Augustus Garland, who served as attorney general of the United States during the 1880s, observed that "this sort of colloquy with the judges and lawyers is the shortest and best way to reach the very heart of the case."[21] That's still true.

At the turn of the twentieth century, mounting cases pressured the Court into changing oral argument yet again. In the early 1900s, the Court divided its docket into "regular" and "summary" cases.[22] Regular cases were allotted one hour per side for oral argument; summary cases (cases thought to be less complex) were given thirty minutes per side.[23] Questioning by the justices continued at this point in time, so much so that other justices reportedly complained. When a colleague peppered counsel with questions during one argument, Chief Justice Edward White was heard to moan, "I want to hear the argument."[24] To which Justice Oliver Wendell Holmes responded, "So do I, damn him[!]"[25] On a multi-member court, occasional frustrations like these are inevitable.

By the 1950s, questioning counsel had become the norm. In one case, justices interjected 237 questions and comments in the course of a two-hour argument.[26] One observer noted, "Contemporary argument is closer in format to the quiz programs on television than to the magnificent speeches of a hundred years ago."[27] That said, the heat from the bench ebbed and flowed. For instance, justices were relatively quiet in the years preceding Justice Scalia's tenure, but his active questioning of counsel set the modern pattern in which the justices talk almost as much as counsel.[28] But despite the uptick in participation from the bench, the clock remained strict. Chief Justice Warren Burger, known for his administrative efficiency, led the Court to cap oral argument at thirty minutes per side in 1970.[29] It stayed that way for fifty years.

In 2020, the COVID-19 pandemic brought change to the Court. For the first time in its history, the Court conducted arguments remotely—but via audio only. To make that work, the Court tried a different format. The justices proceeded in order of seniority, each justice was allocated time to question counsel, and one justice could not interrupt with a question during another justice's slot. COVID brought another historic change to oral argument: it was livestreamed. Before the pandemic, the only way to hear an argument in real time was to physically attend it. Once the building closed, live audio was the only way to keep the proceeding open to the public, at least virtually.

The Court is a tradition-bound institution, so while those changes might not seem significant from the outside, they were major adjustments on the inside. We chose to continue those two alterations—sequential questioning and livestreaming—even after the COVID closures were over. The public appreciated live audio as it dramatically increased real-time access to the argument. Those who don't live in the Washington, D.C., area have to travel—sometimes great distances—to hear an argument in person. And because space in the courtroom is limited, a seat can be hard to come by. With audio available, there is neither a need to travel nor a limit on audience size.

Nor, after COVID, is there a strict cap on the argument time. When the Court returned to the bench in October Term 2021, the fifty-year-old "thirty minutes per side" rule was relaxed. It turned out that remote arguments weren't all bad: in particular, justices valued having uninterrupted time to ask their own questions. The "open floor" model, where any justice could ask questions at any time, was tried and true. To capture the best of both, the Court blended them. The meat of the argument is an open floor and remains governed by time limits, but it's followed by an open-ended cleanup round. One by one, the justices are permitted uninterrupted time to ask counsel any remaining questions. This guarantees that everyone gets his or her questions asked, which necessarily results in longer arguments. Previously, arguments would take about an hour; now, in bigger cases, they run closer to two. That is largely, however, because of the justices. Advocates aren't given free rein to talk until they run out of things to say. Arguments last as long as justices are asking questions.

Just as I recommend that people read Supreme Court opinions, I recommend that they listen to an oral argument. My parents attended the oral argument in *Trump v. Anderson*,[30] which addressed the question of whether Colorado could keep Donald Trump off the ballot on the ground that he had "engaged in insurrection or rebellion against the [Constitution of the United States]"[31] on January 6. (In the end, the Court unanimously held that states lack the authority to make that judgment.) My father is a lawyer; my mother is not. Nonetheless, and somewhat to my surprise, my mother raved about the argument. She followed some of the legal exchanges, but what impressed her most was the attention that each justice paid to the issues. She said that it gave her confidence in the institution to see that not a single justice was unprepared, casual, or focused on the politics of the case. A nonlawyer sister who listened to the livestreamed audio shared a virtually identical reaction. Their feedback pleased me and tracks what I've heard from lawyers who follow the Court more closely: justices work hard to get it right, and oral arguments reflect that.

People often assume that oral argument doesn't matter to the outcome of a case. From my point of view, this is a misconception. When I'm undecided or have only a tentative conclusion, oral argument can move me one way or the other. Occasionally, argument has changed my mind even when I had a relatively strong view before entering the courtroom. And even when it doesn't change my bottom line, argument has prompted me to rethink certain aspects of a case or reframe the path of decision. It's not unusual for a justice to ask an advocate, "If we agree with you, how should we write the opinion?" This question can work out well or poorly for the lawyer. The answer might help us decide a case in a way that avoids obvious pitfalls; alternatively, it might reveal that the party's position is as unworkable as it seems. Because argument is valuable, I always listen to the recording when I am assigned the opinion. (My law clerks wonder why I don't use the transcript, which can be read quickly. The answer is that audio allows me to multitask, so it is background while I cook or run errands.)

Oral argument, besides letting advocates be heard, is an opportunity to hear from my colleagues. We don't confer before argument—the only time that we meet to discuss a case is when we gather to cast votes. Oral argument usually reveals which issues a colleague deems important and—sometimes—the way she is leaning. Questions at argument are not necessarily a reliable gauge of a justice's ultimate position on the merits. Court watchers (including the law clerks sitting in the courtroom) often guess incorrectly, because in the difficult cases that make it to the Court, there are hard questions to ask of both sides.

The chief justice announces the start of an argument, and Justice Clarence Thomas, currently the most senior associate justice, asks the first set of questions. After that, the floor is open, but with a guideline: when two justices start to talk at the same time, the convention is for the junior justice to yield to the senior justice. (Many internal protocols and practices at the Court—and in lower courts too—are governed by seniority.) As a result, some of my questions are asked and answered before I have a chance to speak. But often other questions develop during the course of argument, particularly as the lawyers answer queries from other justices. Most of my questions are of that variety.

After argument, my law clerks gather in my office to hash out the case. All four clerks, not only the clerk principally assigned to the case, are required to know the case well enough to discuss it intelligently and challenge my position. We debate the case from different angles, address various arguments, and probe the weak spots on both sides. I also try to use this as a teaching moment with the clerks, so we talk about the oral advocacy—which lawyers were effective (or ineffective) and why. Many of the clerks are interested in pursuing an appellate practice, so it benefits them to learn what good lawyers do.

After all of this input—the briefs, the research, oral argument, conversations with clerks—it's time to decide how I'll vote and what I'll say at conference. I return to the notes that I wrote before argument and edit them as needed based on subsequent developments. I also test my conclusion with self-reflection. Some cases involve statutes or executive orders that I like from a policy perspective; the opposite is true for others. To counteract my biases, I substitute a different policy into the legal frame. For example, if the question is whether a statute allows an administrative agency to adopt a regulation that I dislike, I imagine the agency using a statute with the same language to adopt a regulation that I like. If a free speech claim involves a message with which I sympathize, I plug in a message I disfavor. Not every case is susceptible to this exercise, but every case is susceptible to this question: Can I look the losing party and any dissenting colleagues in the eye and honestly defend my conclusion as my best understanding of what the law requires?

I expect case preparation to become quicker when I have been on the job for longer. Justice Scalia used to tell his clerks that the preliminary work took much longer in the beginning of his tenure, when he was seeing many issues for the first time. Once he had dealt with recurrent issues under the First Amendment, Fourth Amendment, and so on, he had a comfortable head start when he sat down with the briefs. By that point in his tenure, he had participated in and even written many of the precedents relevant to deciding the case. I have years to go before I'm at that stage, so at this point, preparing for my conference vote consumes a considerable amount of time.

Voting at Conference

Every Friday of an argument week, the justices meet for conference to discuss cases. We sit around a large rectangular table in order of seniority, and only the nine currently serving justices are present. (That, apparently, was difficult for Justice William O. Douglas, who tried to join the conference deliberations even after he had relinquished his seat.)[32] In the relatively rare event of a knock at the door, it is the job of the most junior justice—currently, Justice Ketanji Brown Jackson—to answer it and deliver the message (or a forgotten binder or sweater, as the case may be) to its intended recipient. The person at the door never enters herself.

The justices speak and vote in order of seniority, with the chief justice starting the process. This is different from the practice at the Seventh Circuit, where the most junior judge talked and voted first. I generally like the system at the Court, because it gives me the opportunity to consider and respond to what others have said. The flip side is that it can be frustrating to speak toward the end, because it limits my opportunity to persuade the seven justices who have already voted. (As a junior justice, Justice John Paul Stevens disliked the system for this very reason and advocated for a change of order.)[33] Still, colleagues do listen to those later in line and sometimes adjust their positions after the first round of voting is complete. Conference discussions are respectful and calm, and we do not interrupt one another.

A memo containing opinion assignments circulates at the end of the two-week argument session. At that point, based on the justices' votes across the cases, it is clear how many majority and dissenting opinions will be written, so the chief justice, working with other assigning justices, attempts to equitably distribute the work. My clerks wait eagerly for the assignment list to come around on Friday afternoons, to see both what I get and whether their predictions panned out.

The most senior justice in the majority assigns the majority opinion, and the most senior justice in dissent assigns the dissenting opinion. By virtue of his office, the chief justice holds the highest-ranking seat on the Court, regardless of how long he has served—so the chief justice assigns the opinion for whichever side he is on. If the chief justice voted with the minority, he coordinates with anyone assigning a majority opinion before distributing the assignment list to avoid allocating one justice two substantial opinions from the same sitting. Assignments in the most complex and high-profile cases typically go to the more senior justices, and it is the norm for the assigning justice to keep the highest-profile assignment for herself. For example, in the 2022 Term, cases involving affirmative action and voting rights were among the biggest; Chief Justice Roberts wrote the majority opinions in all of them.[34] That is also true for the highest-profile dissents. For instance, Justice Ruth Bader Ginsburg assigned herself the dissent in *Shelby County v. Holder*,[35] the voting rights case that launched her persona as "the Notorious RBG."[36]

One of the most important factors in an opinion assignment is the author's ability to hold a majority. A justice who expressed an idiosyncratic view at conference might produce a draft that others are unwilling to join—and that creates complications. It might prompt some members of the majority to reconsider their votes, potentially flipping the result. The majority opinion might have to be reassigned to another justice, creating delay and unanticipated work. Or members of the majority might find themselves at an impasse, with multiple draft opinions supporting the judgment, each on a different ground and none garnering five votes. (An opinion that receives only a plurality of votes—more than any other, but less than five—does not set a precedent that binds lower courts facing the same issue or the Court itself in future cases. It therefore does not advance the Court's goal of clarifying the law.) Sometimes, these outcomes are the inevitable result of disagreement or uncertainty that was evident even at conference. Other times, they can be avoided by an opinion that walks the line necessary to keep a majority on board.

Writing the Opinion

When I draft a majority opinion, I'm keenly aware that my task is to present fairly the agreement made at conference rather than to strike my own path. That's not to say that the author lacks discretion. The conference agreement is usually made in broad strokes, so the author inevitably has to decide how to resolve subsidiary issues. But even that must be done with an eye toward what others will accept. I'm writing for a multi-member court, not a court of one.

This task can be tricky. On the one hand, I don't want to lose the majority; on the other, I can't compromise my own principles. Threading the needle can mean relying on one argument rather than another so that more justices can join. This is critical when the majority is slim, because the loss of one vote could turn the opinion into a plurality or even a dissent. But it's important to me even when the margin is comfortable. If I can adjust an opinion to allow more colleagues to join it, I will, so long as the reasoning remains consistent with my own view and others who have joined the opinion agree. Skirting issues is sometimes the price of finding common ground—though it's frustrating to delete points I'd like to make.

Once I receive an opinion assignment, the clerk on the case writes the first draft. I provide some guidance and a rough outline of the opinion's structure. I also highlight any concerns that other justices have expressed, so that the clerk can tailor the initial draft accordingly. After the clerk writes the first draft, she circulates it to her co-clerks for input, makes revisions, and then gives it to me.

After reviewing the clerk's draft, I reread the briefs and relevant law; I also listen to the argument. Then I start writing. I'm usually able to keep at least some of the clerk's work, edited to reflect my style. But I always write portions from scratch—sometimes virtually the entire opinion, sometimes sections of it. This process is important, because the exercise of writing a legal argument reveals whether the analysis is sound. There is an expression that every judge uses at one time or another: "The opinion wouldn't write." The saying doesn't refer to writer's block. It means that trying to explain the argument in writing revealed that the initial conclusion rested on a flawed premise.

I typically begin with pen and paper because I write faster that way. At the keyboard, the ease of selecting and deleting text tempts me to perfect each sentence before composing the next—and it's demoralizing to sit at the computer for an hour with only a few sentences to show for it. I'm less inclined to be obsessive on a legal pad, and it's more efficient for me to establish the flow of the argument with a pen before I start typing. I try to write in a clear and straightforward manner so that a reader can easily follow the argument. Ideally, I'd like the opinion to be accessible to non-lawyers, but because legal analysis is often technical, that doesn't always work. My writing tends to be spare, perhaps to a fault. When I was a law clerk for Judge Laurence Silberman, he once called me into his office and barked, "Amy, don't be afraid of the adverb!" I've tried to take his advice. Still, I favor brief, clean sentences without extra words. My (obviously unattainable) target is more Hemingway than Dostoyevsky.

Depending on the complexity of the opinion, there can be extensive back-and-forth with the principal clerk on the case—we often exchange more than twenty drafts. We also have long conversations throughout the drafting. Our discussions can be high level, addressing legal theories, or quite granular, discussing word choice and verb tense. The writing process can take a few days or several weeks, depending on the complexity of the case and the press of other Court business.

Once I'm happy with the draft, I send it to the other three clerks for input. After more rounds of editing to account for their suggestions, the clerks go through the draft with a fine-tooth comb. They double-check every cited case to ensure it stands for the cited proposition. They check the record to confirm that the facts are accurate. And they review the parties' briefs to ensure the opinion correctly characterizes their arguments. Any discrepancies come to me for resolution.

As this description makes evident, clerks play an important role in this process. Still, the opinion is mine, and clerks learn early on that everything from outcome to word choice is my call, not theirs. I had to learn the same lesson when I was in their shoes. When I was a law clerk, one of the drafts of which I was proudest was one in which I vehemently disagreed with Justice Scalia. Though the justice and I had many debates about the case before it was time to draft, neither of us persuaded the other. (And believe me, I tried.) Obviously, his view controlled, so I retreated to my office to write it up his way. Justice Scalia didn't throw out casual compliments, so twenty-six years later, I vividly remember his praise for the draft. It wasn't a bad ending: I was disappointed that he had rejected my advice but proud to have represented his reasoning well. That's the law clerk's job.

Once I'm finished with the draft, it circulates to the other eight justices. Those who voted with the majority at conference sometimes join outright, sometimes ask for changes, and, in a close case, might wait to see what the dissent has to say. After we circulate an opinion, the clerks closely monitor the votes and celebrate when we cross the threshold for a majority. (That's five votes.) The best days are when "join" memos come in quickly and without requests for changes. Once, when other justices quickly joined a particularly tricky opinion of mine, my chambers celebrated with an impromptu bottle of champagne. More often, there are at least a few requested edits—some simple and others requiring significant work. The latter requests are *not* an occasion for champagne, because after the effort of producing the opinion, reworking it is painful. That said, I accommodate other justices when possible—as everyone does. Suggestions often improve the opinion, and even when I would prefer not to accept them, doing so is a sign of collegiality and respect.

Before I joined the Court, I was sometimes frustrated by an opinion's cryptic language or its failure to resolve fairly obvious points. Now I better appreciate that glossing over issues is often deliberate. If justices disagree about an issue that isn't necessary to the bottom line, it can be omitted from the opinion to keep a majority on board. Or, even if justices don't actively disagree, some may not be ready to commit to a position—perhaps because the briefs or lower court gave it too little attention. So there is often a good reason why the Court says less than a reader might want to know. Yet the story behind opinion language is not revealed until internal deliberations are made public, and that doesn't usually happen until many years after the opinion is published. (Sometimes it never happens—on his deathbed, Justice Hugo Black instructed his son to burn some of his records.)[37] Notes and correspondence are preserved in a justice's papers, which typically remain sealed for a prescribed period following the justice's death—often until the last justice with whom the deceased served is no longer on the Court. Then the library to which the justice has donated the papers (for example, the Library of Congress) typically opens the boxes to readers interested in learning what happened behind the scenes—at least insofar as it was recorded.

I have been talking about opinions that I circulate, but of course I receive them from other justices too. When a draft arrives, my clerks and I read it and discuss whether I should join outright or request changes first. (Another occasion on which the clerks offer input but the decision is obviously mine.) As a rule, I request edits only when I think an assertion is wrong or might confuse the law. Pretty much everything else falls into a category that I tell my clerks is "author's choice." I might think that the opinion could be strengthened with additional arguments or that certain ideas could be better expressed. Maybe I'm objectively right; maybe it's a matter of personal taste. Regardless, no one reads opinions from other chambers with an editor's pen. If I really think there are gaps that the author didn't fill, I can write a concurrence.

Unlike the author of a majority opinion, the author of a concurrence has the freedom to express her own views without worrying about keeping others on board. I write them in a few situations. If I think that lower courts might interpret the majority opinion too broadly or too narrowly, I might use a concurrence to emphasize the scope of the Court's holding.[38] I've also written them to explain my own thinking about an aspect of the majority opinion or to identify areas of the law that could benefit from development by advocates and scholars.[39] And if I refrain from joining part of the majority opinion, I usually write a concurrence to explain why.[40]

If there is a dissent, it circulates after the majority opinion. The principal dissent is assigned, but other justices can add their own dissenting opinions. Like the author of a majority opinion, the author of the principal dissent generally tries to accommodate others in her camp where possible. She has been assigned the opinion to speak for the group, and, like majority assignments, dissent assignments are made with an eye toward equitably spreading the work. This aim is defeated when the assigned justice writes a dissent that others can't join, forcing them to write their own opinions. That said, justices can—and often do—choose to publish their own opinions adding points that are particularly important to them. For instance, Justice Thomas and I both dissented in *Counterman v. Colorado*, a case addressing how the Free Speech Clause applies to threats uttered by a stalker.[41] (We shared the view that the majority's approach gave threats more protection than the First Amendment required.) I wrote the principal dissent, which Justice Thomas joined; he added an opinion, speaking only for himself, that criticized a precedent on which the majority relied.

Justices do not frequently change positions after opinions circulate, but it happens. Flipped votes would be disruptive if they occurred too often. But the case isn't over until the judgment issues and, importantly, until the justice who has authored the opinion has gone through the valuable exercise of writing the analysis. When I was a law professor, I reviewed the papers of Justice William Brennan, Jr., at the Library of Congress and came across a memo that I have recalled as a justice. Justice Brennan had joined a majority opinion written by Justice Scalia—but when Justice John Paul Stevens circulated a dissent, Justice Brennan changed his mind. Apologetically, he told Justice Scalia that he had to withdraw his join.[42] Justice Scalia responded graciously: "If I have any criticism of the process around here, it is that we feel too constrained by our conference vote against being persuaded by a dissent. Go in peace."[43]

Bench Statements

Once an opinion is finalized, it is released in hard copy and on the Court's website. Just before online publication, the author of the majority opinion reads a summary of it from the bench. These "bench statements" are a throwback to an era in which they were the Court's primary mechanism for making opinions public.

In the Court's early days, a justice assigned to deliver an opinion would often—though not invariably—draft a manuscript of it. While that sounds odd to modern ears, the Court had no in-house means of publishing opinions, so they were not officially distributed. Because a polished manuscript was not strictly necessary, the write-up functioned more like a script for the bench announcement, which was the main event. Moreover, the surviving internal correspondence of justices on the Marshall Court suggests that justices rarely circulated draft opinions to one another before announcing them.[44] Authors therefore enjoyed far more leeway than they do today.

The only reason we have copies of the Court's early opinions is that private citizens undertook the task of producing them. When a justice announced an opinion from the bench, members of the audience—including counsel, court reporters, and newspaper correspondents—took copious notes. Court reporters, who were enterprising businessmen rather than employees of the Court, collected these notes and, when available, the justices' own notes to reproduce opinions for sale to the public.[45] When a justice had a complete manuscript to share, the court reporter's task was easier.[46] Given this haphazard process, it is often difficult to evaluate the accuracy of early publications. But by the last quarter of the nineteenth century, the federal government was funding publication, and the Court had a reliable reporting system in place.[47]

Still, bench announcements persisted. And in a practice that sounds more painful to me than days-long oral arguments, the justices read their opinions *in full*—sometimes including footnotes.[48] That continued until 1971, when Chief Justice Burger persuaded his colleagues to deliver summary statements instead.[49]

Given that the public has immediate access to opinions on the internet, bench statements are not the mechanism by which an opinion hits the streets. But for those present in the courtroom, an announcement gives an opinion life that it lacks on paper. And for me, speaking directly to those gathered in the courtroom is a good reminder that opinions have real-world consequences. Everyone in the majority, and the author in particular, has to publicly stand by an opinion, even if it has a tough result. My very first bench statement put me in exactly that position. In *Arellano v. McDonough*, the Court's interpretation of a statute denied disability benefits to a veteran who had missed a filing deadline.[50] The Court was unanimous; the issue was cut-and-dried. But when we entered the courtroom, my heart sank: by coincidence, the courtroom was packed with military lawyers who were being sworn in to the Supreme Court bar. So I was announcing a loss for a veteran in a courtroom full of men and women who were serving in the armed forces. It was bad luck of the draw, and it took discipline to maintain eye contact with the crowd. The episode was a good reminder, though, that the Court's work is not merely academic—it affects real people, often in profound ways.

Announcing the Court's opinion is routine, but justices can also announce dissents. That is rare, done only when a justice is particularly passionate about the issue. For instance, Justice Sotomayor read a dissenting statement in *Students for Fair Admissions, Inc. v. President and Fellows of Harvard College*, which held that race-based university admissions programs violate the Equal Protection Clause.[51] (It is even rarer for a justice to read a concurring statement from the bench, but Justice Thomas did so in *Students for Fair Admissions.*) Justice Kennedy delivered an oral dissent in *Hill v. Colorado*, which rejected a free speech challenge to a law restricting protests outside of abortion clinics.[52] Justice Ginsburg famously wore a "dissent collar" on days that she announced a dissent, so the audience knew one was coming as soon as she entered the courtroom.

One who follows the Court casually might be under the impression that practically every case is decided with the appointees of a Republican president on one side and appointees of a Democratic president on the other. While that breakdown sometimes occurs, presenting it as the norm grossly distorts the Court's work. The statistics of the Court's 2022 and 2023 Terms, during which there were six Republican appointees and three Democratic appointees, offer a snapshot.

In the 2022 Term, the Court was unanimous in about 47 percent of argued cases.[53] That's in line with the average rate of unanimity over the last decade, and significantly above the average percentage of unanimity over the last seventy-five years.[54] About another 9 percent were *almost* unanimous, decided with only a single justice in dissent.[55] So more than half of the cases on the Court's docket were decided in total or almost total agreement. In the non-unanimous decisions from that term, there were twenty different lineups. Only five of the Court's fifty-eight decisions broke down by party of the appointing president.[56]

In the 2023 Term, the Court was unanimous in about 45 percent of argued cases.[57] That's also in line with the average rate of unanimity over the last decade, and again above the average percentage of unanimity over the last seventy-five years. What's more, about another 9 percent were *almost* unanimous, with only one or two justices in dissent.[58] That means that more than half of the cases were decided in total, or near total, agreement. In the non-unanimous decisions from that term, there were nineteen different line-ups, and only eleven cases broke down by party of the appointing president.[59]

In sum, the decision-making process is complex. Sometimes, it takes justices to the same conclusion; sometimes, they land in different places. Either way, all nine justices actively work on the legal analysis from the time the briefs are filed until the decision issues. The nature of the work is captured by the symbol of the tortoise, which appears in multiple spots around the Court. The work is not hasty—instead, it's slow and steady.

A bronze tortoise at the Court. (Collection of the Supreme Court of the United States.)

Chapter 5

LAW CLERKS IN CHAMBERS

IT'S IMPOSSIBLE to describe the decision-making process—or really, life at the Court—without telling you about the law clerks who work for the justices. Their behind-the-scenes job has inspired best-selling fiction. What if a justice falls into a coma and gives his law clerk power of attorney, leaving the clerk to resolve a case involving a weaponized virus?[1] Or if, after the suicide of a judge, a clerk uncovers mysteries about a secret court?[2] What if a clerk is blackmailed and relies on a co-clerk to undo the damage?[3] And maybe a clerk could have changed the course of the internment of Japanese Americans during World War II.[4]

The reality is much less dramatic, but nonetheless exciting. When asked about my own experience as a law clerk for Justice Scalia, I used to say, "All jobs have been downhill since." I recall how it felt as a twenty-six-year-old to walk into the majestic marble building, awe-inspiring in itself; to bump into justices walking in the halls; and to sit in the beautiful courtroom for oral arguments. And those were just the trappings—the substance was no less incredible, though its importance made it far more stressful.

The general job description of a clerk is the same across chambers, though every justice obviously has her own way of doing things. Clerks assist justices in screening cases, preparing for oral argument, drafting opinions, and reviewing opinions circulated by other justices. They therefore have a hand in the process from start to finish, from case selection to the issuance of the judgment. To be clear, every decision along the way, no matter how small, is the responsibility of the justice. But clerks make arguments, raise suggestions, perform research, and coordinate chambers work with administrative offices within the Court. I interact with my clerks almost daily.

The task of reviewing petitions for certiorari—the documents asking the Court to grant review of a case on the merits—is an example. Most of the justices participate in the "cert pool," which divides the work across the clerks from those chambers. In the 2022 Term, for example, the Court considered 4,186 petitions,[5] so each clerk in the pool was responsible for reviewing roughly 149 of them. For each of her assigned petitions, the clerk writes a memo offering a summary, analysis, and recommendation about whether the Court should agree to hear the case. Some justices opt out of the pool, instead tasking their own clerks to review every cert petition. So while the work of screening certiorari petitions is common to all clerks, its execution varies. The same is true for other tasks too: justices make different choices about how to use their clerks in preparing cases and drafting opinions.

Regardless of the details, it is the rare law clerk who finds her job uninspiring. When I wrote pool memos, I was keenly aware that eight Supreme Court justices would read them. (Justice Stevens didn't participate in the cert pool.) It was intimidating to draft and edit opinions for Justice Scalia, who was an excellent—and exacting—writer. I lived in fear of making a grammatical error. But my greater concern was making a mistake of more consequence, like missing something in the record that it had been my job to find. No clerk wants to let her justice down. That has always been true: in the 1939 Term, a clerk for Justice Felix Frankfurter fled town after making a mistake, returning only once he was sure that the justice had forgiven him.[6] In what must have been quite a scene, the clerk literally crawled, humiliated, to Justice Frankfurter, who embraced him.[7]

Still, the stress of the job did not tarnish my experience. The work was important, and I knew that nothing remotely as interesting lay ahead for me as a junior associate at a law firm. I was learning from one of the most talented lawyers and writers in the legal profession. And I was working with other clerks whose company I enjoyed—not only my three co-clerks in the Scalia chambers, but also the other clerks in the building. It was a happy year.

IN SOME RESPECTS, the experience of a judicial clerkship resembles a postgraduate fellowship. Law clerks, particularly in the federal appellate courts, are almost invariably recent law graduates. They typically begin a court of appeals clerkship right after law school; those who clerk on the Supreme Court usually come straight from their prior clerkships, occasionally with an intervening year or two in practice. So law clerks are not seasoned lawyers—they are very much still learning. That's probably a function of the clerkship's historical roots: judges began hiring law clerks over a century ago, when the apprentice model of legal education was still common.[8] Consistent with this model, a one-year appellate clerkship allows novice lawyers an opportunity to hone their analytic and writing skills under the supervision of an expert in the field, alongside co-clerks of similar talent and experience. Clerks also have the opportunity to learn firsthand how the court in which they work operates, which benefits them when they enter practice. All this makes clerking a coveted résumé credential.

Given that clerks participate in important work, you might be surprised that they are so inexperienced. You would not be alone; I get that reaction a lot. A client needing advice on a high-stakes legal problem would hire a senior partner, not the most junior associate at a law firm. Why would judges choose the very greenest lawyers as advisers?

Because clerks neither have nor should expect to have the decision-making role that normally accompanies experience. In law practice, experience brings independence—once a junior lawyer has performed a legal task enough times with supervision, she will rightfully expect to be allowed to do it independently. A senior lawyer will send a subordinate to handle a trial, negotiate a plea deal, or conference with co-counsel. In judicial chambers, by contrast, clerks don't gradually take the reins. They never take the bench, rule on motions, attend conference, or cast a vote. They perform groundwork and give advice, but they never call the shots. The primary qualifications for discharging that role are excellence in research, legal analysis, and writing, all academic skills learned in law school. Matters that require judgment refined by experience—like whether to grant review in a case and how to decide it—are the judge's domain.

The disparity of experience between judge and clerk, combined with the brevity of the job, helps ensure that responsibility is allocated as it should be. It reduces a judge's temptation to rely excessively on the advice of clerks, as well as a clerk's frustration at playing a limited role.

In their ideal form, clerkships blossom into much more than a professional opportunity. Once hired, law clerks become part of the judge's "clerk family." (Justice Scalia affectionately called us his "clerkerati.") Long after the term ends, a clerk remains connected to her judge; it is common to refer to a former Supreme Court clerk as, say, an "O'Connor clerk" or a "Breyer clerk." The same is true of court of appeals clerks (like "Sutton clerks" from the Sixth Circuit) and district court clerks (like "Friedrich clerks" from the District of Columbia). Clerks gather to see their judge, as well as one another, at periodic reunions; the clerks' shared connection to their judge creates a network of friends and acquaintances spanning the judge's years on the bench. Granted, personality differences make some judges less inclined than others to maintain these connections. But clerkships with those who do are viewed as the most desirable. (Clerkships with difficult judges gain the reputation as jobs to avoid.) At its best, the judge-clerk relationship extends beyond its end date into lifelong mentorship marked by affection on both sides.

My own transition to the bench gives a sense of that longevity. Twenty years after my appellate clerkship with Judge Silberman, I was nominated

With Judge Silberman at my Supreme Court investiture. (Photo by Fred Schilling, Collection of the Supreme Court of the United States.)

to a seat on the Seventh Circuit. (By that time, Justice Scalia had passed away.) During my confirmation hearing, Judge Silberman sat immediately behind me, lending moral support. The hearing—my first experience in the rough-and-tumble of politics—was much more aggressive than I anticipated, and I walked out of the hearing room a little shell-shocked. Judge Silberman, by contrast, was exhilarated. Having lived in Washington for most of his career, he was not only comfortable in that milieu—he loved it. He wanted to go over the hearing blow by blow in the middle of the crowded hallway. (I had to duck into a side room to take a few deep breaths first.) His role in the process continued beyond the hearing. After I was confirmed, he traveled to South Bend to administer the oath at my investiture. When I was nominated to the Supreme Court, he was in the Rose Garden, and after I was confirmed, he was present at my swearing-in. To the end, the judge exhibited fatherly concern, calling to make sure that both Jesse and I were taking the need for security seriously as threats escalated. When Judge Silberman died in 2022, his funeral was packed not only with his many friends and family, but also with his many law clerks. He left an indelible imprint on all of us.

That's just a snippet from my own experience, which is repeated throughout the federal judiciary. My experience is shared by many—sometimes down to details. Judge Joan Larsen of the Sixth Circuit, whose court of appeals confirmation hearing was held jointly with mine, sat at the adjoining table, also accompanied by the judge for whom she had clerked.

THE ROLE OF a Supreme Court clerk has not changed much since I worked for Justice Scalia more than two decades ago. Indeed, the substance was the same decades before that, even though it was carried out with typewriters and carbon copies rather than computers and copy machines. Several justices had the experience of clerking on the Court themselves and now oversee their clerks performing the same work they once did. (During the first few weeks I walked into my chambers, which has the same layout as Justice Scalia's did, I found myself instinctively turning left toward the clerks' office, where I used to work, rather than right toward the justice's office, where I now spend my days.) On the current Court, six of the nine sitting justices clerked on the Court (Chief Justice John Roberts; Justices Elena Kagan, Neil Gorsuch, Brett Kavanaugh, Ketanji Brown Jackson;

and me). Justice Byron White (who served from 1962 to 1993) was the first justice to have clerked for another justice.[9] Other former justices—Chief Justice William H. Rehnquist, Justice John Paul Stevens, and Justice Stephen Breyer—also clerked on the Court.[10]

Yet for the first century of the Court's existence, there was no analog to a law clerk.[11] In fact, the justices had virtually no chambers staff at all. The Court had a small number of institutional employees like the clerk of court, the marshal, and the reporter of decisions.[12] But Congress had authorized only one staff member for each justice: a messenger, whose primary responsibility was to run opinions and memos back and forth between the justices' homes, which were scattered across the city.[13] The Court had no building until 1935, so the justices worked exclusively from home, which complicated the exchange of confidential documents—and before the telephone, complicated communication, period.

Justice Horace Gray (1882–1902) was the first justice to hire a law clerk.[14] Desiring help but lacking an official budget, he paid for the clerk out of his own pocket. Continuing a practice he had begun as a Massachusetts state court judge,[15] Justice Gray relied on his half brother, the respected Harvard law professor John Chipman Gray, to select a suitable graduate to work for him each year.[16] Though the Gray clerks were called "private secretaries," their tasks resembled the work of a modern clerk: digesting the briefs, conducting research, debating the merits with the justice, writing first drafts of opinions, and reviewing circulations from other chambers.[17] Nor was the relationship between the justice and his clerks confined to the law. When Justice Gray began courting the daughter of another justice (boldness hard to imagine today), he turned to his clerk, Samuel Williston (later a famous law professor), for advice about the ring.[18]

In 1886, Congress finally appropriated funds for each justice to hire an additional employee. The Court's docket had surged in the wake of the Civil War, and the increased workload spurred pleas for help. Coming to the Court's aid, Attorney General Augustus Garland advised Congress to authorize "a secretary or law clerk" for each justice, emphasizing that cabinet officials and senators had comparable assistance.[19] Congress quickly agreed, authorizing a "stenographic clerk for the Chief Justice and for each associate justice of the Supreme Court."[20] Justice Gray's clerks went on the federal payroll, and other justices began hiring "stenographic clerks" of their own.

In filling this position, some justices—including Justice Louis Brandeis (who had clerked for Justice Gray on the Massachusetts Supreme Judicial Court), Justice Oliver Wendell Holmes, and Justice Benjamin Cardozo—emulated the Gray model. For example, Justice Brandeis (1916–1939) viewed his law clerks as junior partners who worked alongside him.[21] His law clerks conducted extensive legal research, even if that meant traveling to the Library of Congress to find books that the justice would describe from memory by their color and size.[22] In addition, they drafted opinions and then edited and critiqued the justice's revised version.[23] Law clerks assisted Justice Holmes (1902–1932) by performing limited legal research and reviewing cert petitions.[24] And law clerks for Justice Cardozo (1932–1938) reviewed cert petitions and drafted bench memos for oral arguments, though they did not draft opinions.[25] To be sure, the law clerks who served Justices Brandeis, Holmes, and Cardozo performed nonlegal tasks too, but much of their work resembled the work that clerks do today.

Other justices in that period, however, used the appropriated funds to hire secretaries who functioned as true stenographers. This "clerical" model of the Supreme Court clerk dominated in the late nineteenth and early twentieth centuries. It was not until around 1940 that a majority of the justices began to give their clerks real legal work, as Justices Brandeis, Holmes, and Cardozo had done decades earlier.[26] Given the thin historical record, it is difficult to determine the exact duties of these clerical stenographers. Based on the information we have, they probably used shorthand to write down opinions, transcribed those opinions on typewriters, proofread them, and checked citations.[27] In 1905, Justice David J. Brewer (1890–1910) crisply summarized the role of a stenographer: he was "simply a typewriter, a fountain pen, used by the judge to facilitate his work."[28]

Many of the law clerks in the late nineteenth and early twentieth centuries—whether given legal responsibilities, clerical tasks, or both—had legal training.[29] Some of these clerks went to law school during their service and others may have taken side jobs as stenographers and attorneys.[30] Some stayed for a year, while others worked for up to eighteen years.[31] Hours could be long and irregular—a clerk to Justice John Marshall Harlan (1877–1911) met the justice at night after social events and worked until five in the morning.[32] The clerks would work in the homes of the justices and perform tasks as varied as typing and paying bills.[33] Demonstrating the devotion to a justice that was expected of a clerk, it was the norm that he be single.[34] As late as the 1940s, Philip Graham, later the owner of *The Washington Post*, asked his boss, Justice Felix Frankfurter (1939–1962), for permission to get married.[35]

Criteria to clerk for Justice Holmes included the ability to "deal with the certiorari, balance his checkbook, and listen to his tall talk."[36] Holmes joked that he hired new clerks every year because "he liked to continue to tell his fund of stories; this way, he could do so without being accused of repeating himself."[37] While Holmes might seek their advice and they would work on cert petitions, according to Alger Hiss, Holmes's former clerk (later a Soviet spy), "the function of the secretary was rather that of a nineteenth-century private secretary in upper-class British life."[38] They might cut coupons, go for neighborhood walks, tell mystery stories, be assigned to debate the Old Testament with the justice, or—in his old age—drive him to view his future burial spot in Arlington National Cemetery.[39]

Congress authorized the justices to hire a second clerk in the 1920s and added a third in the 1940s, which increased the assignment of substantive work and made the jobs more resemble those of modern-day clerks.[40] Review of cert petitions became a staple of a clerk's day-to-day work.[41] Justices continued to give clerks legal tasks, using them to draft opinions and bench memoranda.[42] Clerks performed nonlegal duties too, like Chief Justice Harlan Fiske Stone's (1925–1946) requirement that they attend his wife's weekly tea receptions and "be agreeable" there.[43] In the 1970s justices received authorization to hire four law clerks, the same number that they employ today.[44] Clerks have come from a variety of law schools, but Harvard and Yale have been the most heavily represented over the years.[45] Former clerks have gone on to successful and often illustrious careers as academics and advocates; they have also served in government as secretaries of state, U.S. attorneys general, U.S. solicitors general, and members of Congress.[46]

While the role of a modern law clerk would be unrecognizable to many of the "stenographic clerks" of the late nineteenth and early twentieth centuries, it would look more familiar to a clerk of the 1960s. By then, it was the norm across chambers for clerks to perform cert work, prepare bench memoranda, and write opinion drafts.[47] Occasionally, however, unique circumstances brought unique responsibilities. Clerks for Justice Abe Fortas (1965–1969) recommended how he should deal with the Warren Commission report and drove the justice to the White House to help President Johnson select bombing targets in Vietnam.[48] More awkwardly, the clerks of Justice John Marshall Harlan II (1955–1971) had to read and describe pornography to the justice in certain First Amendment cases, because Justice Harlan's eyesight was failing.[49]

THE EXPERIENCE OF a clerk, of course, depends to a significant extent on the temperament and habits of her boss. Unfortunately, not all justices have been model supervisors. Justice James McReynolds (1914–1941) forbade clerks from smoking, drinking, or going on dates.[50] The justice's messenger informed a newly hired clerk, "You will also be fired if the justice ever calls up his apartment during the day and finds that you are not there. You cannot eat at the justice's, and you will have to walk six or seven blocks to a restaurant at Eighteenth and Columbia Road."[51] Justice William O. Douglas (1939–1975) was also a notoriously harsh boss.[52]

The experience was quite different for law clerks of Justice Cardozo. As one reported, "When I found a few serviceable statutory precedents from colonial statutes for the Social Security case, the justice acted as though I had just discovered nuclear fission."[53] Justice Frankfurter was famous for the relationships he cultivated with his clerks. Legend has it that he and his clerks would spend hours in chambers debating everything under the sun, including legal history, current events, constitutional law, and music.[54] These arguments, tempered by respect on both sides, reverberated throughout the halls of the Court, and they inspired lifelong friendships.[55] As one former clerk stated of Justice Frankfurter, "It is hard not to reciprocate the affection of someone who cares passionately for you."[56] Clerks of Chief Justice Earl Warren (1953–1969) watched football with him and socialized over drinks.[57] Justice Harlan II's clerks snuck him cigarettes and bourbon as he was dying.[58] After Justice Hugo Black (1937–1971) was widowed, two of his clerks lived with him for a year.[59] Chief Justice Rehnquist (1972–2005) played a weekly game of tennis with his clerks (the ability to play was practically a prerequisite for the job), and he was an avid player of charades when he hosted clerks at his home.[60] Justice White remarked that his criteria were that clerks "would be fun to have around and could get along with me."[61] This extended to athletic competitions; Justice White, a former pro football player, broke several pairs of the clerks' glasses playing basketball in the Court gym—known as "the highest court in the land" because it is located on the building's top floor.[62]

Similar stories of other recent justices and their clerks abound. Justice Sandra Day O'Connor (1981–2006) reportedly loved to play matchmaker, especially for her clerks. One former clerk tells the story of how Justice O'Connor pushed him to propose.[63] Justice O'Connor also routinely took her law clerks on field trips, even fishing with them on the Potomac River.[64] Sharing her passion with her clerks, Justice Ruth Bader Ginsburg (1993–2020) often took them to the opera, sometimes even acting out the dramatic scenes for them before the show.[65] Every year, Justice Anthony Kennedy (1988–2018) and his clerks went to a baseball game with two other chambers.[66] Justice David H. Souter (1990–2009), a gifted storyteller, would share anecdotes most afternoons over coffee with his clerks about his beloved New Hampshire.[67] The upshot is that Supreme Court clerks have a rare—and special—opportunity to see the human side of their justices.

While I was clerking, *Washingtonian* magazine published an article entitled "Clerks Rate Supremes as Bosses."[68] Relying on anonymous interviews with clerks, the author ranked the justices from best to worst.[69] Justice Scalia came in first place. As the article put it, the Scalia chambers was the "intellectual nerve center" of the Court, where, in the words of one clerk, "Every battle is fought out like an Italian street fight."[70] I wasn't the source of the quote, but it's an apt description. Though one clerk took the lead in helping the justice with a case, all four of us were expected to know it well enough to debate it. We gathered in his office while he hammered us with questions, exploring the issues from all angles, which required us to be as articulate as the advocates who presented it to the Court. If Justice Scalia was assigned to write the opinion, the lead clerk wrote the first draft—and then watched it transformed when the justice got his hands on it. Sometimes, that meant watching over his shoulder while he typed his signature lines. He was a master at turns of phrase, not to mention musical references. My term, he used a scene from *West Side Story* in a First Amendment opinion.[71]

We were always eager to go out to lunch with Justice Scalia, but none of us wanted to be the one to invite him. Around lunchtime, the last to make the "not it" sign by touching his nose was charged with asking the justice if he was free. When he was, we piled into the car and headed to his favorite restaurant, A.V. Ristorante Italiano. I had spent a lot of time at A.V.'s the previous year, because it was also a favorite of Judge Silberman's. The restaurant was a dive with character: the walls were lined with signed pictures of movie stars and politicians, and the patio had a replica of Rome's Neptune Fountain. At tables with checkered red cloths, the justice ate anchovy pizza and sipped red wine; we usually skipped the wine (and, for that matter, the anchovies). Conversations spanned family, current events, hunting, and opera. It was difficult to keep up with the breadth of the justice's knowledge and interests—for opera and hunting, I didn't even try.

A.V.'s closed many years ago, so it's not a destination for my clerks and me. Instead, we eat in one of the Court's interior courtyards (in good weather) or the upstairs clerk office (in bad). That office is furnished with couches and chairs that I brought from South Bend, but no table—so we balance food on our laps while talking about family, current events, books, and Netflix queues. We also celebrate birthdays, holidays, the end of term, engagements, births, and other significant events. I keep a stash of champagne on hand so that we can throw together a celebration when happy news unexpectedly arrives. We also go on chambers field trips—we've been to museums, the Virginia countryside, and, when I was on the Seventh Circuit, one of my clerks who was an avid sportsman arranged for us to shoot sporting clays at a nearby range. Every year, Jesse and I host the clerks and their significant others at our home for a New Orleans–style dinner, a tradition we began many years ago when I was a law professor hosting students.

Justices typically hold reunions with their clerks, a practice dating back at least to Justice Stanley Reed in the 1940s.[72] The type of gathering depends upon the preference and personality of the justice, as well as the longevity of the justice on the Court (and the corresponding number of clerks). For example, Justice Scalia hosted an annual black-tie dinner at the Supreme Court; other justices do more casual, family-style events. My traditions are just beginning. For the first few years, we had informal reunions, including one to celebrate the retirement of my longtime assistant, who is beloved by my whole clerk family. Now that the years have expanded the size of my crew, we have shifted to a dinner at the Court. Clerks develop relationships with one another and their justice's family over time, so reunions can continue after the justice passes away.[73] The Scalia clerks still gather.

A nice tradition at the Court is that justices get to know one another's clerks. Each justice has lunch once a term with each set of clerks in the other eight chambers. The justice chooses the location, and, if it involves takeout or order-in, the clerks pick up the tab. The events reflect the preferences of the justice. As a clerk, I particularly remember having sushi with Justice Breyer, tea with Justice Ginsburg, burgers with Chief Justice Rehnquist, and a brown bag lunch with Justice Souter in the Court's cafeteria. Thus far, I have chosen to have brown bag lunches with clerks in the Natalie Cornell Rehnquist Dining Room on the ground floor of the Court, because it is a beautiful room that I want the clerks to see during their year in the building.

JUSTICE LEWIS POWELL said that law clerk selection "was among the most important decisions he made during a term."[74] Indeed it is—and not only because they are important to the Court's work. I consider my law clerks part of my long-term judicial family. Pictures of each class of clerks—from both the Supreme Court and Seventh Circuit—hang on my wall. The relationship lasts long beyond their one year in chambers. Law kicks it off, but affection makes it last.

2024 Barrett Clerk Reunion at the Court. (Photo by Fred Schilling, Collection of the Supreme Court of the United States.)

Chapter 6

DOCKETED

THE SUPREME Court is more than the people who work there—it has its own institutional identity. Most obviously, it has an imposing physical structure: just as the president is associated with the White House and Congress with the Capitol, the Court is visibly tied to a stately building in Washington, D.C. Its existence, though—like that of the other branches—depends not on bricks and mortar, but on the laws that define its power. In this chapter, I'll tell you mostly about the latter. But before I delve into the Court's docket, I'll give you a glimpse of the building that houses the work.

For me, the steps are what I see in my mind's eye when I think of the Court. That's partly because they're striking and partly because of their place in my memory. Most vivid is the role they played in my investiture ceremony. By tradition, the chief justice escorts a new justice down the front steps of the Supreme Court after his or her investiture. When it was my turn, I was mainly focused on not tripping. The chief justice had warned me that bright sun bouncing off the white marble steps makes it difficult to see where one stops and the next begins. That was true—and the last thing I wanted was to topple down the stairs in my high heels for all the camera crews to see. Fortunately, I made it without incident. I met Jesse at the bottom of the stairs, where photographers captured a moment in which we were fortunately both smiling with eyes open and looking in the same direction. That photo sits in our living room along with pictures of our children from family vacations and First Communions.

I had traveled these steps many times as a twenty-six-year-old law

With Jesse after making it to the bottom of the steps. (Photo by Fred Schilling, Collection of the Supreme Court of the United States.)

clerk, most often when heading out for a run. (The steps were much easier to handle in athletic shoes.) I certainly never imagined I would one day walk those steps as a justice. But now, as then, the building awes me.

Finished in 1935, the building was a significant upgrade from the Court's previous quarters. When the federal government moved from Philadelphia to Washington, D.C., the White House (then called the President's House) and Capitol Building were (almost) ready for the president and Congress. No provision, however, had been made for the Supreme Court. The branch of government that Alexander Hamilton described as "least dangerous" was plainly also the least significant.[1] At the last minute, Congress set aside some of its space for the Supreme Court, which bounced around various rooms in the Capitol Building (and, when displaced by the War of 1812, even met in a private home) over the next eight years.[2] Things got a little better after that. Congress built a room in the basement now known as the Old Supreme Court Chamber, where the Court met from 1819 to 1860. Then the Court moved upstairs to the Old Senate Chamber. The Court did not get its own place until it was almost 150 years old.

The Supreme Court Building was the project of Chief Justice William Howard Taft, the only chief justice who also served as president. (Perhaps, having headed two branches, Taft thought it important to underscore that the Court is coequal to the president and Congress.) Now, rather than borrowing space from Congress, the Court stands directly across the street, housed in a beautiful building of its own. Unfortunately, Taft did not live to see the completion of the Court's new home, which was dedicated by his successor, Chief Justice Charles Evans Hughes. It is a sign of the history and continuity of the Court that the sofa in my office once belonged to Hughes. I wound up with it quite by accident: after retrieving furniture from storage for frugality's sake, I discovered that even the Court's hand-me-downs are special.

Now for the docket. While the trappings of the Court have changed dramatically since its early days, its power has always been defined by Article III of the Constitution, which establishes the Supreme Court and authorizes Congress to create other federal courts if it chooses. Article III also describes the judicial power vested in the federal courts—first and foremost, to decide cases arising under federal law. At the same time, however, Congress has significant say-so about how much of that power the federal courts can exercise. The judiciary's structure and docket therefore result from a mix of constitutional and statutory law. That combination answers one of the questions nonlawyers most frequently ask me: How do cases make it to the Supreme Court?

I'LL START WITH a quick look at the structure of the federal judicial system. The Constitution creates the Supreme Court but doesn't specify how many justices serve. The number is within Congress's control and has varied over time. In the beginning, there were six seats, all filled with the nominees of George Washington. (Congress was apparently not worried about tie votes.) It briefly dipped to five during the tenure of John Adams.[3] Then, as the country increased in size, so did the Court. Over the next seventy-four years, Congress raised the number of justices to seven, nine, and eventually ten. That was the peak. In 1866, during the heated politics of Reconstruction, Congress reduced the number of justices to seven to prevent Andrew Johnson from nominating any new members. Since 1869, however, the number has held constant at nine. As prescribed by the Constitution, each justice is nominated by the president and confirmed by the Senate.

The Supreme Court sits at the top of the federal judiciary, which is structured like a triangle: widest at the bottom (involving the most judges deciding the most cases) and narrowest at the top (involving the fewest judges deciding the fewest cases). As it currently stands, Congress has established ninety-four district courts (each state has at least one), thirteen courts of appeals (twelve covering a defined geographic area and one dedicated to specific topics like patent law), and one Supreme Court. The judiciary's caseload is similarly distributed: the district courts hear the most cases, the courts of appeals review a subset of those, and the Supreme Court hears a still smaller subset. So a case filed in the federal system typically starts in a federal district court; the losing party can ask a court of appeals to review the district court's judgment; and the party who loses in the court of appeals can ask the Supreme Court to review the court of appeals' judgment.

Most of the Court's federal cases travel this route. But a handful actually *begin* in the Supreme Court—most commonly, matters in which one state sues another over borders or natural resources. One of my first opinions for the Court dealt with Florida's claim that Georgia consumed more than its fair share of water from interstate rivers and caused harm to the Florida ecosystem.[4] Historically, some of the Court's original jurisdiction cases have involved suits by a state against an individual. In one notable case, the Court addressed whether Texas had seceded from the Union during the Civil War.[5] The short answer is no: as a matter of constitutional law, the relationship between a state and the United States is "indissoluble," so Texas's declarations of secession "were absolutely null."[6]

The Supreme Court also hears cases from state supreme courts—but only on issues of federal law. In our system, states have independent authority to adopt, enforce, and interpret their own laws. For the United States Supreme Court to tell a state supreme court that it misinterpreted its own state law would be an affront to the powers that belong to the state. Besides, why would the federal Supreme Court be better suited than a state supreme court to interpret state law? Unless a state judicial decision turns on a federal question, state courts get the last word.

Certiorari

Both federal district courts and courts of appeals are obligated to decide every case that comes to them, so long as the case falls within their jurisdiction—the range of cases that Congress has properly authorized them to hear. The Supreme Court used to have a similar obligation, but as one court fielding appeals from all over the country, its caseload became unmanageable. In 1925, Congress expanded the Supreme Court's discretionary jurisdiction but continued to require it to hear certain categories of cases. As litigation around the country increased, so did the Court's caseload—and by the 1980s, Chief Justice Burger warned that unless something was done, the Court would not be able to do its job "in keeping with the standards the people of this country have a right to expect."[7] Congress responded by making the Court's jurisdiction almost entirely discretionary.[8]

Whether appeals come from a federal court or a state supreme court, nearly all arrive at the Court via a petition for certiorari—a request that the Court review a lower court's decision. (As I mentioned before, certiorari goes by "cert" for short.) The Court receives thousands of cert petitions a year and grants only a small fraction. In the past few terms, the merits docket—the cases in which the Court grants cert and issues a decision—has hovered at around sixty cases.

Why so few? Given the flood of cert petitions, the Court can't possibly review every case, or even every case that was wrongly decided. To sort them, the Court has adopted standards for identifying the cases that implicate the Court's unique role in the judicial system of the United States.[9] The Court's jurisdiction covers the nation, so it takes cases with national significance. In cases that affect a confined region or particular litigants, the Court typically allows the lower courts to have the last word—even if the last word is mistaken.

What cases have national significance? The clearest case for granting cert is when federal courts of appeals or state supreme courts disagree about how to resolve the same question. The Court's primary responsibility is to ensure that federal law is uniform across the country. Things get unwieldy (and unfair) if federal law dictates one outcome in California and another in New York. So when the courts of appeals or state supreme courts are divided about an issue of federal law, the Supreme Court takes the case to give a single answer that will apply nationwide. For instance, in *Pulsifer v. United States*, the Court resolved a circuit split over the meaning of the word "and" in a federal sentencing statute.[10] (As ridiculous as this issue might sound, *Pulsifer* was a very hard case. Not only did the courts of appeals divide, but the Supreme Court did too—Justices Gorsuch, Sotomayor, and Jackson dissented from Justice Kagan's majority opinion, which I joined.) In *Byrd v. United States*, the Court addressed a circuit split over the Fourth Amendment's application to rental cars.[11] This case was more straightforward for the Court. All nine justices agreed that there is a reasonable expectation of privacy (which triggers the protection of the Fourth Amendment) for anyone with permission to drive a rental car, even if the driver was not on the rental agreement.

Some cases have national significance even in the absence of a circuit split—for example, a state court or lower federal court sometimes decides "an important question of federal law that has not been, but should be, settled by th[e] Court."[12] For example, when a former president was indicted—a historical first—the Court took the case to decide whether he could be prosecuted for his official acts.[13] When a lower court stopped the federal government from pursuing its immigration policy, the Court granted cert to address whether the policy could continue.[14] And when California legalized medical marijuana despite a federal law to the contrary, the Court decided whether Congress had the power to make local medical marijuana use a federal crime.[15]

National significance is not the only factor that matters to the cert process. A decision from the Supreme Court binds every court in the country, and once it decides a case, the Court typically follows that precedent in future cases. Given that a decision has wide and long-lasting effect, it is important for the Court to get it right. To that end, the Court looks for the best case in which to resolve an issue. Questions of national importance are often litigated in different cases around the country. If the case before the Court contains legal or factual quirks that could prevent a clean resolution, the Court will deny cert. Same for a poorly written cert petition—the Court tries to take cases in which lawyers are likely to present the strongest arguments on both sides. And sometimes the Court takes a pass even when a case doesn't present these sorts of obstacles. Multiple opinions from thoughtful judges help the Court make a better decision, so the Court may deny cert to allow time for more courts to weigh in. In the trade, we call that allowing an issue to "percolate."

The upshot is that it is difficult to read much into the Court's disposition of a cert petition. Because the Court hardly ever grants cert simply to correct a mistake, a denial of cert does *not* reflect approval of the lower court's decision. (News coverage sometimes suggests otherwise.) It sets no precedent and offers no guidance to lower courts about the right way to interpret and apply the law. And because the Court tries to optimize its ability to make a good decision, a denial of cert does not necessarily mean that the issue lacks national importance—it can just as easily mean "not this case" or "not yet."

Even the *grant* of cert carries some mystery. By long tradition, the Court has employed what is known as the "rule of four"—it requires only four votes to grant cert. So when the Court takes a case, you should not assume that a majority of the nine justices supported the grant. The Court sometimes decides cases that only a minority of justices wanted to hear.

Given the number of cert petitions (more than four thousand a year), the Court has streamlined the review process. As I mentioned in the last chapter, most justices pool their law clerks together to divide the work of screening petitions across chambers. A law clerk writes a memo analyzing each petition, and justices use these memos to identify the strongest candidates for review. Any justice can list a petition to be discussed and voted on at conference. The petitions that no justice lists—the vast majority—are denied without discussion. Lest that cause concern, it bears emphasis that every petition is analyzed, and the majority are plainly not "certworthy"—in other words, they don't satisfy the criteria for a grant of cert. When not a single justice believes that a petition clears that bar, it would be a waste of time to discuss whether to grant it.

Once the Court agrees to hear a case, it is added to the calendar. An important note about the calendar: a Supreme Court term runs from the first Monday of October to the first Monday of the following October. So each term is named by its start date—for example, "October Term 2024" or "OT 2024" for short.

Emergency Docket

Over the last several years, the Court's docket has swelled with applications from parties who ask the Court to immediately "stay" (the legal term for pause) the effect of a lower court's decision. These applications are filed before the Court decides whether to grant cert and often before the lower courts have finished with the case. The gist of an emergency application is this: "I can't wait for the normal process to play out because the decision below is both wrong and incredibly harmful to me." The issues that have hit the emergency docket in the last few years include clashes between the United States and Texas over the southern border,[16] disputes between various states and the federal government over abortion,[17] challenges to state laws regulating medical treatment for transgender children,[18] and challenges to environmental regulations.[19] And these are just a few of the many applications that the Court has received.

The rise of activity on the Court's emergency docket has garnered attention, because of both the nature and number of the applications.[20] Why the increase in applications for emergency relief? Some commentators point to nationwide injunctions—a growing practice where a single district court prevents the enforcement of a law anywhere in the country.[21] Others suggest that factors outside the Court, including the COVID-19 pandemic and the 2020 election, have simply generated more high-stakes litigation, leading to a greater sense of urgency for emergency relief.[22] In my view, the emergency docket also reflects what's going on in the country—more on that below.

The decision of whether to grant or deny an emergency application depends on settled criteria. An applicant must show (1) a reasonable probability that four justices would grant cert on the legal issue; (2) a fair prospect that the applicant would win on the merits before the Court; (3) a likelihood that the applicant will suffer irreparable harm if the Court denies emergency relief; and (4) that a grant of relief is consistent with principles of fairness.[23] Each of these factors matters, so even an applicant with a very strong argument on the merits of her case might find her application denied. A showing of "irreparable harm" is particularly important, because irreparable harm is the justification for granting *immediate* relief rather than letting the case run its course in the courts below.[24] I have written to emphasize the importance of considering "certworthiness"—the chances that the Court would ultimately grant cert on the regular docket. As my opinion explains, "Were the standard otherwise, applicants could use the emergency docket to force the Court to give a merits preview in cases that it would be unlikely to take—and to do so on a short fuse without benefit of full briefing and oral argument."[25] So, as with the denial of a cert petition, you shouldn't assume that the denial of emergency relief reflects the Court's belief that the applicant has a losing legal argument. More considerations are at play.

Still, the fact remains that some litigants can show irreparable harm from the lower court's order, and many of the issues on the emergency docket are indeed certworthy. In those cases, the Court must make a time-pressured (if tentative) decision about the strength of the applicant's legal position on a difficult, high-stakes issue. It must also decide whether to publish an opinion explaining its decision. On the one hand, an opinion makes the Court's reasoning transparent; that's why opinions are so valuable in cases decided on the merits. On the other hand, a decision on the emergency docket is only a preliminary judgment about the likelihood that the applicant's argument will succeed, not a final resolution of the legal issue. Committing the Court's reasoning to print risks hardening what should be tentative into something more definite.

As long as litigants continue filing emergency applications, the Court must continue deciding them. But the judicial system functions better when litigants and lawyers have the opportunity to fully explain their positions in their briefs, provide the Court the benefit of oral argument, and offer the Court the opportunity to make a deliberative and well-reasoned decision in consultation with one another. The Court does its best to ensure that most cases get the benefit of that process.

THE COURT'S DOCKET underscores that it is a *reactive* institution. It can only resolve disputes that litigants choose to bring; it can't volunteer answers to questions that no one has asked. Because of its role in the judiciary, the Court accepts cases involving issues that, to a greater or lesser degree, are dividing the nation. As a result, the docket of the Court reflects the controversies of the time.

Justice after justice has made this point. Justice Potter Stewart once observed that "the calendar of the Supreme Court will be a fairly reliable mirror of the domestic problems confronting our nation."[26] In response to claims that the Court was engaged in judicial activism, Chief Justice Earl Warren asserted that "[w]e reflect the burning issues of our society, we do not manufacture them."[27] Similarly, Justice Sandra Day O'Connor explained, "Most of the Court's agenda is dictated by external forces: the actions of the other branches of the government, the decisions of the lower courts, and ultimately the concerns of the public. It is these forces, not secret ones within the Court, that frame the bulk of the issues we decide."[28]

Historically, the Court's docket bears this out. Think of the issues that dominated society in a certain period, then look at the docket of the Court. In the aftermath of the Civil War, the Court heard a series of cases challenging public and private segregation.[29] Industrialization transformed the American economy in the late nineteenth and early twentieth centuries, prompting litigation over labor laws, such as maximum hour rules,[30] unionization requirements,[31] and child labor restrictions.[32] Legislation enacted during the administration of Franklin Delano Roosevelt significantly expanded the reach of the federal government; as a consequence, the Court faced a steady stream of cases in which litigants argued about whether the Constitution permitted these changes.[33] During the 1950s and 1960s, civil rights took center stage, and as a result, the Court decided cases involving school desegregation,[34] busing,[35] and the treatment of defendants by the criminal justice system.[36] In the 1970s and 1980s, the movement for women's rights generated cases challenging discrimination on the basis of sex.[37] And whenever the country faces armed conflict—from World War II to the war on terror—the Court can count on challenges to actions taken by the president in the name of national defense.[38]

The docket of the modern Court similarly reflects, as Chief Justice Warren put it, "the burning issues of our society." Restrictions imposed during the COVID-19 pandemic were controversial; as night follows day, litigants filed challenges to vaccine and masking mandates, as well as shutdowns of religious services.[39] The movement for LGBTQ rights has brought significant social change, resulting in cases addressing same-sex marriage,[40] employment discrimination,[41] and, more recently, the intersection of First Amendment rights and public accommodation laws.[42] Social media has changed the landscape of communication and political debate, leading to cases on the content moderation policies of social media platforms and the legal status of government officials' social media accounts.[43] And as Justice O'Connor observed, "[T]he actions of the other branches of the government" affect our docket too.[44] Executive orders issued by presidents on matters like immigration and student loan forgiveness have landed on our docket, as have issues arising out of legislation like the Affordable Care Act.

Controversial cases highlight that the Court walks a fine line. It plays an important role in protecting citizens from unlawful government action; at the same time, it must heed the limits on its own power. There's more to that balancing act than meets the eye, as I explain in the next chapter.

Chapter 7

Judicial Power and Restraint

The judiciary's most significant power—its authority to decide whether a statute is constitutional—is called "judicial review." This authority is not spelled out in the black-and-white words of the Constitution; instead, it is a logical implication of the Constitution's text and structure.[1] Because the Constitution does not explicitly describe judicial review, its propriety and scope were subject to some debate in the Court's early years.[2] Chief Justice John Marshall explained it, and thereby solidified it, in *Marbury v. Madison*, a case decided in 1803.[3] The case—and Marshall himself—is so important that portraits of William Marbury and James Madison hang side by side in the Court's Marshall Dining Room.

Because judicial review checks the work of the elected branches, it can provoke conflict with them. That much was evident right away: After *Marbury* was decided, Thomas Jefferson told Abigail Adams that the case would make the judiciary "a despotic branch."[4] If the authority were unrestrained, I would agree with Jefferson. The power of judicial review gives courts an important role in safeguarding the Constitution, but if exercised too aggressively, it would allow judges to supervise the political branches. Fortunately, the power comes with an accompanying constraint: courts can exercise it only to resolve specific cases, not to announce freewheeling opinions about whether the government has acted unconstitutionally. Thus, the Court cannot exercise judicial review as often as some might want or as others might fear.

⁜

THE DISPUTE BETWEEN William Marbury and James Madison was over a job. At the tail end of his presidency, John Adams nominated Marbury to serve as a justice of the peace in the District of Columbia. On the day before the Federalist government turned over to the rival political party—the Jeffersonian Republicans—the Senate confirmed Marbury, and Adams signed his commission. But when Thomas Jefferson became president, Marbury's commission had not yet been delivered. Nor would it be: Jefferson, frustrated by Adams's batch of last-minute judicial appointments, ordered his new secretary of state, James Madison, to withhold the undelivered commissions.[5]

Marbury filed suit in the Supreme Court, seeking an order that would compel Madison to give him the commission. In the opinion, Marshall focused on two issues. First, did Marbury have a right to the commission?[6] Marshall answered yes. Marbury had been appointed and confirmed in accordance with the law, and the president had signed the commission.[7] It was valid even though it hadn't been delivered. As a result, Marbury was entitled to exercise the judicial office and to possess the commission, which proved his qualifications.[8] Madison had violated the law by refusing to deliver the document or a copy of it.[9]

Marshall's second question was more technical, but also more critical. He asked whether the Court had the authority to decide the case at all.[10] Marbury had come straight to the Supreme Court, invoking its "original jurisdiction," rather than starting in a court below and coming to the Supreme Court on appeal. A federal statute allowed Marbury to do that. The problem, however, was that the statute went further than Article III of the Constitution, which defines the outer bounds of the Court's authority.[11]

Article III permits the Court to exercise original jurisdiction in only a handful of circumstances, but Congress had added a new one.

The case presented fundamental questions about the structure of the federal government. When a statute conflicts with the Constitution, which wins—the statute or the Constitution? Equally important, who decides whether the two are at odds? Marshall explained that the Constitution trumps a statute, and that in the context of individual cases, judges decide whether a conflict exists.

His premise was that the Constitution enacts "the original and supreme will" of the people, making it superior to ordinary legislation.[12] And because it directs the federal courts to decide "Cases" and "Controversies,"[13] they have the power of judicial review. In other words, "[i]t is . . . the province and duty of the judicial department to say what the law is."[14] The judiciary does not simply accept that the legislature or the executive has whatever authority it claims.

In this case, Marshall concluded that the statute expanding the Court's jurisdiction violated the Constitution, and as a result, it was a dead letter. The Constitution is the "supreme Law of the Land"[15] changeable only by constitutional amendment. If ordinary legislation could overcome its text, the document would mean very little. After all, the point of the Constitution is to constrain the government from taking actions that would violate our supreme law. If the legislature oversteps, the act is void. And if an act is void, the judiciary must treat it accordingly. The rule of law requires nothing less.

Practically speaking, this meant that the Court had the authority to determine whether the statute was valid. But because the statute (which gave the Court "original jurisdiction" over the case) was invalid, the Court could go no further.[16] Even though Marbury had a vested right in his commission, there was nothing the Supreme Court could do to force the Jefferson administration to follow the law. Marshall's strategy was masterful. He asserted the Court's power of judicial review while simultaneously acknowledging its limits.

The ancient Greek story of Odysseus and the Sirens offers a vivid way of thinking about the kind of judicial review that the Court exercised in *Marbury v. Madison*—and that federal courts continue to exercise today.[17] While on his journey home, Odysseus is warned that he will encounter the Sirens, mythological creatures who use songs to lure sailors to their deaths. Odysseus knew that he would be tempted by their song to leap overboard. Nonetheless, he wanted to hear them. To protect himself, he instructed his crew to tie him to the mast of the ship, plug their ears with beeswax, and resist his pleas to untie him. The plan worked. When Odysseus and his crew approached the Sirens, he listened, became enchanted, and begged to be released. But his men, safe from the Sirens' song, only bound him tighter. They survived with their ship and lives intact.

The Constitution works similarly. Members of the founding generation knew that democracy can be dangerous—so, like Odysseus, they took precautions. Democratic majorities are tempted to violate the rights of minorities by, for example, silencing offensive speech or overriding civil rights during a security crisis. Or when structural limitations prove inconvenient to their political goals, constituents may press the president or Congress to exceed the limits of their respective powers. Like the ropes restraining Odysseus, the provisions of the Constitution, to which all government officials swear fidelity, are designed to hold them back. Judges, as I will explain, are not always involved in that effort. But when a litigant properly enlists their help, judges function like Odysseus's shipmates. Life tenure, like the beeswax in the sailors' ears, is designed to make judges resistant to the lure of democratic majorities that call for actions that violate constitutional commitments. When that lure overcomes the political branches, judicial review offers another layer of protection.

Granted, this stylized account depicts perfection. When judicial review works as it should, it functions as an important check on political actors; it is one on which our system has historically relied. At the same time, giving judges control of the ropes introduces risk. Does life tenure really function like mythical beeswax, rendering judges consistently impervious to the lure of outside voices? What if judges wrongfully loosen the knots, allowing democratic majorities to act expediently? Conversely, what if they wrongfully tighten the knots, preventing democratic majorities from accomplishing goals they should be free to pursue? And what if the error is in the eye of the beholder, with competing factions of Americans vehemently disagreeing about whether judges got it right?

Echoing these themes, critics often charge the Court with being either too easy or too hard on the political branches. Take a controversial area like gun control. When the Court holds that a firearms restriction violates the Second Amendment, the regulation's supporters charge the Court with wrongfully thwarting democracy. When the Court lets such a regulation stand, gun rights advocates charge the court with shirking its duty to protect constitutional liberties. Everyone wants the Court to uphold the Constitution, but in difficult cases, people disagree about what the Constitution requires.

Given such disagreements, it is important to know that while the Court gets the last word about who wins an individual case, it does not necessarily get the last word about what the Constitution means. To see the point, imagine that the Court decides a case called *Smith v. Jones*. The Court's *judgment* is the formal document resolving who won the case, and the other branches of government can't interfere with it—for example, by ordering the Court to render judgment in favor of Smith.[18] The Court's *opinion*, by contrast, is the written explanation of the reasons for its judgment. The opinion sets a precedent that courts will follow in the future, and in general, Congress, the president, and the states follow it too. But public officials also take an oath to uphold the Constitution, and when they disagree with the Court's opinion about what the Constitution requires, they sometimes assert the right to follow their own interpretation of the Constitution rather than the Court's.[19]

Abraham Lincoln provides a well-known example. Lincoln famously disagreed with the Supreme Court about the status of slavery after the infamous decision in *Dred Scott v. Sandford*, in which the enslaved plaintiff,

Dred Scott, sued for a declaration that he became free by living in a territory where Congress had outlawed slavery.[20] In response, the Court rebuffed Scott's ability even to come to court, insisting that descendants of slaves brought from Africa could not be "citizens" under the Constitution and thus had no right to bring lawsuits.[21] Going still further, the Court declared that Congress could not outlaw slavery in the territories because doing so interfered with slaveholders' property rights.[22] Thus, Dred Scott remained a slave.

Lincoln accepted that the decision bound the specific parties to the case—Dred Scott and Sandford.[23] In other words, he did not contend that the Court's *judgment* could be ignored. But he refused to accept the Supreme Court's *opinion* as conclusive going forward. A few months after the Court decided *Dred Scott* (and a few years before he became president), Lincoln put it this way to a crowd in Springfield, Illinois:

> We believe . . . in obedience to, and respect for the judicial department of government. We think its decisions on Constitutional questions, when fully settled, should control, not only the particular cases decided, but the general policy of the country, subject to be disturbed only by amendments of the Constitution as provided in that instrument itself. More than this would be revolution. But we think the Dred Scott decision is erroneous. We know the court that made it, has often over-ruled its own decisions, and we shall do what we can to have it to over-rule this. . . .[24]

Elaborating on the point in his First Inaugural Address, Lincoln explained that if the Court's interpretation of the Constitution were "irrevocably fixed," then "the people will have ceased to be their own rulers, having practically resigned their government into the hands of eminent tribunal."[25]

President Andrew Jackson had a similar view. When it came to policymaking, Jackson believed both the president and Congress were duty bound to act according to the Constitution as they interpreted it, no matter the opinion of the Supreme Court.[26] One famous example of disagreement arose in the controversy over a federal bank. In *M'Culloch v. Maryland*, the Supreme Court upheld Congress's creation of a national bank as constitutional.[27] By the time Jackson became president, it was time for the bank's renewal, and Congress passed legislation renewing it. But Jackson vetoed the bill. He believed that the bank was not only bad policy but also unconstitutional—even though the Court had already said otherwise. In Jackson's view, "[t]he opinion of the judges has no more authority over Congress than the opinion of Congress has over the judges, and on that point the President is independent of both."[28] Perhaps unsurprisingly, the Court has taken the contrary position that Congress and the president must heed its opinions.[29]

President Franklin Delano Roosevelt had an even more direct clash with the Court. During the Great Depression, Roosevelt led an unprecedented expansion of the federal government. The Court found many of the initiatives unconstitutional.[30] Frustrated, Roosevelt proposed a structural change called court-packing. The plan was for the president to nominate a new justice for each sitting member of the Court over seventy years of age, expanding the Court to a maximum of fifteen justices.[31] The expansion was needed, Roosevelt explained in a fireside chat, because "[t]he Court has been acting not as a judicial body, but as a policy-making body."[32] New justices, he argued, would "save the Constitution from the Court and the Court from itself."[33] Roosevelt's proposal, already controversial, fizzled after the justices changed course. In *West Coast Hotel Co. v. Parrish*, the Court upheld a minimum-wage law nearly identical to one it had struck down just a year prior.[34] (The decisive vote, cast by Justice Owen Roberts, came to be known as "the switch in time that saved nine.")[35] Not long after, Justice Willis Van Devanter, one of the justices who most often ruled against the New Deal, retired. This made space for a Roosevelt appointee, which further calmed tensions.[36] The court-packing plan lost support in the Senate, where it died.[37]

Congress too has occasionally pushed back against the Court. As I explained in the last chapter, Congress controls the jurisdiction of the federal courts, and it has occasionally stripped or threatened to strip the courts of authority to hear cases in certain areas to prevent the Court from rendering an opinion about what the Constitution means. For example, during Reconstruction, Congress acted quickly to protect a statute that split the former Confederacy into military districts pending readmission into the Union.[38] Fearful that the Court would deem the law unconstitutional, Congress limited the Court's jurisdiction while the case was pending.[39] (The Court upheld Congress's authority to impose the limit.) More recently, legislators have considered proposals to limit judicial review of a variety of issues, including school prayer, legislative apportionment, *Miranda* warnings, court-ordered busing, abortion restrictions, the Defense of Marriage Act, and Pledge of Allegiance mandates.[40] A few of these have passed either the House or the Senate, but never both.

And together, the president and Senate have control over personnel. Because federal judges have life tenure, they can be removed only by impeachment. But the president and the Senate can influence the future direction of the courts by appointing and confirming judges who share their constitutional vision. They routinely do just that. For instance, President Reagan emphasized the importance of "judges who would interpret law, not make it."[41] President Clinton, by contrast, highlighted the need for justices who could "translate the hopes of the American people, as presented in the cases before [the Court], into an enduring body of constitutional law."[42]

The Court's power of judicial review is therefore subject to tug and pull with the other branches of government. All three branches have an obligation to interpret and adhere to the Constitution, and while the judiciary's judgment is final as to the litigants before it, the *reasons* supporting its decision are subject to further discussion. As Lincoln observed, frequent rejection of Supreme Court opinions would upend the government; moreover, resistance ought not be motivated by the desire of the political branches to break free of constitutional constraints. Still, it's important to remember that while the judiciary plays an important role in safeguarding the Constitution, its power is not absolute.

The power conferred by Article III is also checked by an internal constraint. A federal court can't answer a legal question just because someone asks it to or even because it would like to. It can only resolve "Cases" or "Controversies," which is the Constitution's language for concrete disputes between opposing parties. This limit drastically minimizes the number of occasions on which any federal court—including the Supreme Court—can offer a legal opinion. Like the power of judicial review, this prohibition on "advisory opinions" is implicit in the Constitution rather than obvious on its face.

The Supreme Court laid the foundation early on in correspondence between John Jay, the first chief justice, and George Washington, the first president. In the summer of 1793, Washington was struggling to stay neutral in the war between France, a crucial ally in the Revolutionary War, and various European monarchies, which the United States had neither the resources nor the will to fight. Maintaining neutrality was tricky business, requiring Washington to carefully navigate the international law of neutrality and America's treaty obligations.

To address the situation, Washington sought help from the Supreme Court. In July 1793, Thomas Jefferson, Washington's secretary of state, asked the justices "[w]hether the public may, with propriety, be availed of their *advice*" on legal questions "of considerable difficulty, and of greater importance to the peace of the U.S."[43] Jefferson concluded by confiding:

> [T]he President would therefore be much relieved if he found himself free to refer questions of this description to the opinions of the Judges of the supreme court of the U.S. whose knolege [*sic*] of the

> subject would secure us against errors dangerous to the peace of the U.S. and their authority ensure the respect of all parties.[44]

Anticipating that the justices would accept the request, Washington's cabinet prepared a list of twenty-nine questions for the Court along the lines of this one: "Do the treaties between the US. & France give to France or her citizens a *right,* when at war with a power with whom the US. are at peace, to fit out originally in & from the ports of the US, vessels armed for war, with or without commission?"[45] In other words, did France have a right to use American ports in its fight against a country with which the United States was at peace?

Washington requested legal opinions untethered to any case or litigants. It might seem like a reasonable ask—wouldn't the Court be a good source of guidance on pressing legal issues greatly affecting national security? Washington may well have thought it wise to get the Court's opinion before he acted, in case the Court later judged his decision to be illegal. Why not save everyone the trouble by clarifying matters at the outset? It's notable too that Washington apparently believed his request to be consistent with the Court's role. He had presided over the Constitutional Convention at which Article III was drafted. The prohibition on advisory opinions could not have been self-evident, or Washington presumably wouldn't have sent Jefferson on a mission to procure them.

The justices declined to share their opinions on Washington's questions. Noting "[t]he Lines of Separation drawn between the three Departments of Government," Chief Justice Jay passed.[46] Congress and the executive, no less than the judiciary, are obligated to uphold the laws of the United States, and, like the judiciary, must therefore interpret those laws. Jay explained that while the Supreme Court *reviews* those determinations when it decides cases, it cannot make such judgments for the other branches in the first instance. To do so, he said, would be to act "extrajudicially."[47] And while Jay did not say it, doing so would also permit the executive branch to shift responsibility for any wrong move to the Supreme Court: if the

United States provoked conflict, Washington could point to the justices. Diplomatically, Jay concluded with an apology:

> [W]e exceedingly regret every Event that may cause Embarrassment to your administration; but we derive Consolation from the Reflection, that your Judgment will discern what is Right, and that your usual Prudence, Decision and Firmness will surmount every obstacle to the Preservation of the Rights, Peace, and Dignity of the united [*sic*] States.[48]

All five justices present at that Court session signed the letter, which was a critical assertion of independence—not only of the judiciary from the executive branch, but also of these five justices from the president who had appointed them.

After Jay's polite refusal, the prohibition on such "advisory opinions" no longer arises in the context of a request like Washington's. Yet private parties seek advisory opinions too—though they do it in the context of lawsuits, not letters.

When the issue first came up, it was not obvious that the same rule would apply when a plaintiff sued a defendant. But the Court, invoking the interchange between Washington and Jay, emphasized that it cannot dispense legal advice in lawsuits either.[49] Article III allows courts to decide "Cases" or "Controversies," which the Court defined as proceedings "for the protection or enforcement of rights, or the prevention, redress, or punishment of wrongs."[50] And lest there be any doubt, the Court emphasized that *Marbury v. Madison* doesn't grant courts "general veto power" over statutes enacted by Congress.[51] *Marbury* holds only that to pronounce judgment in a case, a court has to decide what law to apply—and if the choice is "between a constitutional requirement and a conflicting statutory enactment, the plain duty of the court [i]s to follow and enforce the Constitution as the supreme law established by the people."[52] If there is no dispute between opposing parties, the court has no business assessing the law.

Because of this "case or controversy" restraint, a citizen's fervent belief that the government has acted illegally is not enough to get her in the courthouse door. (If it were, imagine how crowded federal dockets would be.) To challenge a government policy in federal court, a plaintiff must demonstrate that the policy injured her specifically, financially or otherwise, and that there is something that the court can do to make it right—or at least better. A plaintiff who can make that showing has what the law calls "standing" to sue. A plaintiff who can't make that showing is seeking an advisory opinion dressed up as a lawsuit. Rarely a term goes by when the Court doesn't have to address Article III's standing doctrine. George Washington was the first in a long line of people whom the Court has politely turned away.

Injury

The need to show an actual injury is usually the biggest hurdle. *Valley Forge Christian College v. Americans United for Separation of Church and State, Inc.*, decided in 1982, is a good example. After a federal agency donated surplus property to a Christian college, an organization called Americans United for Separation of Church and State sued the government on the ground that the donation violated the Establishment Clause.[53] But the organization had the same problem as any would-be litigant—it needed to show a specific harm to invoke a court's authority under Article III. The group identified its injury as a violation of the right to a government that (in the words of the Establishment Clause) "shall make no law respecting an establishment of religion."[54]

The Court rejected that argument. *Every* citizen has an interest in a government that complies with the law, so the organization's claimed injury didn't distinguish it from any of the other millions of people in the United States who might also object to the property transfer.[55] Moreover, a purely legal objection is not a concrete injury; the plaintiff must be able to point to some additional harm she has personally suffered from the allegedly illegal conduct.[56] For example, a hypothetical nonreligious college that wanted for itself the property that the federal agency gave Valley Forge could show the necessary injury. A bystander critical of the transaction could not.

This distinction between abstract and concrete injuries has played out repeatedly in the Court's cases. A victim of racial discrimination has standing; a bystander who objects to racial discrimination does not.[57] A hiker who frequents a forest has standing to object to its destruction; a hiker who has a general interest in forests does not.[58] A drug company that loses business because the FDA removes restrictions on a competitor has standing; a citizen upset about the FDA's policy does not.[59] The owner of a company has standing to object to how a state calculates the company's tax obligation, but not to object that taxes are generally high.[60]

These limits exist for good reason. Entertaining suits based solely on legal objections would permit the judiciary to exercise general oversight of Congress and the president. Judges could be a roving band of theorists and philosophers, dropping in with binding pronouncements on issues of the day when they—in their sole discretion—deemed it wise. But the Constitution does not assign the judiciary that role, and for the Court to assume it would poison the judiciary's relationship with the other two branches. It is no small thing for a court to hold government action unconstitutional. The judiciary should not shrink from that responsibility. Neither, however, should it antagonize the other branches by reaching beyond actual cases to judge the legality of their conduct.

Remedy

To demonstrate standing, a plaintiff must show not only that the defendant caused her an injury, but also that the court can order the defendant to fix it. The plaintiff can seek compensation (money) or nonmonetary relief (a command that the defendant do or not do something). But the court must be able to render a judgment that orders some kind of remedy. Otherwise, the plaintiff is seeking an advisory opinion—legal analysis with no real-world effect.

Think of it this way: The court's judgment is the main event, and its opinion plays a supporting role. After all, the opinion details the *reasons* for the court's action. If the court takes no action, there is nothing to explain. So while courts can (and do) issue judgments without opinions, they cannot issue opinions without judgments. Justice Scalia once summed it up like this: Article III "requires that the court be able to afford relief *through the exercise of its power*, not through the persuasive or even awe-inspiring effect of the opinion *explaining* the exercise of its power."[61]

Murthy v. Missouri, a case in which I wrote the majority opinion, illustrates this requirement. In *Murthy*, the plaintiffs claimed that various government agencies and employees were violating the First Amendment by pressuring social media companies to suppress their speech—most notably, COVID-19–related posts questioning the efficacy of mask mandates, the wisdom of school closures, and the safety of vaccines.[62] They asked the district court for an injunction ordering the government defendants to stop coercing or encouraging social media companies to suppress free speech.[63] An injunction, however, wouldn't have protected the plaintiffs' posts. By the time they filed suit, the pandemic had subsided, and the government defendants were no longer pressuring the companies—so an order telling them to stop pressuring the companies wouldn't have accomplished anything.[64] Continued restrictions were the independent choice of the social media companies, private actors who had their own content-moderation policies and were no longer coordinating with the government. Thus, the plaintiffs could win only an advisory opinion: a legal analysis with no teeth. While such an opinion might have publicly vindicated the plaintiffs, it is not the role of the federal courts to deliver that kind of victory.

You might be wondering whether the "case or controversy" requirement means that there are some governmental actions that won't ever be subject to judicial review. The answer is yes. But this doesn't mean that the Constitution is thrown out the window—only that the other branches of government get the last word on whether the action is lawful.

Recall John Jay's letter to George Washington: it emphasized that the president, with help from his cabinet, was responsible for determining whether his action complied with America's legal obligations.[65] Nobody doubted for a moment that the president was bound to follow the law. That responsibility has remained constant throughout American history. The federal courts do not have a monopoly on constitutional interpretation. *Every* officer who serves in the executive and legislative branches takes an oath to support the Constitution. When an official action injures someone, the injured person can turn to the judiciary for help. Otherwise, the place for citizens to register objections to government action is at the ballot box. The Court has put it this way:

> An Article III court is not a legislative assembly, a town square, or a faculty lounge. Article III does not contemplate a system where 330 million citizens can come to federal court whenever they believe that the government is acting contrary to the Constitution or other federal law. Vindicating "the *public* interest (including the public interest in Government observance of the Constitution and laws) is the function of Congress and the Chief Executive."[66]

The judiciary neither answers every constitutional question nor rights every constitutional wrong. While *Marbury v. Madison* proclaims that "[i]t is emphatically the province and duty of the judicial department to say what the law is,"[67] that is true only when the judiciary is authorized to speak.

Part Two

The Constitution and the American Experience

Chapter 8

A More Perfect Union

When I joined the Court, I chose to hang a portrait of Abigail Adams, perhaps the most influential woman of the Founding Era, above the fireplace in my office. Abigail did not have a seat at the Constitutional Convention or hold political office—no woman did. But she closely advised her husband, John, through letters when they were apart and conversations when they were together. John Adams was intimately involved in the founding of our country: he was a leader in the Revolution and held many important offices, including the presidency. Abigail chafed at her exclusion from formal participation in government affairs and did what she could to influence the way John handled them. Their many letters to each other reflect her close attention to everything from the conduct of the Revolutionary War to the ineffectiveness of the Continental Congress. John cherished her advice, confiding, "[Y]ou shine as a Stateswoman, of late as well as a Farmeress. Pray where do you get your Maxims of State, they are very apropos."[1]

Abigail's confidence and grit were remarkable for her time. She not only pressed her political opinions; she independently managed her family's farm, finances, and five children (a sixth, Elizabeth, was stillborn). John was frequently away and readily admitted that Abigail was better at business than he was. She kept a hand in two worlds, attending to both the needs of her family and the concerns of government. Sometimes, she felt torn between them. When she married John, Abigail imagined that they would spend their lives in the small town of Braintree, Massachusetts, surrounded by family and longtime friends. It was hard for her to exchange that plan for life in the public eye, where she was never truly comfortable. I can relate.

Abigail reminds me of the sacrifices made to get our nation off the ground. And if she could look down from her portrait, I hope she would be pleased. In one letter to John, she pointedly remarked that women were deeply patriotic despite being "[d]eprived of a voice in Legislation" and "obliged to submit to those Laws which are imposed upon us."[2] Moreover, "Excluded from honours and from offices, we cannot attach ourselves to the State or Government from having held a place of Eminence."[3] That, of course, is no longer true. I can do something Abigail could not: work simultaneously as a mother and a justice of the Supreme Court. Her life, like the Constitution itself, evokes both history and hope.

The portrait of Abigail Adams that is displayed in my office. (Collection of the Massachusetts Historical Society.)

Abigail lived in the Founding Era, a period important to my work. We're still governed by the Constitution that was ratified in 1788, and as I explain in a later chapter, the circumstances surrounding its ratification matter to its interpretation. In resolving constitutional cases, the Court asks questions like, What did the Constitution's language mean to those who adopted it? What problems was the Constitution designed to address? In what follows, I'll tell you a little bit about the latter point—why the constitutional project began and the governmental structure on which the framers settled. But I'll also paint a picture of the framers themselves. What fun would it be simply to march through the document? While describing its content is necessary foundation for the remainder of the book, the Constitution's story is not purely legal, and it was certainly not born in a sterile environment. The Constitution was launched by flesh-and-blood people who achieved something great, despite their many imperfections and messy circumstances. Their work took tenacity and compromise. Success was not foreordained—looking back, it was not even likely. Yet against the odds, the Founding generation produced a document that changed the course of history. What we take for granted—a stable system of government, representative democracy, and the protection of individual liberties—is the result of what fifty-five delegates brought to life in the summer of 1787.

So let's step back in history—before the Louisiana Purchase, Manifest Destiny, the Civil War, Reconstruction, world wars, and the American Century—to set the stage for the American constitutional moment.

THE FIFTY-FIVE MEN who gathered in Philadelphia in 1787 had witnessed a decade in which their new country had declared independence, defeated against all odds the world's most powerful empire, united its states (albeit loosely) under a central government, and begun functioning as an independent nation. At one point, everything must have seemed possible.

But soon after gaining independence, the national government was on the verge of collapse.[4] The thirteen states had little to unite them without a shared enemy.[5] A person in revolutionary America would likely see herself as a citizen of a state first and the union second, if at all.[6] During the war, then commander George Washington asked a group of New Jersey militiamen to pledge an oath to the United States.[7] The soldiers rebuffed the request, insisting that their country was New Jersey.[8]

The states were quasi-countries—and acted like it. Each had its own markets and currencies, customs and loyalties.[9] States with large ports imposed high duties on goods traveling through, paralyzing interstate commerce.[10] Stuck between ports, New Jersey was "a cask tapped at both ends."[11] Trade restrictions were anathema to most Southern states, whose economies depended on exports of tobacco, rice, and indigo.[12]

The Confederation Congress was no use in resolving disputes between states because it was barely functional.[13] The issue was one of design. With the British monarchy fresh in their minds, revolutionary leaders created a central government that lacked any real power.[14] Its founding document, the Articles of Confederation, was more of a friendship pact among thirteen sovereigns than a constitution.[15] Unable to levy taxes, support a standing army, or do much of anything, congressmen stopped showing up for work.[16]

The result was embarrassment.[17] When American merchants in the Mediterranean were overcome by Barbary Coast pirates, the Confederation couldn't afford the ransom.[18] Nor could it counter Britain and Spain when they armed Indian tribes in skirmishes against American settlers in the West.[19] Especially pressing was the war debt. To finance the Revolution, the Confederation borrowed from private creditors and other countries.[20] But without the ability to tax, the government could not raise enough to pay them back.[21] With the country's public credit on the line, almost all of the states agreed to amend the Articles and allow an import tax.[22] Yet New York, rich from its own taxes and reluctant to add more, stopped the effort.[23] The challenge exposed the Articles' fatal flaw: amendment required unanimous consent.[24] A single state could stop the rest from reforming the system.[25]

Just as the Confederation teetered on the brink of financial ruin, farmers revolted in Massachusetts in the uprising called Shays' Rebellion.[26] Desperate from tax hikes and impending foreclosure, vigilantes took over the Springfield courthouse.[27] Wearing their old Continental Army uniforms and sprigs of hemlock in their hats, they accused the state of replicating the British oppressors.[28] The state militia overcame the rebels without much trouble, but the revolt unnerved citizens across the country.[29]

Soon thereafter, the Confederation Congress called for a constitutional convention in Philadelphia.[30] Observers expected relatively modest amendments to the Articles that would maintain a limited central government and significant state sovereignty. States sent their own representatives.

These delegates, while drawn from a narrow band of American society, included overlapping categories of statesmen, politicians, business elite, land speculators, and self-made men.[31] Some were American natives and others were born abroad.[32] Delegates ranged from the young (a New Jersey delegate was twenty-six) to the aged (Benjamin Franklin was eighty-one).[33] The convention included luminaries such as George Washington and Alexander Hamilton, the latter considered by a French minister to be America's greatest statesman,[34] but was missing other marquee names such as Thomas Jefferson, John Adams, Patrick Henry, and Thomas Paine.[35] Still, when it came to education and experience, the delegates were an all-star team.[36]

Philadelphia, however, was hardly a five-star destination. Most of its approximately forty thousand inhabitants were closely packed in an eight-block stretch.[37] While it was the largest American city, the City of Brotherly Love in no way mirrored the great urban centers of its day; London had twenty-five times more residents.[38] Still, Philadelphia had a cosmopolitan feel: it was a center of international trade, the landing spot of immigrants from all over Europe, and the destination of slaves emancipated following the Revolution (Philadelphia was home to roughly two thousand free blacks in 1790).[39] And this was unique—in 1787, just 5.4 percent of Americans resided in places with a population of 2,500 or more.[40]

Although the city was sophisticated for its time and place, a modern visitor to Independence Hall might have requested a refund if she encountered the Philadelphia of 1787. Prostitutes and pickpockets mingled with shoppers and might together observe public floggings.[41] At the market—where a customer could purchase raccoon, opossum, fish otter, bear bacon, and bear's foot—butchers slaughtered animals at their stalls and patrons stood in pools of blood.[42] Marauding dogs and swine wandered the streets, horse corpses rested in common areas, and tanners threw used carcasses into the creek.[43] Contaminated water caused stomach ailments and insects carried diseases.[44] At least one delegate declined to serve due to the risk of smallpox in Philadelphia.[45]

Perhaps to counter the travails of daily life, Philadelphia was home to more than one hundred taverns. Men drank beer and liquor throughout the day and well past dinner.[46] Moreau de St. Méry, a Frenchman critical of American manners, reported that after the women retired for the evening, the men freely relieved themselves in "night tables and vases . . . to make room for more liquor."[47] Many delegates spent their spare time wining and dining with Philadelphia's elite.[48] This was poor entertainment for Virginia's George Mason, who quickly "tired of the etiquette and nonsense so fashionable in this city" and wrote to his son for updates on his farm.[49]

The delegates met in what is now known as Independence Hall, in the same room where the Declaration of Independence had been signed just eleven years earlier.[50] Despite the gravity of events the room hosted, it was not a place of quiet reflection and uninterrupted deliberation. It echoed with the comings and goings of litigants at the Pennsylvania Supreme Court across the hall; onlookers could see inside; and the sound of an outdoor excavation project rattled just one hundred feet away.[51] Traffic was so loud that delegates petitioned the city to regravel the streets.[52]

Adding to the commotion was the jail across the street, the scene of a riot during the convention.[53] From its cells, inmates shouted insults out the windows and begged for money.[54] Nor were these the only Philadelphia residents a luminary of the Revolution might encounter: the delegates' freestanding, outdoor privy accommodated sixteen people and could be used by any passerby.[55]

Although a modern Philadelphia resident might not have recognized her city, she would have been very familiar with the summer climate. Yet in 1787, residents lacked the benefit of air-conditioning. The delegates met six days a week clad in wool (Northerners) and linen (Southerners) from May through September.[56] A perhaps unforeseen consequence of the convention's adoption of a strictly observed rule of secrecy was that the doors and windows of the meeting room were shut.[57] And the room was packed—while nary a comment or telling glance would go undetected, neither would a bodily odor.[58] A New Jersey delegate proclaimed Philadelphia "the warmest place I have been in," and the meeting room must have been even more uncomfortable.[59]

The convention got off to a slow start. James Madison and George Washington were the only out-of-towners who arrived on time for the scheduled commencement.[60] Demonstrating both the difficulties of eighteenth-century travel (it took a month for news from Philadelphia to reach Pittsburgh)[61] and competing governing and economic priorities, the convention did not achieve a quorum for eleven days.[62] The New Hampshire legislature declined to cover its delegates' expenses, so they were forced to pay their own way and did not arrive until late July.[63] Rhode Island declined to participate, period.[64] Maryland's delegates initially refused to serve and never fully engaged (one did not arrive until August 6).[65]

The delay proved beneficial, however, for it allowed the Virginians and Pennsylvanians, who were among the most "active and intellectually gifted" supporters of a new government, to plan ahead.[66] They strategized for almost two weeks before a quorum assembled and the convention launched. Washington was nominated as presiding officer[67]—fitting since he stood over six feet, was still dashing in late middle age, and had arrived in Philadelphia to ringing church bells, firing cannons, and adoring throngs.[68]

Madison, who was prematurely balding, shy, and no more than five feet six inches tall,[69] kept a record of proceedings and did not miss "more than a casual fraction of an hour in any day" of the convention.[70] His notes are our primary window into what happened behind closed doors.

It is from this gumbo of personalities and experiences, all on full display in a hothouse environment over four often unpleasant months, that our Constitution was born. One wonders whether the delegates to the convention, who worked in challenging (and occasionally colorful) circumstances, would be surprised to learn how profoundly "the Miracle at Philadelphia"[71] changed the world.

No miracle would have occurred had the delegates stuck to their charge of amending the Articles of Confederation and preserving the existing state autonomy. It is difficult for a twenty-first-century American to understand how integral state identity was to her eighteenth-century counterpart. The states, which functioned like allied separate countries, had yielded only the slimmest authority to the federal government in the Articles of Confederation. There was neither a judicial nor an executive branch, and the unicameral federal legislature, in which each state had one vote, possessed minimal power. The business of government was handled almost exclusively at the state level.

This had to change if the United States was to succeed as a nation. Yet creating a more centralized federal government required more than a few tweaks to the Articles of Confederation, so the delegates took the momentous step of scrapping the Articles and starting afresh. Their challenge was to create a federal government that was effective, but not so powerful that it threatened individual liberty or banished state autonomy. To say the drafters succeeded is an understatement. In seven articles, they succinctly established the architecture and relationship of the nation's governmental bodies:

ARTICLE I, by far the longest article, created a bicameral legislative branch, consisting of the Senate and House of Representatives, and enumerated the legislative powers.

ARTICLE II established the executive branch, defining the office and duties of the president.

ARTICLE III created a brand-new Supreme Court, authorized Congress to create lower federal courts, and defined the scope of federal judicial power.

ARTICLE IV governed the relationship between the states.

ARTICLE V described the process for constitutional amendment.

ARTICLE VI established the validity of existing federal debts; the supremacy of the Constitution, federal laws, and federal treaties; and the requirement that elected and appointed officials support the Constitution.

ARTICLE VII stated that the Constitution would be valid if ratified by conventions in nine states.

The Constitution's bare-bones, matter-of-fact language masks its genius. The framers managed to navigate the self-interest of each state delegation to create a system of horizontal (separation of powers) and vertical (federalism) checks and balances. This structure satisfied the delegates that their states could be subject to an effective federal government while preserving a sufficient degree of their historical sovereignty. There was no blueprint for this project, because nothing like it had ever been tried. A written constitution that created a centralized federal government with coequal branches while preserving power in sovereign states was a new event in world history.

In many ways, experience had readied the delegates for this project. Three-fourths had served in the Continental Congress, and many in state government too—priming them with political savvy that they brought to bear in the design of the new government.[72] Some had participated in the drafting of state constitutions, provisions of which the framers borrowed. More than half of the delegates had legal training.[73] Because the colonists were British citizens, the delegates were familiar with English government by monarchy and Parliament—and knew well the abuses it allowed. The delegates "were unusually well educated,"[74] and, versed in political theory, they drew heavily from writers like John Locke and Baron de Montesquieu in revising the American system. The initial drafter of the Articles of Confederation, John Dickinson, served as a delegate, and he was ready to replace the failing confederation with a stronger national government.[75] Madison brought more than experience to Philadelphia: months before the convention convened, he confided to Washington that he had been considering "the subject which is to undergo the discussion of the Convention, and formed in my mind *some* outlines of a new system."[76] He proceeded to lay out the plan, which was the culmination of a year's intensive work and presaged some features of the Constitution.[77] Charles Pinckney, a delegate from South Carolina, also came to the convention armed with a draft Constitution.[78]

It took four months of negotiations for the delegates to hammer out an agreement. Even a quick read of the Constitution reveals the number of details they had to settle. Consider just a few: What powers should the chief executive have and how should he be elected? How should judges be picked and how long should they serve? How extensive should the federal legislative power be? What matters should be left to the states? What process should govern ratification and subsequent amendment of the Constitution? Many books have been written about the Constitution's drafting, and I won't attempt to catalog the negotiations here. I'll describe just two of the debates.

One of the greatest clashes was between large and small states and concerned the manner of legislative representation.[79] Large states wanted the number of representatives to be based upon population. They supported the Virginia Plan, which proposed a bicameral legislature with proportional representation in each house.[80] Smaller states, desiring equal representation untethered from population, endorsed a one-house legislature with equal numbers of representatives from each state.

The debate was a power struggle. The Virginia Plan equipped big states to guard their interests at the expense of small states, which could be easily railroaded. Why would Delaware agree to a structure in which it was no longer equal to Pennsylvania? The alternative (sometimes called the New Jersey Plan) solved that inequity but inadequately accounted for the desires of the population as a whole. Why would Pennsylvania, which represented many more citizens than Delaware, agree to have the same voice as its tiny neighbor? The arguments grew fiercer by the day.[81]

Connecticut's Roger Sherman, the second-oldest delegate at sixty-six and the only signer of all the nation's foundational documents, bridged the gap.[82] He proposed proportional representation in one body (the House) and equal representation in the other (the Senate).[83] It worked. In what became known as the Connecticut Compromise, each side got part of what it wanted—the system reflected both respect for the will of the popular majority and the continued importance of individual state identities in the uniquely American form of government.[84] The compromise not only kept the convention afloat; it reflected the logic of federalism.

Another major struggle, also about legislative representation, pitted North against South rather than large states against small. This clash stemmed from the horror of slavery. Southern states wanted to count their large slave populations in determining their representation in the House and Electoral College; Northern states resisted because counting slaves would inflate the power of the Southern states.[85] The Continental Congress had at one time proposed to calculate the tax obligation of each state according to its wealth, and the formula assumed that "the wealth-producing capacity of a slave was roughly three-fifths that of a free person."[86] That proposal didn't pass in the Continental Congress, but the three-fifths fraction resurfaced at the convention.[87] After bitter debate and much negotiation, the delegates chose to count each slave as three-fifths of a person in a state's population total.[88] It was not the only deal that the delegates made regarding slavery: to get South Carolina and Georgia to go along with greater congressional power to regulate commerce, states that would have preferred to immediately outlaw the importation of slaves agreed to permit it for twenty more years.[89]

This compromise prompted one prominent delegate, Gouverneur Morris, to take the floor for "the first abolitionist speech in American political life," condemning slavery as a "nefarious institution" and "the curse of Heaven on the states where it prevailed."[90] Still, the abolitionists in the room never actually proposed abolition. It would have shattered the convention, and everyone knew it.[91] So opponents of slavery swallowed their objections, most believing that slavery would fade away on its own—though this, of course, failed to account for the human suffering that would be endured while awaiting that day.[92]

Hamilton told the New York ratifying convention that without the three-fifths ratio, "no union could possibly have been formed."[93] Be that as it may, at the onset of the Civil War, John Adams's grandson sagely observed, "We the children of the third and fourth generation are doomed to pay the penalties of the compromises made by the first."[94] The consequences of those compromises reverberate still.

GEORGE WASHINGTON WAS the first of thirty-nine delegates to sign the Constitution on September 17, 1787.[95] (Sixteen of the original delegates did not sign.) Yet the work was not done—by its terms, the Constitution was ineffective until ratified by nine states. Given that the Constitution could have been scuttled if roughly one-third of the states had objected,[96] we should not view ratification as inevitable and the state debates as mere mopping up. One Virginia delegate declined to sign the Constitution because he believed that the public would not accept it, and another began drafting his objections before the Constitution had even been signed.[97] The supporters, who called themselves Federalists,[98] had momentum and organization on their side, as well as four months of having considered the issues.[99] Nonetheless, they faced the task of convincing a skeptical public that greatly enhanced federal power was necessary and even desirable.

Given the secrecy of the convention's deliberations, the public must have been stunned to see a document that did not modify the Articles of Confederation, but instead replaced them wholesale.[100] The delegates quickly began the next stage of the process, with a Pennsylvania delegate taking the Constitution upstairs to a session of the Pennsylvania Assembly.[101] Tensions were high: when opponents of the Constitution abandoned the Pennsylvania legislature to deny it a quorum to vote on the call for a ratification convention, a gang organized by Federalists found the missing participants and dragged two of them back.[102]

The positions on either side of the ratification debate are reflected in several hundred essays published from the end of the Convention through late 1788.[103] *The Federalist Papers*, a series of eighty-five essays published in New York City newspapers by Alexander Hamilton (who wrote fifty-one), James Madison (who wrote twenty-nine), and John Jay (who wrote five), made a cogent and compelling case for ratification. *The Federalist Papers* probably had only a small impact on the ratification vote in New York or elsewhere.[104] But they served as a "debater's handbook" for Federalists pleading their cause, and their influence on those who have interpreted the Constitution in the ensuing centuries is hard to overstate.[105] The arguments *against* ratification were advanced by those who became known as Anti-Federalists (a nickname coined by their Federalist opponents).[106] Unlike the essays of *The Federalist Papers*, which were coordinated by their three authors, the Anti-Federalist writings (which number in the hundreds) were published by numerous authors working independently in different states.[107] Although the Anti-Federalists' arguments did not carry the day, they provide valuable context for the arguments that did—and, as we shall see, the Anti-Federalists scored a significant victory in persuading the state conventions to insist on the addition of a Bill of Rights.

Objections to the Constitution ran the gamut. Predictably, Federalists had to defend against the claim that the convention had exceeded its authority by abandoning the Articles of Confederation. They insisted both that producing a new document fell within the letter of the convention's charge and that circumstances justified abandoning the Articles.[108] But even if the convention had exceeded its authority, Madison argued, "does it follow that the Constitution ought, for that reason alone, to be rejected? If, according to the noble precept, it be lawful to accept good advice even from an enemy, shall we set the ignoble example of refusing such advice even when it is offered by our friends?"[109] Plus, "[w]e the People"[110] possessed the sovereign power to form a new government, and if the people exercised that power by ratifying the proposed Constitution through their state conventions, the resulting government would be legitimate.[111]

On the substance of the document, the wisdom of establishing a strong national government dominated discussion. Anti-Federalists identified a litany of risks, including heavy federal taxes, aggressive exercises of federal legislative authority, and prestigious federal courts that would overtake the role of state judicial systems.[112] The overarching concern was that a stronger centralized government would erase the importance of the states. In response, Federalists highlighted the ways in which the Constitution preserved the role of the states, including proportional representation in the House, equal representation in the Senate, proportional representation in the Electoral College, and limits on federal legislative authority.[113] They also stressed that both the ratification of the Constitution and any subsequent amendment are channeled through states: while the Constitution's authority derives from the sovereign people, they exercise it as citizens of states, through a majority vote in state conventions, rather than as citizens of the United States, through a nationwide majority vote.[114] The Federalists did not deny that the Constitution curbed state authority—after all, that was the point of abandoning the Articles. But they underscored the continuing importance of states in the proposed government. This debate about the proper balance between state and federal authority did not end with the Constitution's ratification; it has continued ever since.

Opponents also criticized the Constitution for blurring the lines between legislative, executive, and judicial power. As some understood Montesquieu's theory, a strict separation of powers is what prevents any single person or governmental body from becoming too powerful. The Constitution, however, did not give each branch total dominion in its own sphere. An important innovation was to achieve checks and balances by carefully blending the powers as well as separating them. A few examples: Congress possesses legislative power, subject to a presidential veto; the president heads the military, but Congress declares war; and the president appoints important executive branch officials, subject to the Senate's power of advice and consent. Madison, who was largely responsible for this design of checks and balances, brilliantly defended it in *The Federalist Papers*, insisting that the Constitution's approach to tripartite government was both more faithful to Montesquieu and more protective of liberty than one that siloed legislative, executive, and judicial power.[115]

The ratification debates brought class tensions to the fore. Opponents of the Constitution worried that the new government would entrench an aristocracy of senators.[116] An Anti-Federalist who called himself "Federal Farmer" characterized the framers themselves as "the consolidating aristocracy" whose proposed system concentrated power "in a few hands," rendering a "strong tendency to aristocracy now discernable in every part of the plan."[117] In another tract, he warned that the capital city of the proposed republic would "be the great, the visible, and dazzling centre, the mistress of fashions, and the fountain of politics" that housed the equivalent of a royal court, complete with its hangers-on.[118] The Constitution's defenders protested that the American temperament and structure were inconsistent with European-style "distinctions of rank" and its "honors and offices are equally open to the exertions of all her citizens."[119] They pointed out that the Constitution expressly forbade both the United States and the states from granting any "Title of Nobility."[120] And they resisted the notion that the president would function as an elected monarch—a concern that the drafters shared and tried to address in the document.

Five states (three unanimously) ratified the Constitution within four months of its signing. But as the debate moved to states with stronger opposition—such as Massachusetts, the site of Shays' Rebellion[121]—there would be no more unanimous votes. Massachusetts ratified after John

Hancock presented a plan to adopt the Constitution but include recommended amendments,[122] a formula that six of the remaining seven states followed.[123] Apparently anticipating a loss, Federalists in New Hampshire bought time by moving to adjourn the state's convention before a vote.[124] New Hampshire eventually became the ninth state to ratify the Constitution, making it effective, but by a margin of only ten votes.[125] Rhode Island rejected the Constitution by a lopsided popular vote, 2,708 to 235, after the legislature refused to call a ratifying convention.[126] Following Virginia's ratification (also by ten votes), New York approved the Constitution by three votes after a fierce in-state political battle.[127]

But in the end, all thirteen states (including Rhode Island) ratified the Constitution, with votes closer in some states than others.

Delaware	*30-0*	*December 7, 1787*
Pennsylvania	*46-23*	*December 12, 1787*
New Jersey	*38-0*	*December 18, 1787*
Georgia	*26-0*	*January 2, 1788*
Connecticut	*128-40*	*January 9, 1788*
Massachusetts	*187-168*	*February 6, 1788*
Maryland	*63-11*	*April 28, 1788*
South Carolina	*149-73*	*May 23, 1788*
New Hampshire	*57-47*	*June 21, 1788*
Virginia	*89-79*	*June 25, 1788*
New York	*30-27*	*July 26, 1788*
North Carolina	*194-77*	*November 21, 1789*
Rhode Island	*34-32*	*May 29, 1790*

The state ratifying conventions and the delegates who have been relegated to obscurity are not merely a footnote to the convention: without them, the document would have been a dead letter. Though the fifty-five delegates to the convention drafted the Constitution, the people approved it. And so it belongs to the people, not the framers.

As I'll discuss in the next chapter, the Constitution was not frozen at ratification. It contains a provision allowing amendment, and the people have taken advantage of that process. Still, the foundational document has remained in place. While a modern Philadelphian wouldn't recognize the city of the convention and a delegate wouldn't recognize the city today, both would recognize the structure of the government the Constitution established. The document produced by the "Miracle at Philadelphia," along with its amendments, appears as an appendix to this book.[128]

Chapter 9

A FIRMER FOUNDATION

THE CONSTITUTION that was so important to Abigail Adams remains important to Americans today. It has pride of place in the National Archives, which hosted more than one million visitors in the year before the pandemic limited access. The first time my children visited, they pressed themselves against the glass to get the closest possible look at our founding documents. Maybe they were thinking about my day job; more likely, they were marveling at documents written in fancy, aged handwriting rather than the sleek modern typefaces that they're used to. Jesse and I have also taken our family to the National Constitution Center in Philadelphia, the city where the Constitution was born. The center is not an obscure place that only a Supreme Court justice could love: it attracted one million visitors in its first fifteen months of operation. By design, the center is located near Independence Hall, the location of the Constitutional Convention in 1787. That is my favorite of these destinations. I am captivated by the room where the Constitution was drafted; I imagine the delegates debating while James Madison scribbled his notes. Unsurprisingly, that flight of fancy is better enjoyed on solo visits. It did not impress my teenage sons, who were far more interested in getting to the next stop for Philly cheesesteaks.

Yet Americans do not encounter the Constitution only in buildings like the National Archives and Independence Hall. Relative to other countries, America's devotion to its Constitution stands out.[1] The Constitution has its own dedicated day on the calendar—the date of its signing, September 17—and schools, from elementary to university, hold events to celebrate it. It has been the subject of an award-winning Broadway play,[2] not to mention books,[3] podcasts,[4] and even music.[5] In 2016, the pocket Constitution briefly reached second place on Amazon's bestseller list.[6] American reverence for our foundational document is remarkable. Abraham Lincoln extolled the Constitution as part of "the *political religion* of the nation."[7] That's an apt description. Our country is extraordinarily diverse, but we hold the Constitution in common.

The age of our Constitution is important to its place in the American consciousness. The United States was the first country to have a written constitution, so American reverence for the document has accumulated over generations. Consider that the average constitution is replaced every nineteen years,[8] while we've lived with ours for nearly 250 years. Since our Constitution was ratified, France has gone through five republics, two empires, and two kingdoms—not to mention sixteen constitutions.[9] The longevity of our Constitution is a sign of its success, but it also connects Americans of the present to Americans of the past. The United States has faced immense challenges and undergone drastic changes. Yet through it all, we have remained committed to the fundamental law established by early Americans and handed down through succeeding generations.

That said, the Constitution of today is (of course) not identical to the document ratified in 1788. Along the way, Americans have invoked the Constitution's amendment process to improve it—for impressive as it was, the original Constitution was flawed. Looking through the lens of my own life is revealing. Though I sit on the Supreme Court today, there's no chance I could have served as a delegate to the Constitutional Convention. In fact, every member of my family would have fared poorly in the Founding Era. As women, my four daughters and I would have lacked many of the most basic rights, including the right to vote.[10] My two adopted children, descended from slaves in Haiti, would have had virtually no rights at all.[11] Even my white husband might have been barred from the ballot box. Coming from a modest background, he likely would have lacked the wealth necessary to satisfy the property ownership requirement.[12] And as Catholics, we all would have been disqualified from holding office in many states.[13]

These eighteenth-century realities affected day-to-day living, the existence of "self"-government, and the makeup of the Constitutional Convention. Of the fifty-five delegates to the Constitutional Convention, none was a woman, none was a person of color, all owned property (usually a lot of it), and nearly all were Protestant.[14]

The elimination of these barriers illustrates the Constitution's capacity for change—and the framers' wisdom in leaving us free to make it. Since the people ratified the original Constitution, they have amended it twenty-seven times.[15] Some of the amendments address the nuts and bolts of government—matters like presidential succession, congressional compensation, and whether states can be sued.[16] The lion's share, though, expand the rights of citizens—including the provisions extending the American promise of self-government to the once disenfranchised.[17] As a result, the amendments are provisions that Americans hold particularly dear.

The push for amendment began before the ink on the original document was dry. The Constitution did not initially protect individual rights, because the drafters thought the Constitution's structure—its trademark division of power—offered sufficient protection for individual liberty.[18] As Hamilton wrote, "Why, for instance, should it be said that the liberty of the press shall not be restrained, when no power is given by which restrictions may be imposed?"[19] If no grant of power in Article I authorized Congress to pass legislation infringing freedom, an affirmative restraint was unnecessary. There were other objections too: state constitutions already protected individual rights; it was contradictory to announce protected rights in a country containing slaves; and naming specific rights might preclude the recognition of others.[20]

Yet the people wanted more than constitutional structure to protect their individual rights from the whims of the federal government.[21] A consistent objection raised by the Anti-Federalists, the Constitution's main opponents, was the absence of any explicit protections of individual liberty; indeed, this was "[t]he single issue that united Anti-Federalists throughout the country."[22] The states took the lead in the push for such protection, and many of them ratified on the understanding that a bill of rights would be added after the Constitution became effective.[23]

That understanding was based on trust, because there was no concrete proposal ready to go. James Madison, George Washington, and other supporters of the Constitution worried (with good reason) that the Anti-Federalists would sow chaos by convening a second constitutional convention to take up a bill of rights, which would give them an opportunity to propose structural amendments too.[24] That maneuver would stall the new government before it got off the ground. To head off that prospect, Madison, who had been elected to the First Congress, immediately made a bill of rights his top priority.[25] He gathered the amendments related to individual rights that had been proposed in the state conventions (about seventy-five after duplicates were cut), weighting them based on their number of appearances.[26]

Madison offered nineteen amendments in the First Congress in June 1789.[27] The proposal received a lukewarm reception. Many Federalists dismissed the idea as frivolous, if not intemperate, given that the Constitution's supporters had just run the gauntlet for ratification.[28] Meanwhile, the Anti-Federalists thought that adopting the proposed amendments would thwart their goal of conducting a second convention at which they could try to undo some of the achievements of the first.[29] Due in large part to Madison's tenacity, twelve amendments were passed by the House and

Senate and sent to the states for approval.[30] Between November 1789 and December 1791, the necessary number of states ratified ten of them.[31]

Those ten amendments—collectively called the Bill of Rights—are not only the first added but also the best known. Among them are the freedom of speech, the freedom of religion, protection from unreasonable searches and seizures, the right against compelled self-incrimination, the right to a jury trial, and the right to be free from cruel and unusual punishment—all core liberties that most Americans would be quicker to name than, say, the enumerated congressional powers in Article I or the Privileges and Immunities Clause of Article IV.

Thanks to Madison's efforts, the Constitution now enshrined several core individual liberty and property rights, and the Anti-Federalist threat of a second convention dissipated. Though the achievement was colossal, its reach was not obvious. Thomas Jefferson had to point out to Madison that one benefit of the Bill of Rights was the "legal check which it puts into the hands of the judiciary."[32] The idea that federal courts would review laws for consistency with the Bill of Rights had apparently not occurred to the bill's architect.[33]

Madison initially proposed that his amendments be worked into the body of the original Constitution, not tacked on as a by-the-way coda.[34] He was concerned that a separate list of amendments would become an "ignored appendix" rather than an integrated part of the Constitution.[35] Yet some of the force of the Bill of Rights lies in its presentation as a free-standing list of the protections we enjoy as Americans; Madison's suggestion would have sacrificed this rhetorical and symbolic power.[36]

The Bill of Rights eventually acquired a transcendent status in our republic—one well beyond the conception of its authors. And although the legal effect of the Bill of Rights was not fully anticipated at the time of its ratification, the people's demand for a Bill of Rights nonetheless reveals something fundamental about the American spirit. By adopting the Bill of Rights, the founding generation made the Constitution a more morally laden document. Outside of the Preamble, most of the original Constitution looks pretty dry to most citizens—a lot about how we select our representatives and what they may do with that power, but little about American freedoms. Immediately after we adopted the new Constitution, though, the American people chose to do more to protect our liberty. It wasn't enough that our country be protected by the checks and balances of federalism and the separation of powers. Americans wanted specifics, and wanted them in writing—promises that the federal government would not violate the rights that Americans considered most sacred.

THE BILL OF Rights gave the country its first opportunity to deploy the process of constitutional amendment. The necessary steps are prescribed by Article V, which identifies two routes for constitutional change. Congress may propose amendments if two-thirds of both the House and the Senate agree.[37] Proposing an amendment thus takes the same number of votes as overriding a presidential veto—another one of the Constitution's most conspicuous supermajority requirements.[38] Alternatively, two-thirds of the state legislatures can call for a special convention to propose constitutional amendments, much like the Constitutional Convention that proposed our original Constitution.[39] So far, this last possibility has been only theoretical. We've never had a sequel to the 1787 Constitutional Convention; Congress has proposed all of our constitutional amendments, including the Bill of Rights.[40]

Whether it's two-thirds of both houses of Congress or two-thirds of the states, Article V sets an imposing bar. And that's only what it takes to *propose* an amendment. To actually adopt an amendment, three-fourths of the states must ratify it, either through their legislatures or special ratifying conventions.[41] It's little wonder that amendment is rare—perhaps too rare.

To be sure, the Constitution is much easier to amend than its predecessor, the Articles of Confederation. Because thirteen state legislatures had to agree to any change, no change was ever made.[42] Efforts to amend the Articles died when a lone state stopped the process or exploited its leverage by demanding unreasonable concessions from the other twelve.[43]

Surely more than one state impeded needed changes between 1781 and 1789.[44] But many founders blamed one: Rhode Island. Alexander Hamilton emphasized the delegates' view that the Constitution should be easier to amend than the Articles, hinting that necessary reforms had been stymied by the obstinacy of "a particular State."[45] The identity of that state was no secret. A frustrated Madison informed the Virginia convention that the "petty state of Rhode Island" was "obstruct[ing] every attempt" to reform the Articles; he insisted that a three-fourths requirement would prevent such obstinacy in the future.[46] Other critics were even less diplomatic, with some calling the state "Rogue Island" and hoping that it would be struck out of the Union entirely.[47] Consistent with its reputation as a holdout, Rhode Island didn't send delegates to the Constitutional Convention and was the last of the original thirteen colonies to ratify the new Constitution.[48]

The difficulty of adapting the Articles to new circumstances convinced most delegates to take unanimous consent off the table, sidelining future "Rogue Islands" from impeding progress for the rest of the nation.[49] Yet the appropriate threshold for amendment was vigorously debated and remains a vexing topic today.[50] Yes, the experience with the Articles of Confederation counseled against making amendment too difficult. But other concerns counseled against making it too easy. A readily amendable Constitution imperils many of its safeguards, undermines respect for it, and risks turning it into something that looks more like a statutory code than a framework for government. The founders thus walked a tightrope, balancing "equally against that extreme facility, which would render the Constitution too mutable; and that extreme difficulty, which might perpetuate its discovered faults."[51] The end result was an amendment process that removed the insurmountable obstacle of unanimity but guarded against the whims of temporary majorities and the risk that a few regions of the country would dominate the rest.

At the time, the framers must have thought their approach showed moderation—after all, it was a major departure from the unanimity requirement of the Articles. From the vantage point of the present, however, the framers' compromise might not look moderate enough. One scholar, after analyzing the constitutions of thirty-two countries, determined that the U.S. Constitution was by far the most difficult to amend.[52] Here at home, all fifty state constitutions are more easily changed—forty-one of them with a mere majority vote.[53] As a result, all state constitutions have been amended more frequently than the federal Constitution, an average of about 150 times each.[54] The difficulty of the federal amendment process has prompted commentators from across the political spectrum to call for at least a slightly lowered bar.[55] Such a change might be prudent. Those who regard the process as too onerous often seek constitutional change from the Supreme Court—and seeking change from an unelected body of nine is about as far from the Article V supermajority process as you can get.

Yet despite its difficulty, amendment isn't impossible. In the first chapter, I shared that I keep a picture of my great-grandmother's house on my desk. Reflecting on her experience as I wrote this book was revealing: though the Constitution is difficult to change, it was amended *ten times* during her life. (When she was thirty-five years old, one of those amendments—the Nineteenth—gave her the right to vote.) All in all, the American people have amended the Constitution twenty-seven times. Each of those amendments has marked an occasion on which Americans have rallied together to address a felt need of their time. I'd like to think that if there is another felt need, we can rally together again.

THE FIRST TEN amendments offered an early indication that Americans were not afraid to amend their new Constitution when something was

missing. The ratification of the Bill of Rights in 1791 closed some, though not all, of the gaps left by a document that failed to explicitly protect our foundational liberties.

The Eleventh Amendment illustrates another motivation for change: disagreement with a decision of the Supreme Court. *Chisholm v. Georgia*, which involved money that Georgia borrowed during the Revolutionary War, ignited a firestorm in the young republic.[56] Alexander Chisholm, a resident of South Carolina, sued Georgia in federal court to recover on such a debt; the state refused even to appear, maintaining that its sovereign immunity prohibited it from being sued without its consent.[57] The bottom line? Chisholm had no way of making Georgia pay what it owed. Though Georgia's position might take you aback, it was consistent with the long-standing rule that a government is immune from suit. And in an age when states (and their citizens) were fiercely protective of state prerogatives, this immunity mattered a great deal to Georgia, as well as to the other states. After all, the authority of state governments vis-à-vis the federal government was the hottest topic in debates about whether to ratify the original Constitution.[58]

In a divided decision, the Supreme Court held that Georgia was subject to suit in the courts of the United States.[59] Article III of the Constitution expressly authorized federal courts to adjudicate cases "between a State and Citizens of another State."[60] Because Chisholm was not a citizen of Georgia, the Court reasoned, his suit fell squarely within this language and could proceed.[61] The states had relinquished sovereign immunity, at least from this kind of suit, when they ratified the Constitution.

Georgia was outraged—so much so that its House of Representatives passed a bill authorizing the death penalty for anyone who attempted to carry out the judgment entered in *Chisholm v. Georgia*.[62] In the rest of the country, the response to the decision was similarly swift but fortunately less extreme.[63] One year after the decision, strong majorities in both chambers of Congress—an eighty-one to nine vote in the House, a twenty-three to two vote in the Senate—proposed the Eleventh Amendment.[64] It prohibited federal courts from entertaining such lawsuits and by its terms directly overruled *Chisholm*. There were fifteen states by then, requiring twelve states to ratify the amendment. Congress completed its proposal on March 4, 1794, and the legislature of the twelfth state, North Carolina, ratified it on February 7, 1795.[65] Without telegraphs, telephones, or the internet, the people acted with remarkable dispatch in dealing with a Court decision that they did not like.

One might have expected the brisk pace of amendment to continue, but it slowed instead. Save for the Twelfth Amendment, ratified in 1804 to adjust the procedure for electing presidents and vice presidents through the Electoral College, the Constitution did not see another amendment until 1865—when the people ratified the Thirteenth Amendment, which abolished slavery.[66] That amendment not only required considerable time and a misbegotten Supreme Court decision (*Dred Scott v. Sandford*), but also a bloody civil war.

⁂

THE SPIRIT OF promising Americans more freedoms has largely driven the amending process since the Bill of Rights. True enough, some amendments have been practical. Most Americans, I suspect, do not dearly cherish the Twelfth Amendment's tweaks to presidential elections. But the dominant story in our country has been use of the amendment process to expand individual rights.

This spirit was clearest in the immediate aftermath of the Civil War, which brought the most fundamental changes to the Constitution in our nation's history. We ratified three amendments to the Constitution in rapid succession.

Preeminently, of course, we ended slavery with the Thirteenth Amendment, extending the most basic of liberties to all Americans.[67] This was also the first amendment that directly governs private individuals rather than the government alone. Slavery and involuntary servitude were banned everywhere in the United States, no matter who engaged in the practice.

Reconstruction also brought us the Fourteenth Amendment. Among other things, this amendment demanded that states give all persons "the equal protection of the laws"—a promise quickly deflated by Jim Crow laws, which enforced segregation on the theory that separate facilities were not inherently "unequal."[68] After initially allowing such laws in *Plessy v. Ferguson*,[69] the Supreme Court redeemed both itself and the Fourteenth Amendment's promise—albeit after decades of injustice—in *Brown v. Board of Education*, which ended school segregation.[70] Over time, the Court extended this holding beyond schools to forbid all racial discrimination by the states.[71]

Even beyond its seismic impact on matters of race, the Fourteenth Amendment radically extended the reach of the Bill of Rights. As ratified in 1791, the Bill of Rights restrained only the federal government, not the states.[72] (The First Amendment, for instance, declares that "*Congress* shall make no law respecting an establishment of religion, or prohibiting the free exercise thereof.")[73] The Fourteenth Amendment changed that. Its Due Process Clause prohibits "any State" from depriving "any person of life, liberty, or property without due process of law."[74] In the landmark case of *Gitlow v. New York*, the Court held that the First Amendment's safeguards for speech and the press "are among the fundamental personal rights and 'liberties' protected by the Due Process Clause of the Fourteenth Amendment from impairment by the States."[75] The Court has gradually expanded this reasoning to most other protections in the Bill of Rights.[76] It did so as recently as 2020, when it held that the Due Process Clause required the states to honor the Sixth Amendment's requirement of a unanimous guilty verdict to convict a criminal defendant.[77]

The last Reconstruction amendment is the Fifteenth, which provides that neither the United States nor any state can abridge the right to vote on the basis of race. Like the Thirteenth and Fourteenth Amendments, it gave Congress the power to enact legislation to ensure that states abided by this rule.[78] On the one hand, it was an act of moral clarity that would have been unthinkable a few short years earlier. On the other, the right to vote meant little when so many Americans and courts failed to respect it. Even the Supreme Court thwarted change when, in *United States v. Reese*, it construed the Fifteenth Amendment so narrowly that large numbers of black Americans lacked access to the franchise for many years after the right had theoretically been enshrined.[79]

The Reconstruction amendments teach a hard lesson: the Constitution's superpower (it trumps the will of transient majorities) is also its Achilles' heel (it must withstand pressure from transient majorities). The law, even something as sturdy as constitutional law, is not enough to guarantee freedom. It is effective only if government officials have the courage to enforce it against a hostile citizenry. And we cannot legislate a culture of respect for law into existence. Our constitutional project can succeed only if Americans invest in it.

Since Reconstruction, Americans have frequently used the amendment process to expand the number of Americans who can vote. The Nineteenth Amendment ensured that women could not be denied the right to vote on the basis of sex.[80] The Twenty-Sixth Amendment ensured that no one eighteen years of age or older could be denied the right to vote on the basis of age.[81] The Twenty-Fourth Amendment banned poll taxes,[82] which denied the right to vote on the basis of income. The Twenty-Third Amendment granted the right to vote in presidential elections to citizens of the District of Columbia.[83] And the Seventeenth Amendment—while not directly changing *who* could vote—expanded what the people voted on, by requiring senators be directly elected by the people of each state rather than appointed by state legislatures.[84] All told, five of the twelve twentieth-century amendments have in some way expanded voting rights.[85]

That pattern demonstrates something powerful about the history of American constitutional amendment. A cynic might doubt that those with a monopoly on voting power would agree to share it with others. Granted, convincing Americans to dilute their own voting power has not been easy. Extending the franchise to black Americans took more than a civil war, and the women's suffrage movement involved decades of passionate advocacy by women. But as hard as it may have been, appeals to the American ideal that all people are created equal and have a right to participate in self-government ultimately won out, time after time. The amendment process turned those appeals from abstract to concrete commitments, giving specific legal rights to specific groups of American people.

Those appeals for change came from the people themselves. Many times, well-known leaders were at the forefront, like Madison (the Bill of Rights), John Bingham (the Fourteenth Amendment), or Ida B. Wells and Alice Paul (the Nineteenth Amendment).[86] But the well-known do not hold a monopoly on constitutional change. Considerable credit for passage of our most recent amendment, the Twenty-Seventh, goes to a college student.

In 1982, as a sophomore at the University of Texas, Greg Watson wrote a paper for his political science class about one of the original amendments proposed by Madison—one prohibiting any member of the House or Senate from benefiting from a salary increase until after an intervening election.[87] While several states ratified the amendment soon after Madison proposed it, the amendment languished and, but for Watson's efforts, might have been forgotten entirely.[88] (Some amendments have prescribed time limits for ratification, but the congressional pay amendment did not.)[89] His professor, doubting the viability of an amendment proposed nearly two hundred years earlier, apparently gave him a C.[90] Even after Watson, showing early signs of persistence, appealed the grade, the professor left it in place.[91]

Stuck with a middling grade, Watson refused to let the latent amendment go. Using his own savings, he began a campaign to convince the necessary three-quarters of the states to ratify the amendment.[92] In 1992—a decade after he turned in his college paper—he succeeded when Michigan carried the amendment over the threshold for ratification.[93] That was not the end of the story, at least for Watson. After the Twenty-Seventh Amendment passed, the University of Texas changed his grade to an A+.[94]

That was our last amendment, so the Constitution has now gone for decades without change.

WHAT ABOUT THE failed amendments? The twenty-seven successes constitute a small fraction of the total attempts to amend our Constitution. Since our founding, there have been roughly twelve thousand amendments proposed in Congress.[95] These proposed amendments generally reflect the issues and values of their times. Take the amendment introduced into the House in 1838 that would have barred anyone who had participated in a duel from holding public office.[96] That amendment might seem unimportant now, but it probably felt more pressing then, given that Representative William Graves of Kentucky had just killed Representative Jonathan Cilley of Maine in a duel.[97] Some proposals, though, defy explanation in *any* time. In the 1890s, for instance, Representative Lucas Miller of Wisconsin proposed an amendment to rename "the United States of America" as "the United States of Earth."[98] His stated rationale? That "it is possible for the Republic to grow through the admission of new States into the Union until every Nation on Earth has become part of it."[99] A rather extreme vision of America's future and an ambitious take on Manifest Destiny. But the amendment gained no traction, Miller was not nominated for reelection, and the United States of America felt no need to change its name when Hawaii was admitted to the Union, expanding our nation's borders beyond the continent of North America.

Most of the thousands of failed amendments came and went without ever receiving serious attention from Congress. Six proposed amendments, however, had sufficiently widespread support to command the necessary two-thirds vote in both the House and Senate.[100] But when it came time for state legislatures to approve, they balked.

The first of these six near amendments to the Constitution arguably would have required that there never be fewer than one member of the House of Representatives per fifty thousand persons.[101] It was the only one from Madison's initial list that was never ratified, but had it become effective, it could have radically changed the operation of our federal government. Today, there might be more than six thousand members in the House, instead of the current 435.[102] It's hard to imagine where such an unwieldy body would meet, but it certainly wouldn't be in the current House Chamber of the U.S. Capitol.

The second near amendment, if passed, would have been far less consequential. In 1810, Congress proposed an amendment that would have stripped citizenship from any citizen who received a foreign title.[103] This might have stopped Billy Graham and Steven Spielberg from taking their honorary knighthoods, but it would not have changed much about American political life today.[104]

The third near amendment—known as the Corwin Amendment after its sponsor in Congress—shows that the amendment process can be used for evil as well as good.[105] On the eve of the Civil War, in a desperate effort to prevent Southern secession, Congress proposed an amendment that would have forbidden any future amendment to the Constitution that gave Congress the power to "interfere, within any State, with the domestic institutions thereof, including that of persons held to labor or service by the laws of said State."[106] Put more simply, the amendment would have foreclosed nationwide abolition. Thankfully, it did not receive the requisite three-fourths ratification,[107] and—four years and a civil war later—we amended the Constitution to ban slavery. The near-miss Corwin Amendment confirms that the rigorous process of amending the Constitution can be a blessing.

Opposition to a Supreme Court decision spurred the fourth near amendment. In *Hammer v. Dagenhart*, the Court held that the Commerce Clause in Article I of the Constitution did not authorize Congress to regulate child labor.[108] Congress responded to the decision by proposing an amendment that would give it the "power to limit, regulate, and prohibit the labor of persons under eighteen years of age."[109] Ratification moved slowly, and more than a decade later, the amendment had still not been approved by three-quarters of the states. (In fact, the amendment is technically still pending.)[110] Events overtook the proposal, however, when the Supreme Court, in an about-face, overruled *Hammer v. Dagenhart*.[111] That made amendment unnecessary, and Congress continues to regulate child labor today.[112]

The last two near amendments happened in the 1970s and 1980s. One would have given Washington, D.C., full voting representation in Congress.[113] The other involved the most high-profile debate about a constitutional amendment in my lifetime: the Equal Rights Amendment (ERA). Originally proposed in the 1920s and approved by both houses of Congress in 1972, the ERA states that "[e]quality of rights under the law shall not be denied or abridged . . . on account of sex."[114] The ratification process began swiftly: Hawaii, with the benefit of a six-hour time difference, ratified the ERA the same day it was passed by Congress,[115] and twenty-one other states followed in 1972.[116]

The ERA's opponents, led by Phyllis Schlafly, mobilized slowly. But once energized, they became a national force. They insisted that the ERA would invalidate laws designed to favor or protect women, such as alimony laws and preferences for mothers in divorce cases.[117] Ratifications slowed to a trickle, and five states voted to rescind their ratifications.[118] Ultimately, thirty-five states ratified the ERA before the initial deadline of 1979.[119] This was a breath away from the thirty-eight required for an amendment to take effect. Congress, by only a simple majority in each chamber, then voted to extend the ratification deadline by three years and two months.[120] Though no state ratified the ERA within that time,[121] support for the amendment has never fully evaporated.

⁂

Our original Constitution was one of the most important documents in the history of the world. As Americans, we should be grateful for that shared heritage. But the original Constitution was also flawed. It protected slavery and refused to enfranchise women, minorities, and those without significant property. It did not explicitly protect many liberties we now hold dear. And even on less morally weighty questions, it was not (and could not have been) written to equip government to address all of the challenges of the twenty-first century. By the same token, it's entirely possible, even likely, that our current Constitution does not fully reflect the values and challenges of today—or of ten years from now, much less in one hundred more. The Constitution contains a mechanism for addressing that problem: amendment. The only limit is our ability to reach consensus about what our country should look like.

That said, self-government in the United States is not a matter of keeping all eyes on the Constitution. Far from it. We are governed not only by the Constitution, but also by statutes, and not only by federal law, but by state law too. This mixture of national and regional rules reflects our system of federalism—the subject of the next chapter.

Chapter 10

UNITED YET DISTINCT

YEARS AGO, when I was a full-time law professor, my thirteen-year-old daughter came with me to London, where I was attending an academic conference. We were enjoying tea in a café when we noticed two Englishwomen having an animated conversation at the next table. A pending execution in Texas had made international news, and the women were discussing both the morality of capital punishment and their confusion about why Texas, as a state, could legalize it. Tipped off by our American accents, they recruited us to the conversation. "You're American? Perhaps you could explain to us how Texas can have the death penalty when New York doesn't? Why don't the same rules apply everywhere in the United States?"

I didn't admit that I was a law professor—they might have worried that a lecture was coming. But unable to lose my professorial hat, I offered them the textbook answer: federalism. I explained that under our Constitution, the federal government and the states share authority to govern the same territory. Some matters are committed exclusively to federal control (say, defending the country in a war or printing currency), some exclusively to state control (say, regulating most family law matters), and some lie in an area of overlap (say, protecting consumers from unfair sales practices). For the most part, states have exclusive control over the definition of state crimes and punishments. And the Constitution permits states to impose the death penalty.[1]

Unsurprisingly, my new acquaintances weren't looking for the textbook answer. (So perhaps they would have been right to fear a law professor's lecture.) Rather than learning about *how* our law divides authority between the federal government and the states, they wanted to know *why* we do it that way. Many Americans may have the same question.

Granted, Americans are accustomed to a system in which laws can differ from state to state, even on high-stakes issues. The COVID-19 crisis is a good example: states adopted different policies in response to the pandemic, some more restrictive than others. For instance, Florida reopened schools statewide in August 2020; many California schools remained closed until the next academic year.[2] In July 2021, Florida prohibited school districts from requiring children to wear masks in schools; California required children to wear masks in schools until March 2022.[3]

Though familiar with such variety, Americans might wonder about its value—especially when they vehemently disagree with the course another state (or even their own) has chosen. The heated national debate about school mask mandates and school re-openings illustrates that many Americans care passionately not only about their own state's policies, but also about those of other states. The same goes for many other issues, including the death penalty, abortion, and the curriculum in public schools.

This is not to say that out-of-state critics are busybodies. We are citizens not only of a state, but of the United States too, and we should care about what is happening around the country. But concern for our fellow Americans is distinct from the question of whether we should tolerate differences among states or force all states to go the same way. What's the point of variety? As we have become increasingly mobile, state lines have blurred, and with modern communication, so has the line between local and national news. The founding generation plainly thought states were crucial. But in the twenty-first century, do states matter?

A comparison between the United States and England illustrates an important reason why I think they do: a country the size of the United States could not hang together without political subdivisions. The United States is more than seventy-five times the size and has more than five times the population of England.[4] To put that in perspective, England is roughly the size of Alabama (though it has a much larger population).[5] A national rule in England therefore governs a relatively small territory and far fewer people are bound by it. Consider another contrast. When I was a court of appeals judge, I sat on the United States Court of Appeals for the Seventh Circuit, which covers Illinois, Indiana, and Wisconsin. Combined, those three states have a population of roughly 25 million—about the population of Australia[6]—and the Seventh Circuit is just one of twelve regional courts of appeals in our country.

The United States combines a substantial landmass and abundant population that has few parallels in democratic countries. Think about what a feat it is to keep such an immense and diverse people living under one roof. It is hard to imagine our successfully achieving national consensus on every significant issue, much less every mundane one. Allowing people to organize themselves into smaller political units accommodates differences. Indiana is different from California, Mississippi from New York, and Florida from Oregon. Allowing variations, expressed through state governments, enables our large and diverse country to get along. Local governments offer still more options for variation when variation is due. In the state of my childhood, Louisiana, what made sense for New Orleans did not always make sense for the smaller city of Thibodaux, a little more than an hour away.

The trick lies in deciding when to allow regional differences and when there must be a national rule. What should be national? What should be local? We are, after all, not just fifty states but one country, and some policies must unite us.

Most fundamentally, we are united by the commitments made in the United States Constitution, from which no state (or, for that matter, the federal government) can deviate. We are also bound by federal statutes, which apply nationwide. But the Constitution does not settle every question, and Article I of the Constitution does not permit Congress to set every policy. On the contrary, the Constitution leaves some questions open for state resolution—for example, by protecting only certain individual rights, it leaves the States free to decide whether to recognize others. And Article I simultaneously empowers and constrains Congress by allowing it to regulate some, but not all, policy matters. These limits allow the citizens of each state to adopt policies that may differ from preferences dominant in other parts of the country. They also enable citizens to try different approaches to different problems—what ultimately becomes a form of trial and error for each state to learn from and occasionally borrow. Not everyone knows the best answer for new challenges facing society, whether they concern data privacy, the opioid crisis, jobs, or education. Federalism maintains the healthy but delicate balance between uniformity and diversity.

National Norms in the Constitution

The Constitution is the strongest form of nationally binding law. Some of its provisions concern the structure of government; others concern individual rights. The Constitution delegates some significant powers only to the federal government because the framers thought, quite correctly, that some issues demand a nationally uniform rule. Take foreign relations. The country needs to speak with one voice to other nations. Hence the federal government, through the president and Congress, controls our relationships with other countries, whether in waging a war, negotiating a treaty, or making the most of peaceful international relationships. The Constitution prevents the states from asserting authority in these areas.

Protecting individual rights presents a more complicated picture. The provisions about rights generate the most debate in our national conversations because they have the most visible impact on the lives of Americans. It is harder to get a dinner-table debate going about Congress's constitutional power to regulate patent and copyright, important as it is, than about the First Amendment's guarantee of free speech. Nor are such dinner-table debates limited to well-established constitutional rights like those found in the First Amendment. Americans also talk about rights that the Constitution *should* protect. That is because when Americans feel passionately about a principle of justice, equality, or morality, they often want it secured as one of our fundamental commitments. Sometimes, they are plainly right.

The struggle for racial equality is a case in point. The gravest flaw in the original Constitution was that it allowed regional differences with respect to slavery. The founding generation was incapable of agreeing on a national rule of abolition, and the Constitution permitted—indeed protected—regional differences on the matter. South Carolina, a slave state, was permitted to make a different choice from Pennsylvania, a free one. Freedom for all should have been a fundamental right from the beginning. Instead, it took a civil war and three amendments to secure it—the Thirteenth Amendment, which bans slavery, the Fourteenth Amendment, which prohibits the states from denying any person "equal protection of the law," and the Fifteenth Amendment, which forbids states to abridge any citizen's right to vote "on account of race, color, or previous condition of servitude." These are not matters on which people in individual states should be able to make a contrary choice, and it is a tragedy that they ever did.

Obviously, many other constitutional guarantees properly impose national rules that reflect our fundamental commitments, including the rights to trial by jury, protection from cruel and unusual punishment, and free exercise of religion. But there are other commitments that don't call for uniform constitutional rules, either because they are not sufficiently fundamental or they are not widely shared.

Take Prohibition. Fueled by the temperance movement, the Eighteenth Amendment—which outlawed the manufacture, sale, or transportation of alcohol in the United States—was added to the Constitution in 1919.[7] But as America moved into the Roaring Twenties, teetotaling fell out of favor.

Speakeasies popped up and bootlegging blossomed. Illicit liquor became big business, and the attendant crime far exceeded the vice of drunkenness that the amendment sought to eliminate. Thirteen years after the Eighteenth Amendment was ratified, the Twenty-First Amendment repealed it. It turned out that a ban on alcohol was not well suited to being a fundamental, one-size-fits-all rule—so Americans reverted to the baseline of variety. States and localities could choose to be dry, and some made that choice. Nationwide prohibition, however, was over.

The Eighteenth Amendment is a cautionary tale about the demand for constitutional rules. America is a large, diverse nation, made up of people who differ in many ways—including in regional values and preferences. (To see the point, compare the characters in *Portlandia* to the Texans in *Friday Night Lights*.) Federalism accommodates this variety. Constitutional rules offer critical protection for individual rights by barring local disagreement, as well as efforts to bring about change through Congress. Just like any strong medicine, however, this remedy should be used advisedly. A moral or political principle that is fundamental to a group of Americans does not necessarily rank as fundamental to a stable supermajority. So it was with temperance—and importantly, Americans quickly invoked the amendment process to reflect their changed judgment.

Care in distinguishing between matters properly subject to a national constitutional rule and those left to local variation is important not only in the amendment process, but in constitutional adjudication too. The Supreme Court must enforce constitutional provisions that curb state authority, because no state is free to buck constitutional commitments. At the same time, the Court must be careful not to overread the Constitution to force a national rule. The mistake will please some, but others will chafe against it—sometimes until they convince the Court to correct the error. The American people, not the Court, have the authority to choose the principles that bind the entire nation.

The Due Process Clause of the Fourteenth Amendment—which prohibits the states from depriving "any person of life, liberty, or property without due process of law"—probably generates the most controversy about the Court's role in identifying constitutional norms. The Court has long held that this clause extends special protection to some fundamental rights that, while not mentioned in the Constitution, are nonetheless both "deeply rooted in this Nation's history and tradition" and "implicit in the concept of ordered liberty."[8]

There is a heated debate about whether the Court should be in the business of recognizing such rights. Some have charged the Court with distorting the Fourteenth Amendment by reading the phrase "due process of law," which seems to be about fair procedures, to protect implied substantive rights in a doctrine called "substantive due process."[9] Whatever the merits of these objections as an original matter, the roots of this doctrine extend back more than a century. And importantly, the doctrine is subject to a critical limit: it is not designed to recognize new rights that the Court deems ripe for protection, but rather rights that the American people, diverse as they are, have historically embraced as fundamental to the liberty already protected by the Constitution. The Court has occasionally been accused of straying beyond that narrow band, thereby unlawfully preventing the people from pursuing their preferred policies at the state level.

It's not surprising that the area is fraught, given that it involves rights that are unwritten (enhancing the risk of judicial activism) and hot-button (inflaming passion). The Court has held that the rights to marry,[10] engage in sexual intimacy,[11] use birth control,[12] and raise children[13] are fundamental, but the rights to do business,[14] commit suicide,[15] and obtain an abortion[16] are not. No area of law has provoked more reflection—not to mention heated rhetoric—about the role of the Supreme Court in our constitutional system than substantive due process.

I will say more about these cases in the next chapter. For now, I want to focus on one of their most important themes: federalism. Each case in this area requires the Court to decide whether the asserted right is one protected by a presumptively permanent national rule or one on which the Constitution tolerates regional disagreement. If the asserted right reflects a long-standing, fundamental commitment that a supermajority of Americans hold in common, the Court treats it as fairly encompassed within the Constitution and the people of each state must fall in line. But if the asserted right falls short of that overwhelming historical acceptance, the constitutional default is that the people of each state can resolve the matter as they wish. Alternatively, if the issue is one within Congress's authority, Americans can seek a national rule through the legislative process.

In the absence of a nationally binding rule, state laws, including state constitutions, are a crucial mechanism by which the people actively protect their values. The United States Constitution is not the only game in town—there are fifty others, some of which are even more protective of individual rights. Several western constitutions gave women the right to vote, along with other sex-equality protections, long before the Nineteenth Amendment to the national Constitution was ratified in 1920.[17] Some state constitutions expressly protect not only the "free exercise" of religion but also "a right of conscience."[18] Others explicitly protect a right to "privacy," a word that does not appear in the United States Constitution,[19] and some include a guarantee that the state may not impose "cruel *or* unusual punishment,"[20] while the Eighth Amendment applies only to "cruel *and* unusual punishment."[21] Several states have added protections against extreme partisan gerrymandering.[22] After the Court decided *Dobbs v. Jackson Women's Health Organization*, which held that the Fourteenth Amendment of the United States Constitution does not protect the right to obtain an abortion, voters turned to their state constitutions to set abortion policy. State constitutions also contain all kinds of idiosyncratic guarantees that reflect regional history and concerns: Kentucky bans dueling,[23] Alaska protects local fisheries,[24] New York regulates the width of ski trails on state-protected lands,[25] and Ohio dictates where certain casinos may exist.[26]

While the people of the nation have rarely amended the United States Constitution, the people of the states have amended their state constitutions thousands of times. There is a good explanation for that: state constitutions are far easier to amend than the United States Constitution, and not only because state-level change requires the support of fewer people. While the United States Constitution requires three-quarters of the states to approve any amendment, most state constitutions may be amended by majority vote.[27] Nearly half of the states permit their citizens to engage in "direct democracy," whether through an initiative to amend the state constitution or a referendum to amend or overrule a statute enacted by their legislature.[28] State lawmaking is less cumbersome and often more democratic than its federal counterpart, which allows citizens of a state to more easily secure protection for values that are important to them—even when those values lack the level of national support necessary for a national constitutional commitment.

National Norms in Legislation

The Constitution lays down one set of national norms, but many more are found in federal legislation. That is as should be, for the Constitution, as Chief Justice John Marshall observed, wisely avoids "the prolixity of a legal code."[29] We typically look to Congress, rather than the Constitution, to determine which problems demand a national solution. In the absence of congressional action, the states are largely free to set their own course. If Congress prescribes a national solution, however, no state can contradict it. So, for example, a federal law prohibiting the possession of a drug preempts a state law allowing it.[30] Under the Constitution, federal law is "the supreme Law of the Land,"[31] and any contrary state law is void.

That said, Congress does not have unfettered authority to legislate in any area it chooses. Congress possesses only the authority that the Constitution *grants* it, unlike state governments, which possess any authority that the Constitution does not *deny* them. State authority sweeps widely, reaching matters of economic concern (like taxes and commercial regulations), as well as matters that touch the everyday lives of citizens (like education, housing, and street crime). Congress's authority, by contrast, is confined to an enumerated list, which includes subjects like regulating interstate commerce, establishing federal courts, and imposing federal taxes. And even though some of Congress's enumerated powers are quite broad—like its authority to regulate interstate commerce—none is unlimited. The broad power belongs to the smaller state governments, in which individual citizens have a greater voice.

Debates about the limits of federal legislative power are as old as the Constitution itself. On one hand, the framers knew that a stronger central government was necessary if the United States was to succeed as a nation. That was the impetus for the Constitutional Convention. On the other hand, the framers did not propose to eliminate the power of the states entirely—and the Constitution would not have been ratified if they had. Instead, they struck a balance. The Constitution strengthened the power of the federal government, while allowing the states to retain significant authority.

The charge that the Constitution gave the federal government too much power dominated the ratification debates, and anxiety about the scope of federal power did not recede after ratification. It fueled the formation of America's first political parties—the Federalists, who favored a strong national government, and the Democratic-Republicans, who took a narrower view of the scope of federal power. Prominent Federalists included John Adams, John Marshall, and Alexander Hamilton; prominent Democratic-Republicans included Thomas Jefferson, James Madison, and James Monroe.

An early dispute between these two factions involved Congress's authority to establish a national bank. Given the modern existence of the Federal Reserve, there's no suspense about who won. But the fight was fierce enough to be memorialized in the scene "Cabinet Battle #1" from the hit musical *Hamilton*. Before signing the bill, George Washington solicited opinions on its constitutionality from Jefferson (secretary of state), Edmund Randolph (attorney general), and Hamilton (secretary of the treasury). Their dueling opinions are not just a slice of interesting history. Hamilton's winning argument remains relevant today—so much so that the 1819 Supreme Court case adopting his view, *M'Culloch v. Maryland*, made an appearance in some major cases of the Court's 2023 Term. To understand the scope of federal power, therefore, you have to know about the constitutional reasoning behind the First Bank of the United States.

Jefferson[32] and Randolph's[33] argument against the bank was straightforward: the authority "to create a national bank" does not appear on the list of powers granted to Congress in Article I, Section 8. That list includes powers like the ability to "lay and collect Taxes," "borrow Money," and "regulate commerce." The final, catchall clause of Section 8 grants Congress the authority "[t]o make all Laws which shall be necessary and proper for carrying into Execution the foregoing powers." But one could hardly contend, Jefferson insisted, that a national bank was "*necessary*" to carrying out any of Congress's enumerated powers.[34] Congress could lay taxes, borrow money, and regulate commerce without a national bank. Yes, a national bank might make the exercise of these and other granted powers more *convenient*. But, he argued, the Constitution cannot plausibly be understood to use "necessary" in that loose sense. Such an interpretation would eliminate any limit on federal power, for a creative Congress could characterize anything it wanted to do as "a convenience in some instance or other, to some one of so long a list of enumerated powers."[35]

Unlike Jefferson and Randolph, Hamilton believed that the Necessary and Proper Clause allowed Congress the discretion to establish a national bank.[36] Hamilton began his analysis by stressing that the Constitution should be interpreted with "fair reasoning and construction."[37] For Hamilton, therefore, the task was to discern the most sensible meaning of the term "necessary" in this context. To define it, Hamilton turned to the dictionary, explaining that "*necessary* often means no more than *needful*, *requisite*, *incidental*, *useful*, or *conducive to*."[38] Thus, Hamilton observed, it "is a common mode of expression to say, that it is necessary for a government or a person to do this or that thing, when nothing more is intended or understood, than that the interest of the government or person . . . will be promoted by the doing of this or that thing."[39] Hamilton rejected Jefferson's "restrictive" reading of the Necessary and Proper Clause on the ground that it contradicted the ordinary and natural meaning of the term "necessary." For Hamilton, the critical question was whether the means chosen by Congress—in this case, a national bank—would assist the exercise of any of its express powers. Even though a national bank is not "absolutely" or "indispensably" necessary to effectuate Congress's express powers, it would be useful to exercising that power. So Congress could do it.

Washington sided with Hamilton and signed the bill.[40] Note that when the Bank of the United States was first established, the political branches—Congress and the president—made the call whether the bank was constitutional. The Supreme Court did not get involved until almost thirty years later, when the charter of the First Bank of the United States had lapsed and a second had taken its place. In *M'Culloch v. Maryland*, the Court unanimously upheld the statute creating the bank in reasoning that closely tracked Hamilton's report to Washington.[41] Rejecting the proposition that "necessary" referred to "absolute physical necessity," the Court held that Article I's Necessary and Proper Clause allowed Congress the discretion to choose the means by which to carry into execution its enumerated powers. Here's the famous line: "Let the end be legitimate, let it be within the scope of the constitution, and all means which are appropriate, which are plainly adapted to that end which are not prohibited, but consist with the letter and spirit of the constitution, are constitutional."[42] The Court thus deferred to Congress's flexible authority to deal with new economic problems faced by the fledgling country.

That deference paved the way for a strong and effective national power—*M'Culloch*'s standard remains the law today. Yet while *M'Culloch* laid the foundation, it left open the problem of identifying limits. Put differently, it offered a framework for thinking about federal power but didn't stake out the boundaries. Congress's power is not boundless; if it were, it would effectively swallow the authority of the states. But where is the line?

The Court had few occasions to grapple with that problem during the nineteenth century. In the twentieth century, however, two world wars and a struggling economy prompted a flood of federal law—which, in turn, prompted a flood of litigation. Challenges to federal power peaked during the administration of Franklin Delano Roosevelt. Spurred by the Great Depression, Congress enacted a series of statutes (many creating new federal agencies) to implement Roosevelt's promised "New Deal." The scope of this legislation was unprecedented, as were the constitutional questions that accompanied it. In case after case, the Supreme Court was forced to settle disputes about whether these New Deal statutes exceeded Congress's authority to regulate interstate commerce. In the early years of the New Deal, the Court interpreted the scope of the commerce power narrowly, but it ultimately came to view the power as very broad indeed.

That breadth is best illustrated by *Wickard v. Filburn*,[43] which adopted a capacious understanding of Congress's authority "to regulate Commerce . . . among the several States."[44] (This grant appears in the Constitution's Commerce Clause.) During the Great Depression, Congress tried to stabilize the price of wheat by passing a law that capped its production. After he was penalized for growing more wheat than the law allowed, Roscoe Filburn, an Ohio farmer, protested that the law exceeded Congress's power under the Commerce Clause. Filburn didn't sell the wheat; he kept it to feed his livestock and family. How could this homegrown grain possibly affect interstate commerce? It didn't enter the *intrastate* market, much less the *interstate* market. In fact, it never even left his farm.

Even so, the Court said, activity like Filburn's affected the interstate wheat market.[45] Farmers who fulfill their personal demand for wheat by growing it don't need to buy it. True, the actions of one farmer would have only slight effect on the market. Multiplied by many farmers, however, the effect would be substantial: reduced demand would drive down prices, thereby frustrating Congress's efforts to stabilize them.[46] Because "[h]ome-grown wheat in this sense competes with wheat in commerce," Congress could regulate it.[47]

In the decades after *Wickard*, most lawyers and judges—and perhaps most important, nearly all members of Congress—assumed that Congress's power to regulate interstate commerce was virtually unlimited. Jefferson's fears were apparently realized: the Commerce Clause, boosted by *M'Culloch*'s flexible interpretation of the Necessary and Proper Clause, seemed to wipe out constraints on national power.

In the 1990s and early 2000s, however, the Court emphasized that Congress's commerce power, though broad, is not unbounded. In *United States v. Lopez*, the Court faced a challenge to a prosecution under the Gun-Free School Zones Act, which criminalized the possession of handguns within one thousand feet of a school.[48] The Court held that possessing a handgun "has nothing to do with 'commerce' or any sort of economic enterprise."[49] Unlike the wheat grown in *Wickard*, possessing a gun wasn't "economic" activity, nor did it substantially affect commerce—at least if that test was going to place any meaningful limits on congressional power. Similarly, in *United States v. Morrison*, decided five years later, the Court faced a challenge to a provision of the Violence Against Women Act, which gave victims of gender-motivated violence the right to sue their aggressors in federal court.[50] The Court explained that violence against women, while abhorrent, is not *economic* activity and therefore Congress could not rely on its commerce power to regulate it.[51]

The most recent word on the scope of Congress's commerce power came in a high-profile challenge to the individual mandate in the Affordable Care Act (popularly known as Obamacare). In *National Federation of Independent Business v. Sebelius*, a majority of the justices concluded that the act's demand that each qualifying individual buy health insurance or face a fine exceeded Congress's commerce power.[52]

Unlike the Gun-Free School Zones Act from *Lopez* or the Violence Against Women Act in *Morrison*, the problem in the Affordable Care Act was not the absence of an *economic* regulation. Spending money to buy health insurance certainly counts as economic. The problem was that the mandate regulated economic *inactivity* (the failure to buy insurance) rather than economic *activity* (like the purchase of insurance). And if Congress could require individuals to buy health insurance and regulate them once they entered the market, couldn't it do the same for all manner of products and with respect to all manner of regulatory agendas? Even an individual mandate to buy broccoli for health purposes seemed to be within Congress's power under this theory—for if Congress's power to regulate commerce allows it to require individuals to purchase health insurance, then surely it would allow Congress to require individuals to purchase other commodities too, like vegetables. That expansive view of the commerce power would leave no practical limit on Congress's authority. As five justices saw it, the Commerce Clause allows Congress to regulate commerce—not someone's failure to engage in it.

Each of these cases—*Lopez*, *Morrison*, and *National Federation of Independent Business*—drew a vigorous dissent about the scope of the Commerce Clause. The common theme of these opinions is the need to defer to Congress's judgment about which matters need a national solution. In each case, the dissenters stressed that the regulated activity *could* be said to affect interstate commerce: guns in schools make learning difficult, and the quality of education affects the national economy;[53] violence against women increases spending on medical care and decreases economic activity because of fear;[54] and uninsured individuals affect the overall cost of health care.[55] These connections to interstate commerce are rational, the dissenters insisted, and the Commerce Clause requires nothing more.[56] On this view, the only real limit on the commerce power is Congress's judgment about the wisdom of using it.[57] If Congress shouldn't make people buy broccoli, then we can trust the democratic process to keep it from doing so.[58]

Like Hamilton and Jefferson, then, justices have sparred about the limits of federal legislative power. While the legal issues are different, the underlying problem is the same: allowing Congress leeway to address issues of national concern without effectively erasing limits on its power. That tension is inherent in a federal system like ours, so it's unlikely ever to go away.

Though I've focused on the Commerce Clause, it isn't Congress's only tool. *National Federation of Independent Business* drives home the point. Even though a majority of justices thought that the Affordable Care Act exceeded

Congress's power to regulate interstate commerce, the Court still upheld it. That's because a different majority, led by Chief Justice Roberts, concluded that collecting a payment from those who did not purchase insurance was a permissible exercise of Congress's *taxing* power. Congress's ability to accomplish through its power to tax what it could not do through its power to regulate interstate commerce teaches an important lesson: even when the Constitution closes a door, it sometimes leaves open a window.

Another reliable (if costly) route for securing nationwide compliance with federal policy is Congress's power to spend money to advance "the general Welfare of the United States."[59] Money talks—so when Congress lacks either the ability or political will to forcibly displace state law, it often dangles the carrot of a federal grant to incentivize states to adopt a federal policy. For instance, rather than enacting a national drinking age, Congress conditioned receipt of federal highway funds on the states' raising their own drinking ages to twenty-one.[60] All fifty states took the deal.[61]

States have come to rely heavily on federal funds, so the spending power is a powerful mechanism for nationalizing a norm. To be sure, Congress cannot impose conditions that are entirely unrelated to the grant. Nor can the condition be coercive—for example, the Court held that a congressional threat to *withdraw* Medicaid funds from states that refused to expand their programs was like a gun to the head, given that Congress had already induced states to rely heavily on that money to provide care for the needy.[62] But so long as the conditions are sufficiently relevant, clear, and give states a real choice about whether to accept them, money will usually get Congress where it wants to go. In the spending context, the primary limit on Congress's authority comes from the states' willingness to say no.

MUCH OF CONSTITUTIONAL law involves deciding when to have a national rule and when to leave policy choices to local variation. That may be a matter of determining if Congress has the authority to impose a national policy through federal legislation—that's the debate provoked by the Bank of the United States in the Founding Era and more recently by the Affordable Care Act. Or it may be a matter of determining whether a national constitutional rule precludes *both* the states and the federal government from making a contrary choice—and if not, whether we should amend the Constitution to add one.

Because we have national conversations, it is tempting to default to a preference for national solutions. But we might not want a national rule for every issue, and the Constitution might not guarantee or even allow one. The Constitution does not protect every right, and it limits Congress's power to set nationwide policy. Its structure presupposes that in some areas, individual states will make rules on particular issues to apply in their own geographic spheres, leaving a patchwork of approaches across the United States. That's federalism.

A federal system comes with many well-known advantages. It allows for the coexistence of different values. It promotes experimentation and development. And it permits individuals to "vote with their feet" by moving to the states that better reflect their preferences on issues important to them. Those preferences might involve issues of individual liberty (like regulations on abortion), economic policy (like the absence of state income tax), schooling (like the availability of tuition vouchers), and so on. This approach is especially well suited to a large and diverse nation like the United States. Our republic spans a continent and is home to hundreds of millions of people with a multitude of values. Without some form of subnational government and the localization of some rules, many of the values and viewpoints shared by a discrete minority of the country would be stifled in favor of a national rule. Premature national, constitutional rules cut short the process of experimentation and development, and sometimes they interfere with justifiable and healthy differences in distinct regions of the country.

Of course, accepting the value of federalism does not settle the question of which issues should be local and which should be national. We can all agree that some issues—like curing the evils of slavery—need a national solution. History has proven that for others, like the prohibition of alcohol, we would prefer to live with some state-to-state disagreement. But what about the problems of today? Like many other constitutional questions, this is one we'll have to wrestle with.

I'M FAIRLY CONFIDENT that I didn't persuade the Englishwomen in the café of the virtues of federalism. It might be, though, that you have to experience our federalist system to fully appreciate it. Justice Sandra Day O'Connor, a champion of federalism, made a point of traveling to all fifty states to give public lectures about the Court and the Constitution.[63] I haven't hit that milestone, but when I think about the places I've lived and the states I've visited, the differences in everything from landscape to personality to politics are striking. (Indiana and Louisiana couldn't be more different, but I love the people of both.) The United States has never been a country in which one size fits all; rather, it is an extraordinary mix of national unity and regional difference. A few months after the Constitutional Convention, George Washington told the Marquis de Lafayette, "It appears to me, then, little short of a miracle, that the Delegates from so many different states (which states you know are also different from each other in their manners, circumstances, and prejudices) should unite in forming a system of national Government."[64] The miracle persists.

Part Three

Thinking About the Law

Chapter 11

Can I Have That in Writing?

When I was growing up, my grandmother's shrimp remoulade—a traditional New Orleans dish featuring tangy shrimp on a bed of shredded iceberg lettuce—was a fixture on the family holiday menu. She made it in huge quantities so that there was enough to go around, but no one was allowed seconds. Providing surplus for those gathered—thirteen adults, twenty-nine grandchildren, and guests—would have kept her in the kitchen for way too long.

My grandmother did not use a written recipe—with years of practice, she didn't need one. Nor did my mother, who learned the dish by working alongside my grandmother. So when I asked for the recipe many years later, it took my mom some effort to write it down. Not only did she make the dish by eyesight rather than measuring cup, but she was also accustomed to making it in large quantities, and I planned to make it for a small group of law students. Mom made educated guesses about scaled-down proportions, and mine turned out well—though it was certainly not as good as my grandmother's. I still make shrimp remoulade from Mom's handwritten notes, which I prefer to working from memory.

Writing enables precision and preservation. If my grandmother had committed her recipe to print, I would have had no doubt about the ingredients and proportions. Instead, the content of her recipe, passed down through memory and experience, was subject to uncertainty. It might also have been subject to disagreement: had I consulted my aunts for a second opinion, they may well have quibbled with my mother's formula. Traditions can be maintained orally—I got my shrimp remoulade in the end. But as in a game of telephone, instructions repeated by word of mouth may vary from the original.

Unwritten constitutions, like unwritten recipes, can be hard to pin down.[1] And while codifying a national constitutional document seems unremarkable today, it was an innovation at the founding of our country. The framers were steeped in English law, which consisted of a mix of traditions and legislation that had evolved over the years. But by the time of the Constitutional Convention, nearly all the states had adopted written constitutions,[2] and the framers followed that course instead. The significance of this choice is hard to overstate. In fact, it is no exaggeration to say that the defining feature of American constitutional law is its basis in a concrete document.

Consider just a few things that a written constitution achieves. To start, text makes the terms transparent. Few people are willing to sell a house on a handshake or enter a complex business transaction based on verbal assurances. So too with our Constitution. Each of its provisions is the product of an agreement—some easily reached and others hard-fought. Making the terms explicit in the document protects them from fading memories and strategic denials. And funneling amendments through a rigorous process protects agreements from being easily undone.

Constitutional text also puts people on notice of their rights, thereby enabling them to enforce those rights against the government. If the police unlawfully search someone's home, she can assert a Fourth Amendment violation in a subsequent trial. ("The right of the people to be secure in their persons, houses, papers, and effects, against unreasonable searches and seizures, shall not be violated.") If a city takes someone's property, she is owed compensation under the Fifth Amendment. ("[N]or shall private property be taken for public use without just compensation.") If Congress forces someone to speak, she can invoke the First Amendment and refuse. ("Congress shall make no law . . . abridging the freedom of speech.") Such arguments may not always carry the day, because disagreements often arise about how a constitutional provision applies to particular facts. But there can be no disagreement about whether the right exists in the first place—that much is clear because it's right there in print.

Relatedly, the Constitution's words put government officials on notice of their obligations. The Constitution demands that every state and federal government officer—executive, legislative, and judicial—promise to "support *this Constitution*."[3] This phrase points to an identifiable document composed of concrete commitments. So, for example, members of Congress understand that they cannot pass a law establishing a religion. ("Congress shall make no law respecting an establishment of religion.") A prosecutor who fails to secure a conviction knows that she doesn't get a second try. ("[N]or shall any person be subject for the same offense to be put twice in jeopardy of life or limb.") And state legislators are aware that they cannot enact laws that conflict with federal statutes. ("The Constitution, and Law of the United States made in Pursuance thereof . . . shall be the supreme law of the land . . . any Thing in the Constitution or laws of any State to the contrary Notwithstanding.") Again, there may be disputes about how a constitutional provision applies to particular facts, but in hashing out such arguments, everyone starts from the same place.

Written instructions also promote efficiency. People do not have to constantly reinvent the wheel, which is particularly valuable when it comes to the mechanics of government.[4] The Constitution specifies a minimum age for representatives (twenty-five), senators (thirty), and the president (thirty-five). It prescribes a precise method for passing legislation, down to the detail that the president has ten days, excluding Sundays, to veto a law. It gives the numbers necessary to override a presidential veto: two-thirds of each house, with the first vote coming from the house in which the bill originated. Because these rules are committed to writing, they are not up for debate on a case-by-case basis. Legislators can devote their energy to deciding *what* to do rather than *how* to do it. And while they can change their own in-house rules in response to the pressure of a particular political moment (as the Senate did, for example, by eliminating the filibuster for judicial confirmations), constitutional constraints are more enduring. (If you're curious, the Constitution expressly allows "each House [to] determine the rules of its proceedings.")

Most important, however, is that the Constitution is a particular kind of text: codified *law* subject to specific rules for its adoption and amendment. Article VII states how the Constitution became effective (ratification by nine of the original thirteen states), and Article V prescribes the process necessary to change it (proposal by two-thirds of both the House and Senate or two-thirds of the states, followed by ratification by three-quarters of state legislatures). Neither of those formal processes could be easily imposed on unwritten traditions. Codified law has staying power. And given the rigor of the amendment process, codified *constitutional* law is unusually sturdy.

The Twenty-Second Amendment, which limits presidents to two four-year terms, illustrates the distinction between a conventional practice and a constitutional commitment. George Washington set a valuable precedent by retiring after his second term in office, and for nearly a century, every president observed that convention.[5] It began to crack in 1880 when Ulysses S. Grant sought (but failed to secure) the Republican nomination for a third term. Then in 1912, Theodore Roosevelt made it to the general election with a bid for his third term.[6] He lost that race, but decades later, his cousin Franklin Roosevelt successfully ran *four* times.[7] Perhaps stability of leadership was particularly appealing during the uncertainty of the Great Depression and World War II. But however happy voters had been with Franklin Roosevelt, the prospect of unlimited presidential terms made them nervous. Long-serving leaders might start to resemble dictators.[8] And once the two-term convention had been breached, Americans knew that it would not constrain future presidents. So in 1947—two years after Franklin Roosevelt's death—Congress proposed the Twenty-Second Amendment, which provides that "[n]o person shall be elected to the office of the President more than twice."[9] By 1951, the amendment had passed the threshold for ratification, giving it the status of a formal constitutional rule. That clear imperative—now memorialized in our binding law—leaves no room for second-guessing.

MAKING THE TWO-TERM limit part of the Constitution's text entrenched it, which was the goal. But while entrenchment protects a constitutional commitment, it also raises difficult questions about fairness to future generations. What if, a century later, voters living in a time of upheaval prefer the continuity of a third- or even fourth-term president? The Twenty-Second Amendment bars that option, even though those voters had no voice in the ratification process. Such concerns become even more acute in the context of the original Constitution, ratified in 1788, or the Bill of Rights, ratified in 1791. Why should we follow law made by people long dead, particularly when they lived in a different world and many of them held prejudices we reject?

Many critics have made this point, and when I was teaching constitutional law, it is an objection that my students frequently raised. They were in good company, for Thomas Jefferson raised it too. In a 1789 letter to James Madison, Jefferson wrote, "The earth belongs always to the living generation. . . . Every constitution, then, and every law, naturally expires at the end of 19 years."[10] As he saw it, "one generation is to another as one independant [*sic*] nation to another."[11] So if Jefferson had designed the Constitution, the United States (or whatever name subsequent generations chose to give it) would entirely reinvent itself every nineteen years—or a bit longer, if we adjust generational length to account for modern lifespans.

Jefferson's objection has surface appeal: Who would agree to be bound by the dead hand of the past? On reflection, though, the critique doesn't pan out. Jefferson is surely right that each generation has charge of its own fate. At the same time, America is not a country in which one generation is like "an independent nation" from the next. We live in a continuous society, and this continuity presupposes the ongoing validity of laws made by preceding generations.[12] Those laws do not derive their force from the command of a dead mouth—we're not taking First Amendment marching orders from James Madison. Those laws derive their force from our continuing acceptance of a legal system in which we treat the law on the books as effective until we change it through the agreed-upon processes.[13]

Doing so is in our best interests. If you doubt me, think about what an approach like Jefferson's would mean in practice. As Jefferson recognized, the "dead hand" objection logically applies not only to the Constitution, but to *all* law. So taking up his suggestion would mean wiping the slate clean at regular intervals—no more Constitution, statutes, or regulations, at either the state or federal level. The government would have to repeatedly start from scratch, and that chronic instability would create both domestic upheaval and national security risks. I am unaware of any democratic country that has adopted such an unstable and impractical approach.

Importantly, accepting law made by prior generations doesn't lock us in. Our ability to change the law preserves the democratic character of our government. We can repeal old statutes and enact new ones. We can amend the Constitution. In fact, we could even scrap it and start over, much like the founding generation scrapped the Articles of Confederation and replaced them with the Constitution. The Constitution's text expressly anticipates this possibility by providing for a convention if two-thirds of the state legislatures call for one.

Granted, it's difficult to imagine pulling off a wholesale re-do of our fundamental charter. We should be grateful that we have inherited the Constitution we have, because in our current, polarized environment, I'm not sure that we could agree on a new one. Making laws, constitutional or otherwise, requires working with others to find common ground; it demands the ability to compromise and persuade. If Americans aren't up to that task—if our fissures run so deep that constitutional change isn't possible—then the fault lies with us, not the Constitution. We would be defaulting to the vision of the past because we can't envision a future together. And that state of affairs would reflect not that we are bound by the past, but that we are paralyzed by the divisions of the present.

Being controlled by the "dead hand" of the past is one common objection to our codified Constitution. But even if sticking with the Constitution is consistent with a commitment to self-governance, some object that our codified Constitution is too rigid. Unwritten traditions can shift with relative informality, and by design, the Constitution—which sets limits on what legislatures are permitted to do—is harder to amend than a statute is to enact. That makes government less nimble. When pressing public policy issues arise, the Constitution limits the ways in which the government can address them.

It's important to recognize that some degree of inflexibility is the point of committing a constitution to print. Writing fixes the terms, which makes breaches easier to spot and rules easier to enforce. Because the Constitution ranks first in the hierarchy of our law, it trumps any conflicting law, including statutes and regulations at both the federal and state levels. And because the Constitution is hard to amend, neither legislatures nor agencies can brush it aside in pursuit of a preferred policy, no matter how pressing it may seem. The upside is stronger resistance to pressures that arise in the heat of the moment. A legislature can't squelch unpopular speech, a guilty defendant is entitled to a fair trial and a jury of her peers, and even the most admired president can't serve for life. Entrenching commitments is the point of any constitution that trumps ordinary law.

Still, the Constitution is not a straitjacket, and we wouldn't be living with it two centuries later if it were. Two features of the Constitution allow the government to adjust to changed circumstances. First, the Constitution does not consist exclusively, or even mostly, of hard-and-fast rules—it also employs more flexible standards. Second, the Constitution's brevity leaves most matters to be worked out through the democratic process, which responds more easily to change.

Rules and Standards

One of the first things every first-year law student learns is the difference between "rules" and "standards." Rules are black-and-white commands, no questions asked. They are to be applied mechanically and predictably. Sometimes, rules might seem like they are too broad in one situation, or too narrow in another—leading to curious or even unjust-seeming results in particular applications. But the inflexibility of rules ensures that there will always be a clear and predictable result. Standards, by contrast, ask more open-ended questions. They require someone, usually a judge, to look holistically at a variety of factors to determine whether an open-ended requirement is triggered in a particular circumstance. An open-ended standard doesn't give very specific guidance about how it applies in borderline cases. But the flexibility of standards allows for the exact contours of a legal rule to adapt to unpredictable new circumstances—some wiggle room here, some wiggle room there.

Our Constitution has its fair share of both rules and standards. It's hard to get more black-and-white than the two-term limit or the requirement that the president be at least thirty-five years old. Elsewhere, however, the document employs more flexible standards. Article I authorizes Congress to make laws "necessary and proper" for carrying its powers into execution, giving Congress flexibility to make decisions like what laws are "necessary and proper" for regulating interstate commerce. Before a state takes "life, liberty, or property," it must give "due" process of law, a standard that varies by situation—more stringent procedures protect a defendant standing trial for a capital crime than a student facing suspension from public school.

It shouldn't be surprising that constitutional standards generate more debate than constitutional rules. It's hard to imagine a closely divided Supreme Court case about whether someone was old enough to be president of the United States—the answer will always be clear. So if the framers were just trying to provide clear answers and constrain future decisionmakers, then we would think that they would have preferred rules to standards throughout the document.

But they didn't, because for some matters, we're better off with flexibility. For instance, try to come up with a set of rules that perfectly explains when police officers can enter a private home. Can they get a warrant based on an anonymous tip? Because they saw suspicious activity in the front yard? For that matter, do they always need a warrant? What if there is a hostage inside the house? A bomb? If they get a call from a frantic child? If they think a suspect is about to destroy incriminating evidence? Does the answer change if they know the bomb or the hostage is in one of ten different houses, but they don't know which?

The Fourth Amendment does not directly answer any of these questions. Instead, courts have spent decades figuring out on a case-by-case basis whether individual searches are "unreasonable." Through that process, they have developed a body of law balancing the rights of citizens to be protected from government intrusions with the needs of government to keep people safe. Fleshing out this guarantee in the context of specific factual situations surely works better than using an exhaustive set of rules drafted in the 1700s, because no lawmaker could have anticipated, much less accounted for, the varied range of law enforcement searches that would occur over the centuries.

The framers could have taken a similarly flexible approach to the presidential age requirement. For example, they could have said that the office may be occupied only by an individual of sufficient years to have obtained the necessary wisdom, giving future generations the ability to decide if any given thirty- or forty-year-old was ready to be president. But the framers chose a hard-and-fast age requirement of thirty-five years instead. By mixing rules with standards, they placed some questions beyond debate from the beginning, while permitting others to be adjudicated on a case-by-case basis. Rigidity and flexibility each have value—and fidelity to the text means that a judge must not try to transform standards into rules or vice versa.

Legislation

The Constitution does not purport to address every issue, and it would quickly have become obsolete if it did. It is notably spare: from the Preamble to the end of the Twenty-Seventh Amendment, the Constitution is fewer than eight thousand words and takes little more than half an hour to read. Compare Germany's (more than twenty-five thousand words) and South Africa's (more than forty thousand). By contrast, the United States Constitution is short enough to be printed in a lightweight pocketbook copy. And it is truly portable—I was charmed to learn that the late senator Robert Byrd used to wave a pocket Constitution while shouting "Make way for liberty!" as he rolled through the Capitol in his wheelchair.[14]

By virtue of its brevity, the Constitution leaves most problems of modern society—including the substantive rules for regulating technology, health care, and the environment—to the nimbler and present-tense democratic process. If the Constitution did too much, governments would lack the needed flexibility to make trade-offs based on the problems, values, and resources of the current moment. The Constitution is static; legislation responds to change.

Consider environmental law. The Constitution says nothing explicit about the environment—and anything it had said in 1787 would be hopelessly out of date. But Congress has repeatedly used the powers the Constitution grants it to address environmental problems. The Clean Air Act and Clean Water Act regulate our nation's air and waters, each with its own complex scheme that combines direct regulation of polluters with cooperative efforts with state governments.[15] The National Environmental Policy Act sets an aspirational environmental policy of the United States, which is implemented through regulations.[16] The Comprehensive Environmental Response, Compensation, and Liability Act seeks to clean up hazardous waste sites around the country.[17] And these statutes are just the tip of the iceberg. There are many more federal statutes, a multitude of federal regulations, and a body of state law too.

Of course, many statutes provoke controversy, and those disputes often lead to constitutional challenges. A persistent problem in such cases is distinguishing between matters entrenched in our fundamental charter and those left to the legislative process. On the one hand, the Court must enforce the Constitution's commands; on the other, they must not infringe on the democratic process by entrenching issues that the Constitution leaves open. Overreading the Constitution blunts the benefit of its brevity.

The classic example in American constitutional law of the Supreme Court's over-constitutionalizing is *Lochner v. New York*, decided in 1905.[18] In that case, an employer challenged a state law that prohibited the employees in his bakery from working more than sixty hours a week. The Court acknowledged that states have general authority to regulate behavior to promote the health, safety, and general welfare of their citizens. But it said that employers also have the right to contract with their employees (and they with their employers)—a freedom protected by the Fourteenth Amendment's Due Process Clause, which forbids a state to deprive a person of "life, liberty, or property without due process of law." The Court held that under this clause, a legislature cannot interfere with the right of contract without a compelling reason to do so.[19] Applying that standard, the Court concluded that the maximum-hours law was unconstitutional because it was unnecessary to "safeguard the public health or the health of the individuals who are following the trade of a baker."[20] All occupations carry at least some health risk, the Court observed, yet "are we all, on that account, at the mercy of legislative majorities?"[21]

The case drew vigorous dissents. Any "right to contract" is not explicit in the Constitution, but rather implicit in the word "liberty." (Unlike, for instance, the right of free speech, which the Constitution spells out.) The dissenters chided the majority for using this capacious word to thwart the will of the legislature.[22] The Constitution is "made for people of fundamentally differing views,"[23] Justice Oliver Wendell Holmes pointed out, and legislatures have wide latitude to pass statutes promoting the public interest.[24] By second-guessing legislative judgments, he said, the Court had overstepped. Justice John Marshall Harlan, in his own dissenting opinion, summarized the problem this way:

> No evils arising from such legislation could be more far-reaching than those that might come to our system of government if the judiciary, abandoning the sphere assigned to it by the fundamental law, should enter the domain of legislation, and upon grounds merely of justice or reason or wisdom annul statutes that had received the sanction of the people's representatives.[25]

In short, the dissenters insisted that legislation is constitutional so long as it is rational, even if the Court thinks it undesirable.

By 1937, the dissenting view had prevailed, and the *Lochner* era—a time during which the Court frequently invalidated economic and social legislation—was over.[26] As this reversal of course reflects, there is good reason to be skeptical about an approach that reads a broad standard like "due process of law" (which, by its terms, aims at procedural fairness) to foreclose an entire category of legislation in a heavily contested area of public policy. Nearly every statute—including criminal statutes, health regulations, and environmental laws—affects someone's liberty. Courts owe deference to legislative majorities in determining how to handle economic and social problems. The Constitution has survived in large part because it does not freeze an answer to every contentious question.

The existence of unwritten rights remains a point of tension in interpreting our written Constitution. (These implied rights are usually called "unenumerated rights," because in contrast to the guarantees in the Bill of Rights, they are not listed in the Constitution.) The end of the *Lochner* era marked an important shift, and since then, the Court has generally been much more restrained in its treatment of the Due Process Clause. As a rule, it gives legislatures wide berth, upholding a statute so long as it can be regarded as a rational means of pursuing a legitimate state interest. But it continues to recognize some "fundamental rights" that, while not expressly mentioned in the Constitution, are largely insulated from infringement by democratic majorities.[27] The Court's twentieth-century cases were not always consistent in defining fundamental rights. By 1997, however, the Court had synthesized its precedent to articulate a definitively high bar: a right is fundamental only if it is "deeply rooted in this Nation's history and tradition" and "implicit in the concept of ordered liberty."[28]

By design, the Court's test for recognizing implied fundamental rights is backward-looking, not forward-looking. *New* constitutional rights are the province of legislation or the Article V amendment process. The Due Process Clause implicitly encompasses only those rights that Americans have traditionally embraced—rights *already* so etched in our society that they "go without saying." Only then can a right be treated as one that a supermajority of Americans has implicitly agreed to place beyond the reach of the ordinary legislative process. The cases define the category to include the rights to marry, to engage in intimate conduct, to procreate, to direct the upbringing of one's children, to use contraception, and to resist forced medical procedures.

To assess whether a fundamental right exists, the Court insists on a "*careful* description of the asserted fundamental liberty interest."[29] The point is to determine whether Americans have historically and widely agreed about the asserted right, not whether Americans agree generally on the importance of liberty—of course they do, but "liberty" and its limits mean different things to different people. If "liberty" broadly means "freedom" when it comes to implied rights, then the Due Process Clause would function as a virtually empty vessel through which the Court could constitutionalize myriad value judgments. The disciplined, backward-looking approach imposed by our precedent is the best way of reconciling the judicial recognition of unwritten rights with our written Constitution.[30]

Washington v. Glucksberg, which addresses a claimed "right to choose a humane, dignified death" illustrates what it means to follow the "careful description" requirement.[31] In that case, a group of doctors and terminally ill patients, along with an organization called Compassion in Dying, challenged a law rendering someone guilty of a crime "when he knowingly causes or aids another person to attempt suicide."[32] The plaintiffs grounded the asserted right to die in a general right of bodily autonomy. But the Court squarely rejected that broad formulation: "That many of the rights and liberties protected by the Due Process Clause sound in personal autonomy does not warrant the sweeping conclusion that any and all important, intimate, and personal decisions are so protected."[33] Assessing whether a fundamental right exists requires a "*careful* description of the asserted fundamental liberty interest," the Court explained.[34] The right question, then, is not whether history and tradition support a general right to bodily autonomy; it is whether history and tradition support a "right to assisted suicide." And given long-standing and countrywide criminal prohibitions on assisted suicide, it can't be said that the American people considered it to be an implied yet deeply entrenched constitutional right.

Glucksberg emphasizes the Court's reluctance to add to the narrow category of unenumerated rights that it has already recognized. Without text as a constraint, judges can easily slip into naming fundamental rights based on the values of people they know and respect rather than the values of the vast and diverse American citizenry. (It's human nature, after all, to think that the values held by you and your fellow travelers are both right and dominant.) Requiring that a precisely described right be supported by history and tradition gives the Court at least some objective measure of what a widespread swath of Americans hold dear. "[The Constitution] is made for people of fundamentally differing views," as the dissent stressed in *Lochner*.[35] If the Constitution places a matter beyond the reach of democratic majorities, the Court must vigilantly and fearlessly enforce that choice. Otherwise, the Court must leave the matter to the democratic process, which requires citizens to persuade one another rather than a handful of Supreme Court justices.

These points animate the Court's reasoning in *Dobbs v. Jackson Women's Health Organization*, which holds that the Constitution leaves the regulation of abortion to the democratic process.[36] (I joined *Dobbs* and encourage you to read both the majority and dissenting opinions rather than just my explanation of them.) The text of the Constitution doesn't mention or address abortion or any other medical procedure, so the right to obtain an abortion, if it exists, must be an implied fundamental right. To have that status, this specific right must be "deeply rooted in this Nation's history and tradition" and "implicit in the concept of ordered liberty," as *Glucksberg* explains. It bears emphasis that abortion does not have the status of a fundamental right simply because it has some relationship to the rights to have sex and use contraception. Each of these rights is analyzed distinctly, consistent with the requirement that implied fundamental rights be assessed with specificity. Moreover, *Roe* and our subsequent abortion precedent emphasized that abortion is different from other sexual privacy rights because it terminates "life or potential life,"[37] which makes it a "unique act."[38]

The evidence does not show that the American people have traditionally considered the right to obtain an abortion so fundamental to liberty that it "goes without saying" in the Constitution. In fact, the evidence cuts in the opposite direction. Abortion not only lacked long-standing protection in American law—it had long been forbidden. It was criminal in the vast majority of states when the Fourteenth Amendment was ratified in 1868 and still prohibited in a substantial majority when *Roe* was decided in 1973.[39] *Roe*, therefore, did not pull an outlier state law into line with an overwhelming national consensus; rather, it overhauled abortion laws across America. By contrast, even in 1965, "the Connecticut statute at issue in *Griswold v. Connecticut*," which recognized an unenumerated right to use contraception, "was an extreme outlier."[40]

Getting ahead of the American people came at a cost. Justice Ruth Bader Ginsburg, herself a supporter of abortion rights, observed nearly twenty years after *Roe* that the case may have "halted a political process that was moving in a reform direction," "prolonged divisiveness," and "deferred stable settlement of the issue."[41] Almost fifty years after *Roe*, when *Dobbs* was decided, abortion remained a contentious, hotly debated issue that caused significant rancor in American politics. Against this background, it's impossible to say that a supermajority of Americans has traditionally considered abortion access so obviously fundamental to liberty that the Constitution protects it even without explicitly saying so. The complicated moral debate about abortion stands in dramatic contrast to widespread American support for liberties like the rights to marry, have sex, procreate, use contraception, and direct the upbringing of children—other implied rights that our cases have ranked "fundamental" under the Due Process Clause. Because a right to abortion is not "deeply rooted in this Nation's history and tradition,"[42] the *Dobbs* opinion explains that it was an "exercise of raw judicial power" for *Roe* to treat the right as constitutionally protected.[43]

The justices who dissented in *Dobbs* advanced a different vision of both the Due Process Clause and the Supreme Court's role in interpreting it. They resisted the Court's precedent limiting unwritten, fundamental rights to those with the pedigree of history and tradition. As they saw it, interpreting the Due Process Clause is not a matter of identifying and implementing fundamental rights to which Americans have *already* (though implicitly) agreed. Instead, "the majestic but open-ended words of the

Fourteenth Amendment—the guarantees of 'liberty' and 'equality'"—invite "evolution in their scope and meaning."[44] "And over the course of our history," the dissenters argued, "this Court has taken up the Framers' invitation,"[45] as it should with respect to abortion.

This approach self-consciously puts the Supreme Court, rather than the American people, in charge of placing rights outside the ordinary democratic process. If the Due Process Clause expressly assigned the Court the role of creating some as-yet unnamed rights that are important enough to be placed outside the power of ordinary governance, I would agree that the Court has not only the authority but also the responsibility to engage in that task. But that task does not belong to the Court; on the contrary, the Court's role is to respect the choices that the people *have agreed upon*, not to tell them what they *should agree to*. That is why the Court insists on a "careful description" of the "asserted right" and evaluates it with a backward-looking assessment of the long-standing history and tradition of this country.[46] My dissenting colleagues conceded that this test would not show overwhelming nationwide support for a right to abortion.[47] Instead, they argued that the test should not apply.[48]

As I said at the outset of the chapter, one of the benefits of a written constitution is that both citizens and government officials are on notice of the Constitution's demands. There may be fierce disagreement about how a textually expressed right applies in a particular case, but there can be no disagreement about whether the right exists in the first place. Unenumerated rights complicate that picture, because there is room for threshold disagreement about the existence of the right itself. Using historical tradition as a guide minimizes that threshold disagreement and better harmonizes the Court's long-standing recognition of implied fundamental rights with our written Constitution.

Over-constitutionalizing areas of dynamic policy debate can come at great cost to both flexibility and democracy. It deprives legislatures of flexibility to respond to social changes. It puts those decisions in the hands of courts, which are ill-suited to make them. It inhibits democracy by thwarting the ability of citizens to bring about their preferred policies on these issues. And it eliminates the possibility of regional variety by imposing a nationally uniform and effectively permanent rule that the people of every state must follow. Thus, while courts must not hesitate to enforce the Constitution's commitments, they also must be careful not to overread what the Constitution requires. They must respect the Constitution's balance between rigidity and flexibility, between what has been decided in the past and what has been left for the present and future.

A WRITTEN CONSTITUTION represents a trade-off. We gain greater protections for our constitutional structure and individual rights but lose the flexibility of a system governed solely by unwritten tradition or ordinary legislation. To my mind, the trade-off is worth it. That's not to say that our document strikes the perfect balance. As I discussed in the chapter on amendments, there are good arguments for making constitutional change a little easier to accomplish. But those are not arguments for *abandoning* a written Constitution. Particularly in a country of our size and diversity, foundational ground rules enable the government to run smoothly and fortify the civil rights of minorities. Our Constitution reflects America's aspirations, but it is not a merely aspirational document. It is, first and foremost, a legal text, and therein lies its force.

Chapter 12

PAST MEETS PRESENT

AFTER MY grandparents died, their house, which had been built by my great-great-aunt, remained in the family. No one had sorted through the crowded first-floor storage (there are no basements in New Orleans) until Hurricane Katrina flooded the house in 2005. The water filled the first floor and rose into the second, where my grandparents' piano sat in the living room. Though the piano has been restored, Katrina's imprint remains in a faint water line a few inches from the bottom. The piano now sits in my living room, and though it's getting old, I can't bring myself to replace it.

When the water receded, my uncle and cousin went to the house to survey the damage. At the foot of the stairs lay my grandfather's sea bag, a hefty duffel he used during his naval service in World War II. Made to resist water, the bag had mostly preserved its contents—including 674 letters that my grandparents wrote to each other during the war. He spent most of the time on a ship in the Pacific Ocean, though his long stretches at sea were punctuated by a few brief leaves. (On one trip ashore, he spotted Betty Grable.) My grandparents met shortly before my grandfather enlisted, and the correspondence chronicles their courtship.

My aunt meticulously transcribed the letters, and once the project was finished, she and my uncle selected a collection for publication in a book (named *The Sea Bag*) given to my grandparents' children, grandchildren, and great-grandchildren. The story is mostly for our family, though another uncle, a musician, shared it publicly by composing a beautiful piece called "The Katrina Letters," which blended music with lines read aloud from my grandparents' correspondence.

Of course, the letters are more than a sum of their lines, and understanding them requires the reader to look beyond the words on the page. The circumstances under which my grandparents wrote them provide important background. Her letters are newsy, full of stories about daily life in wartime New Orleans. His are almost entirely introspective, offering few details about daily life on the ship. Without knowing some historical context, I might attribute this contrast entirely to differences in personality—she was vivacious; he was more circumspect. While that's surely part of the explanation, there's also more to it: my grandfather's letters had to make it past the ship's censor, who ensured that no inadvertently revealed detail would endanger the ship if the letter fell into enemy hands. So one reason my grandfather talked so much about his thoughts and feelings is that he couldn't talk about much else. Had I been unaware of the looming censor, I would have misinterpreted his omissions.

Understanding the letters also requires deciphering the meaning of unfamiliar words. Some are easy to figure out from context—like *Cimarron*, the name of his ship. A dictionary is necessary for others—like "gedunk," which, I discovered, refers to both the canteen on a navy vessel and the snacks sold there.[1] His more oblique references invite educated guesswork. In one letter, my grandfather cryptically mentioned an "occasion" that left him looking "comical" with a shaved head. He apologized for being unable to disclose more. Maybe this should be taken at face value—he shaved his head and kept the details quiet. But my uncle's research suggests that this was probably a reference to a traditional "Crossing the Line" ceremony, a ritual initiation of rookie sailors making their first trip across the equator. Experienced sailors wore costumes, and a senior officer (often dressed as King Neptune) presided.[2] Describing the occasion would have given away information about the ship's location; hence, my grandfather couldn't talk. It seems a likely explanation for his shaved head, though we'll never know for sure.

Reading the letters as a collection also reveals themes unsaid but evident. At the outset, my grandfather was far more smitten than my grandmother—or at least far more willing to say it. As he pushed the relationship along faster than she wanted it to go, she expertly deflected his declarations of affection with lighthearted replies. Her tone was so perfect that she was able to keep the relationship going without overcommitting. Who knew that my grandmother could have given me excellent dating advice? As my uncle put it, "[S]he adroitly manage[d] him."[3] My grandfather was weary of war and the monotony of the ship; my grandmother responded with just the right balance of sympathy and optimism. She never chided him to slow down, back off, or snap out of it. But she got her point across all the same.

The letters showed me that my grandmother was both deft in relationships and a very talented writer. The revelations about my grandfather, though, touched a deeper chord. His familiar affection and warmth were there. Yet while I had seen only his strength, the letters revealed his

My grandparents, who wrote the World War II letters, holding up a baby gift for their first child, my mother.

vulnerability. My grandfather didn't know whether he would get the girl—or even survive the war. When I read the letters, I knew the story's end. When he wrote them, the future was unseen.

⁂

The Constitution is hardly as personal or accessible as my family's collection of World War II letters. But it, like the letters, is rooted in a particular moment in time; it too is a historical text with an important backstory and unfamiliar words. To understand the Constitution's separation of powers, it's useful to have some background, such as knowledge that the founders both broke from and borrowed from the English law that had previously governed them. You'll need outside sources to define some of the words—unless you're already familiar with phrases like "letters of marque and reprisal," "bills of attainder," and "Corruption of Blood." Some of the Constitution's more cryptic references call for investigative work and educated guesses. What are the "privileges" and "immunities" of Americans? They seem to refer to something special, but what? And reading the Constitution as a whole reveals themes unstated but evident: the Constitution never uses the phrases "separation of powers" or "checks and balances," but read as a whole, the document makes clear what its drafters were up to.

Interpreting the Constitution isn't always easy. It's difficult for us to grasp the world that the founders inhabited, much less to apply a centuries-old document to a world that they could not have foreseen. They knew the United States as a fledgling country that might fail; we know it as an international power with borders stretching from the Atlantic to the Pacific. They traveled by carriage and communicated by post; we have electricity, airplanes, and the internet.

So why bother? Does interpreting the Constitution today require us to understand its historical meaning? Is it even possible to do so? And assuming that we can determine what the document meant when it was originally adopted, how can we apply it to the problems of the modern world?

Though none of these questions is easy, I think the answer to all of them is yes. This approach to the Constitution is called "originalism," and it emphasizes the primacy of the Constitution's historical meaning. In this chapter, I explain why I think that this approach is right and how it works in practice.

To INTERPRET ANY text, you must determine what it communicates, and to determine what it communicates, you must understand what the words meant to those who used them. Interpretation requires more than consulting a dictionary, because there is a distinction between the meaning a text will bear and the meaning it was designed to express.

A simple analogy illustrates the point. There is a famous scene in Shakespeare's *Macbeth* in which Lady Macbeth, sleepwalking, frantically rubs her hands together while crying, "Out, damned spot! Out, I say!"[4] I could quote that language while treating a stain on a tablecloth. But I would be using the words differently from Lady Macbeth, who was referring not to a visible stain, but to the symbolic stain of her guilt for her role in assassinating King Duncan. Same words, different reference. To understand what Lady Macbeth was communicating, we need to consider her lines in the context of the scene—indeed, in the context of the whole play. In my example, I co-opted the lines to convey my own message.

You can draw a distinction between original meaning and possible meaning in the context of the Constitution too. Consider the Sixth Amendment's Confrontation Clause, which provides:

> In all criminal prosecutions, the accused shall have the right . . . to be confronted with the witnesses against him.

In *Crawford v. Washington*, the Court observed that the phrase "witnesses against him" bears three plausible meanings: it could be read to refer only to witnesses "who actually testify at trial, those whose statements are offered at trial, or something in-between."[5] The facts of *Crawford* show why the choice between these definitions matters. Michael Crawford stabbed a man, allegedly in self-defense. Though his wife, Sylvia, did not testify at his murder trial, the prosecution played the jury a statement recorded by detectives who had interrogated her after the stabbing. Sylvia's recorded statement contradicted Michael's version of events; Michael argued that admitting it violated the Confrontation Clause because he had no opportunity to cross-examine her.

If the clause guarantees only the right to cross-examine witnesses who take the stand, then Michael's argument necessarily fails, because Sylvia didn't testify. If the clause guarantees the right to cross-examine anyone whose out-of-court statement is introduced at trial, then Michael's argument necessarily succeeds, because the prosecutor introduced Sylvia's out-of-court statement. If the clause means something in between those two positions, then Michael's argument *might* succeed, depending on the circumstances under which Sylvia gave the statement.

To choose among the three plausible meanings, the Court examined the original meaning of the clause.[6] Because the confrontation right originated in English common law, the Court started with English sources like legal treatises and court decisions.[7] It then turned to American sources like the decisions of colonial courts, the declarations of rights adopted by many states after the Revolution, the ratification debates about the United States Constitution, and early court decisions interpreting the scope of the confrontation right.[8] The Court concluded that the right was designed to protect defendants from the prosecutorial practice of taking testimony from a witness outside the presence of the accused and then introducing the statement at trial with no opportunity for cross-examination.[9]

Based on this history, the Court decided that the phrase "witnesses against him" has the third plausible meaning: it refers to any witness who gives a *testimonial* statement, whether in or out of court.[10] (In a later case, the Court defined "testimonial" statements as those given when "the primary purpose of the interrogation is to establish or prove past events potentially relevant to later criminal prosecution.")[11] And, the Court continued, the "right to be confronted" tracks the right as it existed in 1791: if a witness is unavailable to testify at trial, then her testimonial statement is admissible only if the defendant had a prior opportunity to cross-examine her.[12] Sylvia's statement was testimonial, given during a police interrogation rather than in casual conversation with a friend or neighbor.[13] Because Michael had no opportunity to cross-examine her, he won his case.[14]

Now, the *Crawford* Court could have used criteria other than the original meaning to interpret the phrase "witnesses against him." Instead of asking what the clause meant at the time of its adoption, the Court could have asked, "Which of these interpretations seems most sensible?" To answer that question, it could have considered factors like the relative burden of each interpretation on prosecutors, social science studies about the effectiveness of cross-examination, how court systems in other countries protect defendants from the risk of unreliable testimony, the tradition of cross-examination in the United States, and whether Americans today place a premium on the right. After weighing such factors, the Court might have reached a different conclusion than it did in *Crawford.* For instance, it might have concluded that the phrase "witnesses against him" covers only witnesses who take the stand at trial—not witnesses who, like Sylvia Crawford, testify during police interrogations. The Court might have decided that a narrower interpretation strikes the right balance between an efficient criminal justice system and protecting defendants from mistaken or untruthful testimony.

Whatever its merits, this narrow interpretation of the clause differs materially from its original meaning. Like my quotation of Lady Macbeth ("Out, damned spot!"), this hypothetical Court could claim consistency with the Sixth Amendment's words, but not with the meaning those words were designed to communicate. That raises an important question: Should we care? Maybe the original meaning unduly hampers prosecutors, while the pragmatic approach is both fair and efficient. Is the Court obligated to stick to the original meaning, even if it thinks an alternative interpretation would work better?

Yes. In my view, departing from the original meaning differs in degree but not in kind from departing from the text outright. It is easy to see why a court can't legitimately interpret the Sixth Amendment to apply to "all civil proceedings" when its text states that it applies to "all criminal prosecutions." Yet shifting from the original meaning to a new interpretation (say, by narrowing the meaning to a right to cross-examine only witnesses who take the stand rather than any witnesses who give testimony) also changes the content of the law. It just does so more modestly, by taking language that communicates one thing and repurposing it to mean something else. Note too that departures from historical meaning can contract rather than expand individual rights; Michael Crawford would surely prefer the original meaning to my hypothetical update.

For what it's worth, no justice in *Crawford* endorsed the hypothetical approach that I sketched above. Justice Scalia wrote the majority opinion and was joined by Justices Stevens, Kennedy, Souter, Thomas, Ginsburg, and Breyer. Chief Justice Rehnquist and Justice O'Connor agreed with the result (that Sylvia Crawford's confession should be excluded from evidence) but read the history differently. As this lineup reflects, all justices consider history relevant, even though they do not all identify as originalists. So far as I know, that has always been true. Even Justice William Brennan, Jr. (who served on the Court from 1956 to 1990), an outspoken critic of originalism, acknowledged that justices "look to the history of the time of framing and to the intervening history of interpretation."[15] He insisted, however, that "the *ultimate* question must be, what do the words of the text mean in our time."[16]

The primary difference between originalism and other approaches is that originalists treat historical meaning as determinative, while nonoriginalists sometimes prioritize other considerations, such as the purposes or values underlying a constitutional provision.[17] For instance, Justice Brennan famously described the Constitution's "text [a]s a sparkling vision of the supremacy of the human dignity of every individual," and took as his interpretive guide the "concepts of human dignity" as transformed by modernity.[18] Justice Stephen Breyer considers the original meaning of the text, but he "normally tr[ies] to emphasize the need to read the text as informed by the provision's purposes, even if doing so points toward a different result."[19]

Why do originalists reject such approaches? I like Professor Steven Smith's answer: because "what counts as *law*—as valid, enforceable law—is what human beings enact, and that the meaning of that law is what those human beings understood it to be."[20] If you start, as I do, from the premise that the Constitution's enacted text is law, then the question for the judge is how to interpret it. And the answer depends on the meaning of the language that the lawmakers employed—not on the perspective of some other lens.

It bears emphasis that a provision's original meaning does not resolve every case. The Court must still apply the provision to the facts in front of it, and that can generate differences of opinion. For example, justices may disagree in a Sixth Amendment case about whether a particular statement qualifies as "testimonial."[21] Or they may have different views about how to implement a broad constitutional guarantee. For instance, they may agree that, as an original matter, the First Amendment permits some state regulation of speech but disagree about how to measure whether challenged regulations pass muster.[22] Still, the antecedent question is *what the law is*; for an originalist, the answer turns on what the language conveys.

WHAT HISTORICAL EVIDENCE does the Court consider when it identifies the original meaning of constitutional text? For provisions ratified in the late eighteenth century, it consults a variety of sources, including Founding Era state constitutions; materials from the Constitutional Convention, including the notes of James Madison; *The Federalist Papers*; *The Antifederalist*

Papers; records of debates in the state ratifying conventions; and legal treatises such as Blackstone's *Commentaries*, which has been cited by the Supreme Court some five hundred times.[23] For amendments ratified after the Founding Era, the Court considers sources from the relevant period. For instance, when interpreting the Fourteenth Amendment, which was adopted in 1868, the Court considers Reconstruction-era sources, including debates about the amendment in the Congress that proposed it.[24]

The goal in consulting historical sources is to determine how informed members of the public would have understood the provision at the time it became law.[25] How was language used at the time? (Dictionaries from the period can help.) Did the provision memorialize a right already known to law? (We saw that with the Confrontation Clause in *Crawford*.) What problems did the lawmakers and ratifiers understand themselves to be addressing? (The Fourteenth Amendment, for instance, addressed the states' continued discrimination against former slaves.) What were the points of disagreement and points of compromise? (For example, in what became known as the Madisonian Compromise, the Constitution created "one Supreme court" but left the existence of lower federal courts up to Congress.)

People sometimes describe originalism as a search for "the framers' intent." That's a misconception. The goal is *not* to gaze into the minds of the framers to determine how they intended the Constitution to apply in particular circumstances. If a judge must decide whether it violates the Free Speech Clause to make flag burning a crime, she should not try to channel James Madison, imagining how he would resolve the problem. Could the judge peer into Madison's mind to capture his thoughts? (That mystical undertaking makes me think of the enchanted Pensieve used by Harry Potter to magically recover memories.) What if Madison could not have foreseen the problem? (Can anyone say what Madison would have thought about free speech and the internet?) And even if Madison had a definite opinion about a given issue—say he wrote it down in a private journal—why should his opinion have controlling weight? The people ratified a text, not the private beliefs of Madison (or anyone else) about how the text would apply.

Besides, those involved in the debates about the Constitution's drafting or ratification—even active participants like Madison—might have been wrong about how the Constitution applies to a particular set of facts. When a commitment is general, it's particularly easy to be mistaken about its consequences. Here's an illustration from everyday life: a New Year's resolution to follow a healthy diet. After happily making that commitment, I might be dismayed to learn that many foods I thought were healthy (say, flavored yogurt, protein bars, and sports drinks) are full of empty calories. Tough luck. If I'm serious about the resolution, I must let those foods go—even if I initially thought I could keep eating them. Those who make a constitutional commitment can similarly harbor mistaken expectations. For example, drafters and ratifiers of the Equal Protection Clause might have thought that the clause permitted a regime of "separate but equal" racial segregation. Tough luck. The commitment to equality controls, not anyone's expectations about how the commitment would apply.

People deviate from resolutions not only because of mistakes, but also because of human weakness—in politics as well as in diets. Recall the analogy of Odysseus tied to the mast: government officials will be drawn toward actions that are inconsistent with the Constitution. Early adopters of a commitment are not immune from this temptation,[26] and the Sedition Act of 1798 is a case in point.[27] Signed into law by President John Adams, the act (among other things) made it illegal to "write, print, utter, or publish . . . any false, scandalous and malicious writing or writings against the government of the United States, or either house of the Congress of the United States, or the President of the United States, with the intent to" (among other things) "bring them . . . into contempt or disrepute."[28] The Federalists, the political party in power, thought this prohibition was necessary to enforce loyalty to America during a quasi-war with France.[29] Controversial even at the time, this law is now widely regarded as an infringement of the freedoms of speech and press.[30] In the heat of the moment, however, President Adams and the Federalists in Congress convinced themselves otherwise. It would be a mistake to conclude that the First Amendment permits the government to enact such a law just because members of the founding generation did it.

None of this is to say, of course, that expected applications of the Constitution are *irrelevant*. Take my New Year's resolution to follow a healthy diet. If my list of go-to foods includes chicken and eggs, an observer can safely conclude that "healthy," in my case, is not synonymous with "vegan." So too with the Constitution: early and expected applications can shed light on the scope of a constitutional commitment. The critical point, though, is that they cannot control constitutional meaning. The commitment is embodied in a text, and only the text itself is binding.

My tour of these sources might lead you to wonder, Can judges really do it? After all, they are lawyers, not historians. Are they capable of sorting through historical materials to make judgments about the Constitution's original meaning?

To start, it's worth noting that methodological disputes are not about *whether* to use history—they are about how much weight to give it. From the Founding Era to the present day, the Court has taken the Constitution's original meaning seriously.[31] Given that history has long been a standard tool of constitutional interpretation,[32] declaring it off-limits would be a radical shift. The system has long assumed that judges are competent to deal with historical materials.

That said, judges—including originalist judges—do not function as historians. They do not write accounts of historical events or biographies of historical figures, nor do they draw from the wide range of sources on which historians rely. They use sources that are almost exclusively *legal*, such as cases, legal treatises, statutes, state constitutions, and debates about how to draft and whether to ratify the Constitution. And while considering how history bears on a constitutional issue has scholarly elements (as all judging does), it occurs in the context of a practical enterprise (as all judging is). The goal is to resolve a dispute between parties about how to interpret and apply a constitutional provision, not to offer a pathbreaking account of the past. Courts analyze legal issues using legal sources, and for that they are well equipped.

To put the use of history in perspective, consider the wide range of subjects with which judges routinely deal. Federal judges are generalists, not specialists.[33] During my years as a law professor, I taught and wrote about issues related to the federal courts and constitutional law, including how to interpret statutes and the Constitution. While that expertise was helpful when I became a judge, it was only part of my new portfolio. Federal judges encounter practically every area of law, including environmental law, antitrust, bankruptcy, employment discrimination, labor law, criminal law, copyright, patent, admiralty, and tax. And the adventure goes beyond new areas of law. One of the cases I heard on the Seventh Circuit involved a patent for a "sperm-sorting technology" that "enables cattle breeders to determine the sex of calves by separating a sample of bull semen into X-chromosome bearing and Y-chromosome bearing sperm cells."[34] Environmental cases have required me to be conversant with matters like the Environmental Protection Agency's "methodology for setting emissions limits" on states that "significantly contributed to ozone pollution in downwind States."[35] To interpret the statutory phrase "single function of the trigger," I had to learn the inner mechanics of a firing cycle for a semiautomatic rifle.[36]

All to say that, for better or for worse, judges deal with a wide range of subject matter. As for me, I'm more at home with a historical source like *The Federalist Papers* than with technology for breeding cattle.

Though history is well within a judge's bailiwick, it's not a cure-all for legal uncertainty. It would be nice if there were a magical index, where the entry on a topic (Sixth Amendment, Confrontation Clause) pointed directly to a source (Blackstone's *Commentaries*, volume 5) containing the definitive answer to an interpretive question ("The Confrontation Clause guarantees the right of the accused to cross-examine all witnesses, even those who make testimonial statements outside the courtroom"). But legal reasoning rarely follows such a direct path, especially in cases that make it to the Court. Judges do their best to determine what historical sources reveal about the law's meaning, but the sources can leave room for disagreement.

Justices Scalia and Thomas are well-known originalists, yet they didn't always interpret constitutional text the same way. For example, they had different views about the original meaning of a defendant's Sixth Amendment right to confront the witnesses against her. (Justice Thomas interprets it to reach only relatively formal out-of-court testimony; Justice Scalia understood it more broadly.)[37] Similarly, Justices Thomas and Gorsuch have disagreed about the original meaning of the Double Jeopardy Clause.[38] (Justice Thomas understands it to prohibit successive prosecutions by the *same* government; Justice Gorsuch understands it to prohibit successive prosecutions, period.) These two justices have also divided over the meaning of the Appropriations Clause.[39] (Justice Thomas interprets it as a relatively loose constraint on Congress; Justice Gorsuch interprets it to be more exacting.) I was on the Court when that case was decided, and I agreed with Justice Thomas.

While I wish it were otherwise, hard cases are not like math problems: everyone will not necessarily agree on the right answer. Judges don't always see eye to eye about what statutes mean, what judicial precedent requires, the implications of the constitutional structure, and so on. History is no different. And like any legal source, it can be misused by judges who overclaim or cherry-pick.

The upshot? I'm not an originalist because I think that history yields easy answers or prevents bad judging. I'm an originalist because I think that it's the right way to think about law.

⁂

Now for the question that many find to be the most perplexing: How can old text deal with new problems? Take the First Amendment. Ratified in 1791, it promises that the government "shall make no law . . . abridging the freedom of speech." In 2022, the Court resolved a free speech challenge brought by a high school cheerleader who was disciplined for a Snapchat post.[40] How can text adopted by men who wore breeches apply to a cheerleader's use of a social media app?

Here is where the genius of the founders comes in. As I explained in the last chapter, the Constitution is written at varying levels of generality. The First Amendment uses relatively broad terms. It doesn't list the specific forms of speech that existed at the time, such as books and pamphlets; instead, it protects "speech," which refers to the communication of ideas rather than the form of the communication. So "speech" easily covers news conveyed on social media (and by text, email, and so on), not only by criers in the town square.

Kyllo v. United States, decided in 2001, illustrates how the Court applies historical text to modern technology.[41] The Court had to decide whether it is a "search" under the Fourth Amendment for the government to use a thermal-imaging device to detect relative amounts of heat within the home. (The agents suspected that the homeowner was using high-intensity lamps to grow marijuana indoors.) Because the agents involved could use the thermal-imaging technology without physically entering the property, the government argued that the scan did not qualify as a "search" within the meaning of the Fourth Amendment. The Court rejected that argument. It noted that the original meaning of the Fourth Amendment term "search" was "[t]o look over or through for the purpose of finding something; to explore; to examine by inspection; as, to *search* the house for a book; to *search* the wood for a thief."[42] Relying on Founding Era usage, the Court concluded that "search" covered the thermal-imaging scan. It explained:

> We think that obtaining by sense-enhancing technology any information regarding the interior of the home that could not otherwise have been obtained without physical "intrusion into a constitutionally protected area," constitutes a search—at least where (as here) the technology in question is not in general public use. This assures preservation of that degree of privacy against government that existed when the Fourth Amendment was adopted.[43]

Thus, the Court applied the original meaning to current circumstances, thereby ensuring that the entrenched constitutional protection didn't erode over time.

The argument that old text is irrelevant to modern problems would have substantial force if the Constitution demanded fidelity to "the framers' intent" about how individual provisions would apply. There is obviously no way to know what the framers would have thought about thermal imaging technology, Snapchat, or any number of other modern innovations. Being governed by thought experiments would be both unworkable and undemocratic. But as I explained above, the original meaning of the text controls, not anyone's expectations about how it would apply. The world has changed, and will continue to change, in ways that eighteenth-century Americans could not anticipate. Throughout the generations, however, the Constitution's commitments endure.

HAVING READ THIS far, you might be surprised by my concluding point: a case does not invariably begin with an analysis of the Constitution's original public meaning. The Court resolves cases within a system of precedent, which means that it presumptively follows cases decided in the past rather than rewinding the clock to study each problem anew. For example, after the Court decided *Crawford v. Washington*, subsequent Sixth Amendment cases did not revisit the question whether the Confrontation Clause applies to all testimonial statements. Instead, those cases took *Crawford*'s holding as a given and addressed whether particular statements qualified as testimonial—such as a report prepared by a lab technician,[44] the assertions of a domestic violence victim to a 911 operator,[45] and statements made by a dying gunshot victim to police in a parking lot.[46]

The practice of following precedent is called "stare decisis"—which, translated from Latin, means "stand by the thing decided."[47] Stare decisis has been part of our system since the beginning,[48] and its benefits are evident.[49] It's efficient, because courts don't have to continually analyze issues from scratch. It makes the law stable and predictable, enabling people to rely on it. And consistency encourages confidence in the judicial process—if the Court repeatedly analyzed the same question, chances are that it would not always come up with the same answer. Ordinarily, then, the Court sticks with the first answer it gives.

To be sure, stare decisis is only a presumption; the Court can and does fix mistakes. In fact, *Crawford* itself corrected an error: it overruled a case that allowed the admission of any "reliable" out-of-court statement.[50] While reversing course is the exception to the rule (hopefully, serious errors are too), it happens every term. The Roberts Court, of which I am a part, has overturned precedent roughly once per term.[51] When Earl Warren was chief justice between 1954 and 1969, the Court overturned precedents roughly two and a half times per term. The rate increased to three cases per term during the years of the Burger Court but has declined ever since.

For present purposes, though, the point is that no justice, originalist or not, reinvents the wheel in every case. Justices take the law as they find it, unless a case presents the question whether to overrule precedent.[52] And even then, justices do not analyze the issue as if they were writing on a blank slate. In determining whether to overrule precedent, they consider a series of factors, including the nature and degree of the error, whether the precedent has proven to be unworkable, whether it has been undercut by subsequent legal or factual developments, and whether overruling it would unduly upset the interests of those relying on the previous decision.[53] The Court does not overrule precedent lightly, or simply because current justices disagree with the judgment of their predecessors.

Because originalists operate within this system, the theory's effect is muted when there is precedent on point; it has greater impact when the Court is presented with a new issue. Justice Scalia was asked on more than one occasion whether his judicial philosophy required him to overrule all cases that deviated from the Constitution's original meaning. His stock answer: "I am an originalist. I am a textualist. I am not a nut."[54] I feel the same way.

LAST CHRISTMAS, I went to my grandparents' house, along with a collection of aunts, uncles, siblings, and cousins. After surviving Katrina, the house had suffered more damage in a recent hurricane, and the current owners had decided to tear it down and sell the lot. Kindly, they allowed us to let ourselves in to say goodbye. We walked through the stripped-down interior, swapping stories as we stepped over debris. When we were done, we stood on the sidewalk and toasted the house—and my grandparents—with wine poured in red plastic cups.

There is a sense in which prior generations remain with us, even after they're gone. That's true in families, and of the Constitution too.

Chapter 13

All About Words

The Supreme Court's role in interpreting the Constitution is the one that grabs the most headlines. Its statutory cases, however, also deal with subjects that significantly affect the lives of Americans. In just the last few terms, the Court has addressed the liability of social media companies under an anti-terrorism statute,[1] limits on a union's right to strike,[2] an agency's authority to forgive billions of dollars of student loan debt,[3] and an agency's authority to impose COVID vaccine requirements.[4] All these cases involve legislation rather than the Constitution, but they are no less important to Americans. And statutory cases arise more frequently—which makes sense, given the amount of legislation on the books. While the Constitution tops out at 7,591 words, the United States Code, the compilation of federal statutes, takes up fifty-four volumes and four appendices.[5]

That contrast, while jaw-dropping, reflects the constitutional design. The Constitution is deliberately bare-bones, setting out only the framework of government and the rights of citizens. Congress, working within that framework, adopts the details of national policy on matters as varied as the economy, the environment, crime, health care, immigration, national security, and taxes. After Congress enacts a statute governing such an area, disputes inevitably arise about how the statute applies in the real world.

Resolving such disputes falls to courts, which must discern what Congress conveyed in the language it chose.

What does that task involve? The basic rules of statutory interpretation are simple: "(1) Read the statute; (2) read the statute; (3) read the statute!"[6] Following this advice often yields an easy answer. But some cases are tougher, especially those that make it to the Supreme Court. In this chapter, I'll address a problem that has long vexed judges, not to mention the law students who read their opinions. What if the most reasonable reading of the text is at odds with what seems to be the most sensible way to apply the statute? Should the Court follow the text of the statute anyway? Or should it do what it thinks Congress would have wanted instead?

An example from everyday life illustrates the problem. Imagine that I give my children a strict order never to open the door to strangers. Then, after I leave the house, a police officer rings the bell. What should the children do? A police officer is presumably not the kind of stranger I had in mind when I announced the rule. Suddenly, my straightforward instruction requires a judgment call. The children must decide whether my words contain an implicit exception for law enforcement.

Courts face similar problems all the time. Some judges handle them by prioritizing a statute's purpose over its textual details.[7] Congress can't possibly anticipate, much less spell out, every situation to which a statute will apply. So, the theory goes, Congress would want judges to adjust the text to ensure that the practical outcome in a case is consistent with the statute's larger goals. A purpose-focused judge faced with my hypothetical might reason that the children should open the door because my overall purpose is safety, and a police officer is a safe visitor. In fact, refusing him entry might make the children *less* safe if the police officer is there on a safety-related mission. For judges in this camp, the limits of language and foresight make it rigid for anyone following instructions, including a judge, to stick to words alone. When text stands in the way of what Congress would have wanted, the text should give way.[8]

My guess is that this approach is very attractive—and might even seem obviously right—to many people, particularly at first blush. Indeed, it was at one time the dominant approach to statutory interpretation, and retired justice Stephen Breyer continues to support it.[9] I am more persuaded, however, by the theory's critics. While privileging purpose over text has intuitive appeal, it is plagued by serious flaws.

Here's one: it's not possible to know what Congress "would have wanted." Even a simple example like my police officer illustrates the point. Maybe I would want the children to answer the door for law enforcement. But the opposite is plausible too. I might want the instruction to hold because of the risk that the visitor is an impostor. Or I might want the door to stay shut to keep my children out of the business of making judgment calls. Even if I'm okay with the police officer, what about the water meter reader or the Amazon driver? Opening the door to exceptions (so to speak) could make the children less safe overall. So maybe I meant exactly what I said: Never open the door to strangers.

Switching from family rules to the United States Code makes things even more complicated. If it's difficult to discern the intent of one person who has given a simple instruction (like me to my children), it's all the more difficult to discern the intent of a majority of 435 members of the House, a majority of 100 members of the Senate, and a single president with veto power.[10] Statutes are difficult to pass and reflect the views of hundreds of different actors with a range of views about how a statute should apply to a particular set of facts.[11] Whose views count? Those of committee chairs? Sponsors? Members whose votes were most in doubt? Each legislator has her own understandings about how (and to what degree, at what cost, and with what trade-offs) the statutory language accomplishes her policy goals.

There are also many issues that few, if any, supporters of the bill anticipated at all. Consider a case that arose under the Americans with Disabilities Act, which aims to eliminate discrimination against persons with disabilities.[12] To that end, the act requires certain entities to make "reasonable modifications" that would allow the disabled to participate "unless the entity can demonstrate that making such modifications would *fundamentally alter* the nature" of the activity.[13] In *PGA Tour, Inc. v. Martin*, the Supreme Court had to decide whether allowing a disabled golfer to ride in a golf cart during a competition—rather than walking the course, as tournament rules required—would "fundamentally alter" the game of golf.[14] (The Court held that the statute entitled the golfer to use a golf cart.)[15] Is that an issue that members of Congress actually thought about in 1990 when they passed the Americans with Disabilities Act? Would it be fruitful for a judge to ask herself how the House majority, Senate majority, and president would have defined the essential attributes of golf, had they considered the question? Or to ask, even more specifically, whether the House majority, Senate majority, and president would want the PGA Tour to allow the disabled golfer to ride in a golf cart?[16]

Questions like these simply aren't answerable. A collective body can express its collective intent only in the language it chooses; any effort to figure out what Congress *really* wanted or *would* want in a given situation is pure guesswork.[17] Rather than trying to get into Congress's mind, an interpreter should take Congress at its word. The best way to glean Congress's collective intent is to ask what a reasonable person would have understood this language to mean. Members of Congress voted on this text, which was also presented to the president. Whatever unexpressed intentions or expectations some legislators may have had, the text is the common denominator—the bill's supporters agreed on that much. So what does the text convey? The objective meaning, rather than the subjective intent, controls. This principle might sound familiar, because the same rule applies to constitutional interpretation, as I discussed in the last chapter.

In straightforward cases, the objective and subjective perspectives will lead to the same place. (So, for example, if a stranger selling magazines knocks at the door, everyone will agree that my rule prohibits the children from opening it.) But in hard cases, the two perspectives can yield different results. (That's the police officer: the rule says "*no* strangers," but surely Mom would want me to open the door for law enforcement.) In situations like these, courts taking the objective approach to statutory interpretation stick to the ordinary meaning of the words, while those taking a subjective approach are willing to depart from the ordinary meaning to better serve Congress's presumed intent.

United States v. Locke, decided in 1985, is a classic illustration of the contrast between text-based and intent-based interpretation.[18] *Locke* involved a statute that required a claim to be filed "prior to December 31."[19] A claimant, taking this to mean "before the end of the year," filed *on* December 31.[20] The question whether this claim was timely divided the justices. Justice Thurgood Marshall, writing for the majority of the Court, concluded that the claim was late because "*prior to*" December 31 plainly means *before* December 31—in other words, by December 30.[21] The language might be awkward, and most people might think that a deadline of December 31 makes more sense. "But," he explained, "the fact that Congress might have acted with greater clarity or foresight does not give courts a *carte blanche* to redraft statutes in an effort to achieve that which Congress is perceived to have failed to do."[22] Courts must honor Congress's choice, even if the claimant's reading seems like a better policy.

In dissent, Justice Stevens, joined by Justice Brennan, protested that the statute's "text cannot possibly reflect the *actual intent* of Congress."[23] Justice Stevens thought "[i]t would be fully consistent with the intent of Congress to treat any filing received during the 1980 calendar year as a timely filing for that year."[24] And he expressed "no doubt that Congress would have chosen to adopt a construction of the statute that filing take place by the end of the calendar year if its attention had been focused on this precise issue."[25] Thus, he would have held that the filing was timely on the theory that Congress's "actual" intent was both discernible and controlling.[26]

Intent-based arguments like Justice Stevens's were once common. Every law student who studies statutory interpretation reads *Church of the Holy Trinity v. United States*, an 1892 case in which the Supreme Court announced that "a thing may be within the letter of the statute and yet not within the statute, because not within its spirit nor within the intention of its makers."[27] Translation: the text forecloses this interpretation, but Congress didn't mean what it said.

These are the facts: Holy Trinity Church, located in New York City, hired as its rector a British citizen named Reverend E. Walpole Warren.[28] Unfortunately for the church, a recently passed federal statute made it illegal to assist the immigration of noncitizens hired to perform "labor or service of any kind" in the United States.[29] A straightforward application of the statute's text led readily to the conclusion that the church owed a hefty fine. But the Supreme Court refused to adopt this straightforward reading, finding it unimaginable that Congress intended to preclude a church from bringing its minister of choice into the country.[30] The statute was designed to limit the "influx of . . . cheap unskilled labor," not the valuable "labor or service" of "brain toilers" like Christian ministers.[31] Congress's intent was at odds with the statutory text, the Court claimed, so intent carried the day.

Students read *Holy Trinity* because it so clearly expresses the interpretive approach long dominant in the federal courts. But they also learn that *Holy Trinity*—once a key precedent—has not been cited favorably by a Supreme Court majority, much less relied upon to turn the outcome of a case, in over thirty years.[32] Though it used to be conventional wisdom, the claim that legislative intent can outright trump statutory text has largely fallen by the wayside.[33]

In my view, fidelity to statutory text is required by the constitutional structure. Enacting a law requires compromise—there is no other way for a bill to cross the finish line.[34] It must command a majority in both houses of Congress (which means navigating committee rules, floor votes, and the threat of filibuster); the House and Senate must reconcile their bills to reflect agreement on the same language; and the reconciled bill must have either the support of the president or enough votes to overcome the veto. At every step, choices are made that affect the contents of the bill. For example, a statute's proponents might give up some of what they want to secure the bill's passage. (So a bill designed to address climate change might permit some fossil fuel production to secure the vote of a senator from a coal-mining state.)[35] Or drafters might use vague language because competing factions could not agree on all of the specifics. (So a bill barring certain cases from being filed in federal court might not specify what should happen to cases that are already there.)[36] And in every instance, Congress draws lines, because no statute "pursues its purpose at *all* costs."[37] (For instance, the Americans with Disabilities Act requires newly constructed buildings to be "accessible to and usable by" disabled individuals, but it does not require existing buildings to retrofit their facilities to the same extent.)[38] Extending a statute to better accomplish its purpose takes the statute further than a majority of Congress, not to mention the president or a veto-proof majority, chose to go.

After all, Congress does not just choose an *end*—it also chooses a specific *means* of accomplishing that end. As the Court has explained:

> Congress may be unanimous in its intent to stamp out some vague social or economic evil; however, because its Members may differ sharply on the means for effectuating that intent, the final language of the legislation may reflect hard-fought compromises. Invocation of the "plain purpose" of legislation at the expense of the terms of the statute itself takes no account of the processes of compromise and, in the end, prevents the effectuation of congressional intent.[39]

A judge who tweaks the text to improve its fit with statutory purpose risks undoing the very compromises that made the passage of legislation possible.[40] There is no way for the judge to know whether its new, supposedly improved version would have made it into law. What *did* make it into law, for better or for worse, is the text on which Congress voted. The Court has driven home that point in case after case.[41]

The shift from the primacy of legislative intent to the primacy of statutory text happened largely through the efforts of judges and scholars who call themselves "textualists," Justice Scalia foremost among them.[42]

Textualists advanced the arguments I summarized above: that legislative intent is unknowable and adherence to the statutory text is required by the constitutional structure.[43] Their critique of "purposivism" (the name given the approach epitomized by *Holy Trinity*) has had a significant impact on the way federal judges approach statutory text. To be sure, not all judges consider themselves to be textualists. Nonetheless, as Jonathan Molot, a professor at Georgetown Law School, has explained, "The broad appeal of textualism's underlying premises has led judges who do not consider themselves adherents to heed textualism's warnings about the pitfalls of strong purposivism and to alter their approach to statutory interpretation."[44] Today, few judges assert the authority to make friendly amendments to statutory text. As I discuss below, however, disagreement remains about a narrower issue: whether judges can choose an awkward (but still plausible) meaning to harmonize the statute's text with its apparent purpose.

Legislative History

Any discussion of the role of legislative intent would be incomplete without touching on legislative history. If statutory interpretation really comes down to divining the purpose of the legislature, where better to look? To the casual observer, it might even seem like the best place to find out what Congress was trying to say. Over time, and particularly beginning in the middle of the twentieth century, courts tried that approach. They treated legislative history materials—committee reports on bills as well as floor statements and the like—as windows into what Congress had "really" been thinking. In 1940, the Court declared that it would rely on any source that might be an "aid to [the] construction" of a statute,[45] and things were off to the races. The more heavily the Court relied on legislative intent in interpreting statutes, the more heavily it relied on legislative history.

By the 1970s, reliance on legislative history had gotten out of hand. In one case, the Supreme Court proclaimed that because of ambiguity in the legislative history, "it is clear that we must look primarily to the statutes themselves to find the legislative intent."[46] The Court indicated no awareness that such statements reflected a statutory interpretation culture gone awry—too often statutory text was a side show rather than the main event. The result was a system in which courts, however well-meaning, were thwarting the democratic process in an effort to do what they thought Congress "really" wanted, regardless of what Congress actually said.

The flaws in using legislative history became evident over time. For starters, courts were treating a statute's legislative history as if it were legally binding—even though only the *statute* was passed by both houses of Congress and presented to the president for potential veto.[47] But even when used as an interpretive tool, legislative history is an unreliable gauge of what a statute means.[48]

The problems with legislative history are well-known. I'll mention three. First, legislative history materials (particularly committee reports) are produced by and large by staff members, who in turn often work with favored interest groups.[49] It is therefore naïve to assume that assertions in legislative history represent the considered views of the legislators to whom they are attributed; they can just as easily reflect the hopes of self-interested groups about how a statute will apply to their industries or areas of concern. Moreover, points tucked into the legislative history may well be items that one side of the legislative debate didn't have the votes (or at least feared it didn't have the votes) to put in the text itself.[50]

Second, legislative history sometimes qualifies as legislative fiction. Members can insert words into the *Congressional Record* that were never actually uttered in the run-up to the bill's passage. In one case that made it to the Court, the briefs cited a supposed colloquy among senators, complete with phrases like "If I might interrupt."[51] It turned out that this "discussion" was inserted into the *Congressional Record* after the fact—it never actually happened.[52] Such later-added statements have long been par for the congressional course,[53] and efforts to curtail such practices have proved ineffective.[54]

Third, using legislative history is like "looking over a crowd" at a cocktail party and "picking out your friends."[55] Both sides pepper the legislative history in the hope of influencing courts, which means that there's often something in the record for everyone.[56] (When I taught statutory interpretation, the students who had worked in Congress were the students most skeptical of legislative history.) If the history contains statements going both ways, it's not reliable. Plus, as I've explained, members of Congress may have different views about how a statutory provision should apply to particular circumstances, and there's no reason to treat the views of one member or a faction of members as representative of the majority in both houses of Congress. That principle does not change if members insert their views into the legislative history.

Just as the move toward textualism resulted in vastly reduced reliance on a statute's purpose instead of its text, it resulted in a dramatic decline in reliance on legislative history.[57] It wasn't long before a majority of the Court would say, "[J]udicial reliance on legislative materials like committee reports, which are not themselves subject to the requirements of Article I, may give unrepresentative committee members—or, worse yet, unelected staffers and lobbyists—both the power and the incentive to attempt strategic manipulations of legislative history to secure results they were unable to achieve through the statutory text."[58] While the Court occasionally cites legislative history,[59] it has nothing close to the influence it once did. Now, it is typically invoked as a data point or to provide background rather than as the primary justification for a decision.[60] This limited use of legislative history keeps it in its place.[61]

So far, I've explained that guesses about what Congress "would have wanted" or "really intended" can't overcome the text, even if the evidence of Congress's supposed intent is found in legislative history. But my students always ask the obvious question: What if a statute contains a true mistake?

Must a textualist follow the language off a cliff? No. Sound interpretation includes the correction of true blunders—those that would be obvious to any skilled speaker of the language. Written by human beings, statutes occasionally contain mistakes. (In the business, we call these "scrivener's errors.") But to be correctible by a court, the mistake must be *obvious.* To get a sense of how obvious, think about a speed limit sign warning that "VIOLATORS ARE SUBJECT TO A MINIMUM FIND OF $200." Would enterprising drivers think that they could earn cash by speeding? No—they would recognize the typo. As Justice Scalia remarked, he was willing to "go along" with correcting such mistakes "only because the intelligent reader would understand the meaning that way."[62]

Such blatant missteps in statutes are extremely rare, but they do happen. The Louisiana legislature once passed a statute authorizing litigants to impeach the testimony of their opponents "in any unlawful way."[63] Applying the rule, the Supreme Court of Louisiana took "cognizance of the fact—which is obvious—that this substitution of the word 'unlawful' for the word 'lawful' was an accident" and announced that it would read the law as it had appeared in the predecessor statute, which allowed impeachment "in any lawful way."[64] Another good example is an amendment to Arkansas law dealing with certain powers of municipalities that finished by saying that "all laws . . . are hereby repealed."[65] Plainly, the state legislature didn't mean to repeal all law and return Arkansas to a state of nature; instead—as the Arkansas Supreme Court readily concluded—the amendment repealed only conflicting legislation on the same subject.[66] Our Court too has confronted at least one scrivener's error: an evidentiary rule in which Congress omitted the word "criminal" in front of "defendant."[67] Because the statute was nonsensical without that qualification, the Court read the statute to include it.[68]

Mistakes like these are correctible. But in the context of statutory interpretation, "mistake" is a very narrow term. Recall *United States v. Locke*, which dealt with a statute requiring claims to be filed "prior to December 31." Some people might call that language a "mistake," reasoning that Congress surely meant to say "*by* December 31." But did it? That's hardly obvious, because, as the Court said in that case, all deadlines are arbitrary.[69] Nor is language a mistake simply because it leads to an odd or unexpected result. Recall *Holy Trinity* and the ban on immigrant labor. Discussing the statute with a friend over a cup of coffee, a judge might express her view that Congress made a "big mistake" by drafting the statute broadly enough to include ministers. But once the judge dons her robe, that's not the kind of "mistake" she can blue-pencil. The term "scrivener's error" refers to a slip of the pen, not inartful drafting or a failure of foresight. It is therefore a category distinct from the larger debate about when courts can stretch language to make it better account for Congress's purpose. Take comfort in the fact that courts can correct scrivener's errors, but don't overestimate the reach of that power.

ON ONE LEVEL, then, textualism has swept the field, and the days of preferring the spirit to the letter of a statute are over. As my colleague Justice Elena Kagan observed in a lecture honoring Justice Scalia, "We are all textualists now."[70] At the same time, the debate between purposivists and textualists simmers below the surface. Even if it is not acceptable to out-and-out depart from statutory text, as the Court used to do, is it appropriate to stretch the text beyond its most natural reading to get to a result that the judge thinks more sensible? Occasionally, the Court has answered yes.

Scholars have given this approach names like the "new purposivism"[71] and the "New Holy Trinity."[72] Unlike adherents of old-school purposivism, these newer purposivists work within the text. Unlike textualists, however, their interpretive lodestar is not necessarily the best meaning of the words as they would be understood by an ordinary person. Instead, judges employing this approach are willing to adopt an awkward meaning if they think that doing so will make the statute more consistent with its apparent purpose. You might think of it as "purposivism lite."

A frequently cited example of this phenomenon is the Court's decision in *King v. Burwell*,[73] a complicated case involving the terms on which Congress authorized the federal government to provide subsidies to taxpayers for purchases of health insurance plans under the Affordable Care Act (popularly known as Obamacare). Despite its complexity, *King v. Burwell* is worth considering because it deals with a statute familiar to every American, and the Supreme Court's role in interpreting the statute was well publicized. Indeed, when the case arrived at the Court, many argued that the viability of the Affordable Care Act hung in the balance. *King v. Burwell* highlights the tension between competing theories of statutory interpretation in a context that Americans know and care about.

The Affordable Care Act changed health care law in significant ways.[74] Among the prominent and popular reforms was the requirement that health insurance plans not turn away or charge higher prices to those with preexisting conditions. Perhaps the heart of the act, though, was its establishment of health care "exchanges" (basically marketplaces) for the purchase of health insurance plans, accompanied by government subsidies (in the form of tax credits) to make these plans more affordable.[75] Critically, the subsidies were available only for plans purchased on one of the exchanges. That condition was express in the statute, as were Congress's plans for setting up the exchanges. The states were supposed to be at the forefront. But Congress also planned for the contingency that not all states would choose to participate. In that event, the statute provided that the secretary of health and human services "shall . . . establish and operate such Exchange within the State."[76] These interlocking features appear straightforward: the states would establish the exchanges, and if they chose not to, the federal government would do it instead.

Now comes the problem: the text allowed subsidies only if the purchaser bought an insurance plan through "an Exchange established by the [purchaser's] *State*."[77] On its face, this language ruled out subsidies for plans purchased on other exchanges—namely, those established by the federal government in states that chose not to create them. And since (contrary to widespread expectations when the statute was passed)[78] dozens of states chose not to establish exchanges, it looked like many millions of people wouldn't be able to get the benefits envisioned by the statute. The act was supposed to make health insurance accessible to everyone by providing financial assistance to those who needed it. Without the subsidies, those who lived in nonparticipating states were left out.

So the Internal Revenue Service adopted a regulation—based on the original statutory text—making the tax-credit subsidies available for health insurance purchased on an exchange "regardless of whether the Exchange is established and operated by a State . . . or by [the federal government]."[79] This regulation teed up the issue in *King v. Burwell*: whether a statute limiting subsidies to purchases made on exchanges "established by a State" permitted subsidies for purchases made on exchanges established by the federal government.

The Court said yes. It began by stating that a contrary result would produce other interpretive oddities in the extremely complex statute.[80] (I will spare you the march through this thicket.) Most of all, though, the Court emphasized that limiting subsidies to state exchanges would thwart the statute's accomplishment of its basic purpose.[81] Accordingly, the Court concluded that "the context and structure of the Act compel us to depart from what would *otherwise be the most natural reading* of the pertinent statutory phrase."[82] Note that the Court didn't say that it was actually overriding the text. While this interpretation surely turned on the statute's spirit, the Court insisted that the interpretation was consistent with the statute's letter. That insistence is important, because it shows that the Court today is not where it was in the heyday of purposivism, when it asserted the authority to openly break from the statutory text. Still, the Court was willing to strain the text by adopting a less natural interpretation, revealing that purposivism retains some gravitational force.

I was not on the Court when it decided *King v. Burwell.* As a law professor, however, I wrote an article expressing the view that the dissent had the better of the argument.[83] The dissent maintained that despite the Court's strenuous efforts to show otherwise, the statutory text and structure didn't justify treating an exchange established by the federal government as one "established by a State."[84] As for the Court's insistence that the statute's overall purpose demanded that reading—well, the Affordable Care Act, like all statutes, had multiple purposes, which it pursued through specific means.[85] Congress certainly wanted to expand health insurance coverage by providing generous tax subsidies. But it also wanted to involve the states in administering the system, which it did by limiting subsidies to taxpayers in states that established exchanges. As written, the act offered the states a bargain: if a state set up and administered an exchange, then the federal government would provide generous subsidies to its taxpayers.[86] "So even if making credits available on all Exchanges advances the goal of improving health care markets, it frustrates the goal of encouraging state involvement in the implementation of the Act."[87] The Court's decision—rather than implementing both Congress's decision to provide subsidies *and* its decision to require states to participate if they wanted their citizens to get health insurance subsidies—let those nonparticipating states off the hook. They were able to get the benefits of the program without paying the political and financial costs of fully opting in. One can only speculate on how the nonparticipating states would have responded had the Court interpreted the statute to forbid subsidies to their taxpayers—pressure from state citizens denied the subsidies might have prompted nonparticipating states to change course.

To my mind, *King v. Burwell* illustrates the difficulties of emphasizing a statute's purpose at the expense of the most natural interpretation of its text. When the Court settles on a single congressional purpose to drive textual interpretation, it risks upsetting the compromises and trade-offs that underlay the legislation itself. The consensus that text controls is a welcome development. In my view, however, courts must be careful not to allow an atextual purposivism to sneak in through the back door.[88]

⁂

Statutory interpretation is hard. Good judges grapple all the time with difficult cases—like *King v. Burwell*—and do their best to settle on the correct interpretation. Judges sometimes disagree on what a text means (though the public might be surprised at how frequently court decisions are unanimous). But we shouldn't be surprised by that, because judging—as its name reflects—requires judgment. And judges acting in good faith sometimes will simply understand a text differently. I am reminded of George Bernard Shaw's quip that England and America are divided by a common language. While judges sometimes divide over the interpretation of the same language, textualism works to ensure that the debate is about what Congress *actually* did and not about judicial speculation about what it *wanted* to do. And that, by and large, is what judges are trying to figure out.

Chapter 14

DON'T TAKE IT LITERALLY

I HAVE TAUGHT a seminar in statutory interpretation for about twenty years. Every year, a majority of students happily signs on to the proposition that the text alone is the law. But many of those newly minted textualists also believe that textualism is context-free literalism. I like to show the class a picture of a green, gas-guzzling truck parked in front of a sign that says "RESERVED FOR GREEN VEHICLES." I then ask the students whether a textualist would conclude that the owner of the truck has violated the parking regulation. A surprising number of them say no. That, however, is a serious misunderstanding of textualism, which interprets language in context. An ordinary English speaker would understand that the phrase "green vehicles" on a parking sign refers to something like "low emission vehicles." In this context, it would be a mistake to interpret the sign's use of the word "green" as referring to paint color.

A rigid translation from one language to another vividly illustrates why literalism fails.[1] When I was in college, I spent a summer in France with the goal of becoming fluent in French. One evening at dinner, my host asked if I wanted more food, and I responded, translating literally, "Je suis pleine"—"I am full." I was very proud of myself for responding in French. But my sentence was greeted with uproarious laughter—and not, as I initially assumed, because I spoke French with a distinctive southeastern

Louisiana accent. It was much worse than that. I learned that in French, the phrase "je suis pleine" means "I am pregnant." While that phrase did come up with some frequency later in my life, it was definitely not what I was trying to communicate at the time.

As a budding French speaker, I was unaware of the nuance. Language involves conventions shared by those who speak the language. As I've explained in my academic writing, "[Language] cannot be understood out of context," and literalism, even when accompanied by the most sophisticated dictionary in the world, "strips language of its context."[2] Fluent speakers of language are not literalists, and neither are good judges.

Because textualists are not literalists, they don't come to the job of statutory interpretation "armed only with a dictionary."[3] As John Manning, a leading textualist scholar and former dean of Harvard Law School, explains, "[D]ictionary definitions of words will often fail to account for settled nuances or background conventions that qualify the literal meaning of language and, in particular, of legal language."[4] Even nonlegal examples show why.[5] One dictionary defines "vehicle" as "a means of carrying or transporting something."[6] So is a grocery cart a "vehicle"? It fits the literal definition, but it's hard to imagine asking for a "vehicle" at the local supermarket. Here's another example: a "bachelor" is "an unmarried man."[7] So is a Catholic priest a "bachelor"? The term doesn't quite fit, because it evokes a man who is eligible for marriage. Final example: "furniture" means "movable articles used in readying an area (such as a room or patio) for occupancy or use."[8] Does a piano count? Maybe to a moving company or an interior designer, but I doubt it's a go-to description for people who play. In sum, a dictionary entry is often a decent starting point, but it's not an answer key.

Justice Scalia frequently invoked the case *Smith v. United States* to make this point.[9] In that case, the defendant had been charged with the "use" of a firearm "during and in relation to . . . [a] drug trafficking crime."[10] The defendant attempted to trade an unlawful automatic weapon for two ounces of cocaine.[11] The question for the Court was whether that trade constituted "use" of the weapon within the meaning of the statute.[12] The majority (from which Justice Scalia dissented) cited multiple dictionary definitions of the verb "to use" and concluded that "[a]s the dictionary definitions and experience make clear, one can use a firearm in a number of ways," and that it fell within the common meaning to say that someone "uses" a firearm when he trades it for drugs.[13] The Court thus upheld an enhanced sentence—an additional thirty years' imprisonment—for the defendant because he had "use[d]" the gun during a drug-trafficking crime within the meaning of the statute.[14]

In dissent, Justice Scalia explained that the fact that a word *can* be used a certain way does not mean that it is *ordinarily* used that way or that it was *in fact* used that way in a particular context.[15] In his view, the majority's reliance on multiple, broad dictionary definitions of what "use" could mean violated the "fundamental principle of statutory construction (and, indeed, of language itself) that the meaning of a word cannot be determined in isolation, but must be drawn from the context in which it is used."[16] In typical fashion, he offered a memorable illustration:

> When someone asks, "Do you use a cane?," he is not inquiring whether you have your grandfather's silver-handled walking stick on display in the hall; he wants to know whether you *walk* with a cane. Similarly, to speak of "using a firearm" is to speak of using it for its distinctive purpose, i.e., as a weapon.[17]

This isn't to say, of course, that dictionaries are useless—it's simply a warning against overstating their value.[18] (Nor is it to say that other features of the statutory structure did not support the majority's interpretation. It was a hard case.) Dictionaries are evidence of a word's possible meaning, but they don't, by themselves, pinpoint the word's meaning in context. For that, courts should follow the advice of Judge Frank Easterbook, a prominent textualist (and my former colleague on the Seventh Circuit): they should listen to "the ring the words [of the statute] would have had to a skilled user of words at the time, thinking about the same problem."[19]

The ring of the words drove the result in *Wooden v. United States*, which was decided during my second term.[20] In that case, the Court faced a law mandating a fifteen-year sentencing enhancement for offenders with three or more prior convictions for violent felonies "committed on *occasions different from one another*."[21] Wooden burglarized ten storage units in a row at the same facility on the same night and had ten burglary convictions to show for it.[22] Those convictions counted as violent felonies.[23] But were the crimes committed on *different* occasions or as part of the *same* occasion? The dictionary did not settle the question, because it allowed for both possibilities.[24] An occasion is commonly defined as an "event, occurrence, happening, or episode."[25] It is possible to treat the burglaries, which happened sequentially, as ten distinct events or episodes—that's what the government wanted us to do.[26] On the other hand, the burglaries, which were closely related in time and place, could also be treated as part of a single overarching event—that was Wooden's position.[27]

Relying on ordinary usage, the Court, in an opinion written by Justice Elena Kagan, sided with Wooden. Colorfully, Justice Kagan asked how "an ordinary person (a reporter; a police officer; yes, even a lawyer)" would characterize the burglaries:[28]

> [Such an] observer might say: "On one occasion, Wooden burglarized ten units in a storage facility." By contrast, she would never say: "On ten occasions, Wooden burglarized a unit in the facility." . . . She would, using language in its normal way, group his entries into the storage units, even though not simultaneous, all together—as happening on a single occasion, rather than on ten "occasions different from one another."[29]

In everyday conversation, drawing the temporal line separating one occasion from another is "straightforward and intuitive."[30] Take a wedding, which "often includes a ceremony, cocktail hour, dinner, and dancing."[31] A guest would not describe these four sequenced events as four different occasions; rather, they are part of the same occasion: the wedding. To be sure, there will be cases that are harder than Wooden's. But resolving them is not a matter of deciding whether the crimes were committed sequentially rather than simultaneously. It depends on whether the crimes were so closely related that an ordinary speaker would consider them to be part of the same event. "In law as in life," Justice Kagan explained, "it is usually not so difficult to identify an 'occasion.'"[32]

Unfortunately for judges, some statutory terms show up in law but *not* in life. In that event, deciphering a term is not so "straightforward and intuitive." For instance, I once wrote an opinion analyzing whether a private arbitration panel qualified as a "foreign or international tribunal" under a particular statute.[33] That's not a phrase that comes up at cocktail parties, and the dictionary definition of "tribunal" didn't much help. The word could be used narrowly, to refer only to governmental bodies, or broadly, to refer to both governmental and private bodies. But there are a number of cues on which lawyers rely in interpreting statutes, including the statute's structure and its fit with related laws; factors like these indicated that Congress had used "tribunal" in its narrower sense. Sometimes, as in that case, interpreting the statute as a skilled user of language means interpreting it as a skilled user of *legal* language—one familiar with the conventions of interpreting law.

Regardless of whether terms are commonplace or technical, discerning their ordinary meaning is not a mechanical exercise. Those who take an oversimplified view of textualism imagine that it works like Google Translate or ChatGPT: a judge punches in a word or query, and—voilà!—out pops the result.[34] If interpretation worked that way, one could expect every judge to interpret a text in exactly the same way. But popping words into a machine does not require judgment; construing language in context does. Skilled users of language don't always agree on what language means in context. In recent years, the Court has divided on whether a fish is a "tangible object" (it isn't);[35] whether a statute's coverage of 100 or 200 tons of emission of air pollutants can be understood to mean 100,000 tons or more (it can't);[36] whether the term "compensation of interpreters" covers written as well as oral translations (it doesn't);[37] and whether a floating home is a "vessel" (it isn't).[38] Viewed in isolation, these words might seem easy to define. In the context of the particular statutory schemes, however, the answers were not self-evident.

Such uncertainty is not reason to lose faith in the process. My point is simply that no approach to interpretation, including textualism, is a right-answer generator. Given the complexity of both language and legal problems, we should not be surprised that in difficult cases, judges aiming at the same target—ordinary meaning—sometimes land in different places. Acting in good faith, judges do the best they can with the tools they have.

WHAT ARE THOSE tools? Most important is the statutory context, because words are colored by their surroundings and the backdrop against which they were enacted. Thus, judges consider factors such as how the words fit with words and phrases; how they fit within the overall structure of the statute; and whether context suggests a specialized meaning, much like the phrase "green vehicles" refers to "low emission vehicles" on a parking sign. Notably, all judges, including textualists, consider the statute's purpose as part of its context.[39] For textualists, though, statutory purpose can only illuminate—not overcome—the text's ordinary meaning.

The rules of grammar are front and center more often than you might think. I once wrote an opinion devoted entirely to connecting a restrictive adverbial phrase to the terms that it modified.[40] (The statute was so awkwardly worded that I described the task as "enough to make a grammarian throw down her pen.")[41] That case was not an anomaly. Important cases have turned on whether a word functions as a noun or a verb,[42] the applicability of the "last antecedent rule" (the rule that the correct antecedent is usually the nearest reasonable one),[43] and whether a modifying clause applies to every noun in a sentence.[44] In one lawsuit about overtime pay for truck drivers, millions of dollars rode on how to interpret the absence of a comma.[45]

I don't want to sound too technical about it—the Supreme Court does not grade Congress's work. As the Court once put it, we don't sit "as a panel of grammarians; but neither do we regard ordinary principles of English prose as irrelevant to a construction of those enactments."[46] That about sums it up. Congress communicates in English, so the conventional rules of English grammar presumptively apply.[47] When they don't, it's usually because the format of a statute does not lend itself to the grammatical precision expected of narrative prose. They are often written in outline form, with sections, subsections, and even subsubsections. Yet having read hundreds of papers as a professor, I can attest that questionable grammar does not always prevent writers from getting their point across. Judges can usually understand Congress's work, even if a professor might rate it a C. Looking past grammatical oddities is sometimes the path to identifying the statute's most plausible meaning.

In addition to rules of grammar, courts deploy rules called "canons of interpretation" to assist in the interpretation of statutes. Canons are traditionally classified as either "linguistic" or "substantive." The former apply patterns of speech to statutes, and the latter instruct courts to interpret statutes in light of certain values. Federal courts have applied canons since they began hearing cases, and many are rooted in English sources that long predate the founding of our country.[48] So while lawyers (especially law professors) debate the utility of canons, they're not going anywhere anytime soon. They are a staple of our interpretive tradition.

Linguistic canons bear fancy labels but capture ordinary concepts. "Expressio unius est exclusio alterius," which means "the expression of one thing implies the exclusion of others," is a standard example.[49] If I tell my daughter that she can spend her birthday money on clothes, books, or roller skates, and she spends it all on candy, I will think (and she will know) that she violated my directions. In context, the list was exclusive. But the "expressio unius" canon is just a rule of thumb, because speakers do not intend for every list to be exclusive. If I ask my husband to go to the grocery store to get bread, milk, and fruit, and recognizing we're out of cereal, he picks up Cheerios too, I won't think that he violated my wishes. In context, the list was *not* exclusive. Legal language works similarly. If Congress goes through the trouble of specifying items in a list, there is good reason to think that the list is a closed set, especially in the formal context of lawmaking. Still, context can defeat that presumption. Like all English speakers, then, judges must decide when canons like "expressio unius" apply. Linguistic canons are helpful, but—like dictionaries and rules of grammar—they cannot be applied robotically.

Linguistic canons have the uncontroversial goal of helping a judge identify the statute's most natural meaning. Substantive canons work differently. Rather than capturing the "ring the words would have had to a skilled user" of the language,[50] as linguistic canons aim to do, substantive canons single out certain values for protection. For instance, the rule of lenity promotes fairness to the accused by instructing courts to construe ambiguous criminal statutes against the government.[51] The rule of constitutional avoidance promotes judicial restraint by counseling courts to interpret statutes, where at all possible, to avoid raising serious constitutional questions.[52] There are also substantive canons protecting Indian tribes and structural principles like federalism. The list goes on.

Substantive canons come in different strengths. Some break the tie between two equally possible interpretations.[53] The rule of lenity is typically understood this way, as is the canon favoring Indian tribes. In one case, for example, a man challenged his conviction for running an illegal lottery scheme.[54] After finding ambiguity in the text of the money-laundering statute,[55] the Court applied the rule of lenity, noting that "the tie must go to the defendant."[56] In another case, the Court held that Yakima County, Washington, could not impose a land-sale tax against tribal members of the Yakima Nation.[57] The statute was susceptible to "two possible constructions,"[58] so the principle that "[s]tatutes are to be construed liberally in favor of the Indians" tipped the scale.[59]

Other canons are heavier-handed. Rather than breaking a tie between equally plausible interpretations, they instruct a judge to adopt a less natural reading to avoid a disfavored result.[60] For example, it is an "ordinary rule of statutory construction that if Congress intends to alter the 'usual constitutional balance between the states and the Federal Government,' it must make its intention to do so 'unmistakably clear in the language of the statute.'"[61] Congress must speak with similar clarity if it wants a statute to apply retroactively, to provoke a serious constitutional question, or to subject the federal government to suit by private litigants. How do these more aggressive canons work in practice? The following are examples.

In the 1970s, the National Labor Relations Board attempted to exercise jurisdiction over attempts to unionize the employment of teachers at Illinois and Indiana Catholic schools.[62] The text of the statute granted the board jurisdiction over all employers with only eight exceptions, and church-operated schools were not on the list.[63] Most naturally interpreted, then, the statute appeared to allow the board to exert authority over religious entities. If that interpretation prevailed, however, the Court would have to confront serious constitutional questions under the First Amendment's Religion Clauses. To sidestep these thorny questions, the Court applied the constitutional avoidance canon: because Congress had not *clearly specified* that the board could regulate church-run schools, the Court declined to interpret the statute to grant the board that authority.[64] Faced with a choice between a constitutional close call and a less natural statutory interpretation, the Court chose the latter.

Atascadero State Hospital v. Scanlon is another example.[65] In that case, Scanlon sued a California state-run hospital for illegally denying him employment because of his disability.[66] The hospital argued that the Eleventh Amendment shielded it from the lawsuit because it was a state-run institution.[67] If the hospital was right, Scanlon was out of luck. But Scanlon had a good counterargument. Federal law allowed "*any* recipient of Federal assistance" to be sued for employment discrimination. Congress can override the Eleventh Amendment, and Scanlon argued that the phrase "any recipient" was broad enough to include states receiving federal assistance.[68] So, Scanlon said, the Eleventh Amendment didn't shield the hospital after all.

Despite the force of that argument as a matter of the text, Scanlon lost. One of the federalism canons requires Congress to speak clearly if it wishes to subject states to lawsuits by private litigants. Because Congress did not specifically mention the states, the Court held that they were not included in the otherwise broad statutory language.[69] The hospital was immune from Scanlon's lawsuit.

Here's a case with colorful facts: *Bond v. United States*.[70] Carol Anne Bond, a microbiologist from Pennsylvania, learned that her best friend, Myrlinda Haynes, was pregnant as a result of a love affair with Bond's husband.[71] Bond wanted revenge, so she smeared arsenic, as well as a chemical used for cleaning lab equipment, on her (former) friend's doorknob, car, and mailbox.[72] The chemicals caused a minor burn on Haynes's thumb.[73]

Normally, if someone assaults her neighbor she will be charged with a state crime, because the states enforce most criminal laws in our system of government. But in this case, federal authorities charged Bond with violating a federal statute that prohibits the possession and use of *chemical weapons*.[74] The question before the Supreme Court was whether this statute applied to Bond's conduct.[75] On one hand, most Americans associate "chemical weapons" with World War I trench warfare or Russian spy assassinations, not a local love triangle turned nasty.[76] On the other hand, the statute didn't use the phrase "chemical weapon" in its purely ordinary sense. The statute set out a specific definition of "chemical weapon," and the skin irritants that Bond employed fell squarely within it.[77]

Enter another federalism canon, this one requiring Congress to speak clearly if it intends to override the normal balance of federal and state authority. If taken at face value, the definition of "chemical weapon" would intrude into the state's traditional authority to prosecute local crimes. The

Court explained, however, that the statute's "general definition does not constitute a clear statement that Congress meant the statute to reach local criminal conduct."[78] The canon narrowed the statute's facially broad language so that Bond's conduct was out.

Cases like these often provoke disputes about whether the Court has used a substantive canon to distort the language beyond what its meaning will bear. (Recall that a canon applies only if the alternative interpretation is *plausible*.) For example, several justices lambasted the majority in *Bond* for conducting a "gruesome surgery" on the text of the chemical weapons law,[79] and in the case about labor law and Catholic schools, the dissent protested that the majority's interpretation was "not fairly possible."[80] But regardless of whether the Court gets it right in any individual case, the broader point holds: there are cases in which external values like federalism counsel a judge to adopt something other than the most natural interpretation of the text. "Instead, if the better reading leads to a disfavored result (like provoking a serious constitutional question), the court will adopt an inferior-but-tenable reading to avoid it."[81]

Adopting an inferior reading of a statute is in tension with textualism's core tenet that a judge must follow the ordinary meaning of the text wherever it leads. That provokes an uncomfortable question for a textualist judge: Must she forgo use of the substantive canons, no matter how long they've been around?

I wrote an academic article about this in my prior life, and my attitude now is consistent with my conclusion then: a textualist judge should proceed with caution.[82] Most, if not all, of the substantive canons are deeply grounded in precedent, and here (as in other areas of law) that is reason enough to follow them. That is basic to our system of precedent and the doctrine of stare decisis. But adding new substantive canons to the judicial tool kit is a different story. There might be narrow circumstances in which the Constitution authorizes courts to protect constitutional values by adopting substantive canons—I explored that topic in the article. Even if the courts possess that power, though, they should be wary about exercising it.

Part of the beauty of textualism is in the discipline that it imposes on the judge to follow the law wherever it leads; judges should therefore resist adopting new canons as an escape hatch from text that takes them to an undesirable place. After all, the appeal of the destination often lies in the eye of the beholder.

⁂

THIS DISCUSSION OF judges' interpretive tool kit may sound abstract, but its present-day applications are very real. *Biden v. Nebraska*, a high-profile case about a program to forgive student loans, demonstrates practically all these tools in action.[83]

In 2022, the Biden administration established a program to cancel $430 billion in student loan debt.[84] Six states challenged the loan forgiveness plan as unlawful.[85] The administration argued that a 9/11-era bill, the Higher Education Relief Opportunities for Students Act of 2003 (nicknamed the HEROES Act), granted it the authority to "waive or modify" the statutes and regulations governing federal financial assistance programs when the secretary of education deemed it "necessary in connection with a . . . national emergency."[86] The administration deemed the COVID-19 pandemic to be a national emergency requiring student debt relief.[87] The case turned on whether the $430 billion plan was a "waiver or modification" under the HEROES Act. In 2023, the Court decided that the administration lacked statutory authority to carry out its loan forgiveness plan.[88] The Court's opinion, which I joined, used several of the interpretive tools previously discussed in this chapter to support the Court's reasoning.

The Court began by examining the text of the statute. The administration claimed that the loan forgiveness plan fell within its statutory authority to "waive or modify" the laws governing student loan programs.[89] (Importantly, the authority was not to waive or modify *the loans themselves*.)[90] The Court started with dictionaries and past cases to define the word "modify."[91] Modification of a statute or regulation means to make "*modest* adjustments and additions to existing provisions," not to create "novel and fundamentally different" programs.[92] The administration's plan was plainly more than a "modification"—the Court said that the plan sought to "modify" student loan programs in the same sense that "the French Revolution 'modified' the status of the French nobility."[93] Nor did the government's "waiver" authority justify the plan, because the government did not (and could not) identify any statutory provision that it was waiving.[94] The loan forgiveness plan was neither a "modification" nor a "waiver" of the statutory and regulatory scheme; it was a rewrite. This straightforward textual analysis meant that the administration had exceeded its legal authority.

Next, the Court rejected the proposition that the statute's purpose could be used to stretch the language of the law. The purpose-driven argument went as follows: Congress passed the HEROES Act to grant the secretary of education substantial emergency management powers.[95] The pandemic was a genuine emergency. Therefore, the Court should give the statute its broadest possible reading, one permitting "'the most substantial kind of change' imaginable."[96] The Court correctly rebuffed this purpose-driven argument, which, in direct contradiction to the statutory text, would have granted the secretary nearly "unlimited power."[97]

If anything, the Court explained, the breadth of the secretary's claimed power cut in the opposite direction. To support this point, the Court invoked a canon: the major questions doctrine.[98] When an administrative agency seeks to exert power of "vast economic and political significance," the Court looks for a clear congressional statement granting such vast authority.[99] The absence of such a statement is reason for the Court to doubt that Congress empowered the agency to settle such a major question rather than retaining the authority for itself. That principle applied to the "sweeping and unprecedented" loan forgiveness program, which sought to eliminate $430 billion in student loan debt and affected 43 million borrowers.[100] One would expect Congress to speak clearly if it was giving the secretary of education a virtually blank check—yet the HEROES Act said nothing of the sort.

The major questions doctrine has provoked controversy—so much so that the canon has made the news.[101] Legal scholars and some of my colleagues have critiqued it as a new, strong-form substantive canon—one instructing courts to adopt an inferior (though still plausible) interpretation of a statute to enforce the principle that Congress should make major decisions itself rather than delegating them to administrative agencies.[102] I don't think the major questions doctrine is new, because the Court has invoked it for decades.[103] But if it's a strong-form canon, it—like all such canons—is in tension with textualism insofar as it pushes courts to adopt something other than the most natural interpretation of the text.

I take this critique seriously, but, as I wrote in a concurring opinion in *Biden v. Nebraska*, I respectfully disagree with those who characterize the major questions doctrine as a substantive canon.[104] In my view, the doctrine illustrates the interpretive guideline that I explained at the outset of this chapter: ordinary meaning depends on "the ring the words would have had to a skilled user of words at the time, thinking about the same problem."[105] A skilled speaker of English would not understand unexceptional words to grant exceptional authority.

In my concurrence, I used this example to illustrate the point: imagine that a parent gives a babysitter her credit card with instructions to "make sure the kids have fun" while she is away for the weekend. Onlookers would surely be surprised if the babysitter thought she had authority to spend thousands of dollars taking the children on a multi-day excursion to an out-of-town amusement park. In the ordinary course, "make sure the kids have fun" means permission to go on more modest outings to places like a movie theater or pizza parlor. If the parent wanted to greenlight a trip of that magnitude, we would expect her to speak more clearly.

As I see it, the major questions doctrine grows out of similar commonsense principles. In our system of separated powers, we expect Congress to legislate on "important subjects" while delegating away certain "details" to administrative agencies.[106] Thus, we "expect Congress to speak clearly if it wishes to assign to an agency decisions of vast 'economic and political significance.'"[107] Rather than counseling a court to adopt a *less* plausible interpretation, the major questions doctrine points a court toward the *more* plausible one. It reflects "the familiar principle that we do not interpret a statute for all it is worth when a reasonable person would not read it that way."[108]

Biden v. Nebraska nicely illustrates the tools of statutory interpretation in action. It also demonstrates that statutory interpretation is an evolving field with active debates about the proper role of certain methodologies and tools like the major questions doctrine. These debates are worth understanding, because they shape judges' reasoning (and ultimately our decision-making) in the many matters of public importance that come before federal courts.

INTERPRETING STATUTES, LIKE interpreting the Constitution, can be difficult, but the complications are of a different sort. Courts generally deal with statutes that are much younger than the Constitution, so understanding their language and context does not typically demand a deep dive into history. But because statutes are often more detailed than the Constitution, untangling their language more frequently requires judges to deploy tools like grammar and canons of interpretation. The task of statutory interpretation might sound simple. (Recall the rules: "(1) Read the statute; (2) read the statute; (3) read the statute!")[109] Sometimes, however, deciphering the words is much harder than advertised.

CONCLUSION

OVER A year after I joined the Court, a friend asked me to tell her honestly, without rattling off an answer, whether I liked my job. She didn't have to worry about my rattling off an answer, because I didn't have one ready. Life was so full that I hadn't had time to engage in much self-reflection. At that point, there were still boxes to unpack; even now, there are a few unfilled picture frames hanging on an out-of-the-way wall. (Jesse jokes that the smiling strangers whose stock photos came with the frames are starting to feel like family members.) After more time, I still don't have a simple yes-or-no answer—but I think that's because it's not quite the right question. While I've thought about other jobs in terms of whether I like or dislike them, this one is different. Describing a seat on the Court that way makes it sound, at least to my ears, like the most important thing is what I get out of it. But for a judge, that's the least important thing. A seat on any court is oriented toward public service. Sometimes, it is rewarding; other times, it is costly. It is always, however, a privilege.

I'll end the book where I began it: with the picture of my great-grandmother's house. Her life inspires not only grit but also gratitude. Her strength and unwavering faith made its mark on my grandfather (author of the World War II letters), his daughter (my mother, matriarch of the sprawling Coney family), and, indirectly, me. No generation starts afresh; each is shaped by its predecessors.

So too for Americans. The founding generation launched the Constitution, but each succeeding generation has taken custody of it. So far, none has scrapped the document and started over, as the founding generation did by replacing the Articles of Confederation with the Constitution that governs us today. Instead, each generation has continued the project, thereby leaving its mark on the next. I'm grateful for the constitutional order we have inherited.

The Court is part of this long-running order. Justices today face the same challenges as those who have served in the past. The constitutional oath has not changed—nor has the difficulty of living up to it. Tension between the Court and the political branches has existed since the beginning. And because, as Justice Potter Stewart observed, the Court's docket is "a fairly reliable mirror of the domestic problems confronting our nation,"[1] the Court has often found itself facing cases involving the most contentious issues of the time. Such cases impose pressure because of the mismatch between the desires of the public and the duty of the justices: the public cares much more about the result than the reasoning, yet the justices must decide every case based on the reasoning rather than the result. Whatever the Court decides, it makes enemies.

This historical pattern is not the sign of a flawed system. It reflects the lived experience of an independent judiciary operating in a government committed to the separation-of-powers principle and the constraint of written law. While the intensity of the challenges faced by the Court ebbs and flows, the challenges themselves will never disappear. Throughout, the job of every justice is to do his or her best by the law.

Where does that leave us? I hope I've conveyed the Court's important role in preserving the rule of law. Citizens should insist that justices discharge their duties in good faith and consistently with their oath; in deciding cases, justices must faithfully follow the law that the people have enacted. For more than two centuries, the Court has discharged that role.

Like the other branches of government, the Court has experienced both shining moments and spectacular failures. Overall, however, the Court has functioned as a source of stability in the United States.

But the Court cannot maintain America's commitment to the Constitution by itself. When I described the limits on the judicial power, I emphasized that officials in the executive branch and members of Congress make the first, and often the final, judgment about whether government action is constitutional. The same is true for state officials, state legislators, and state courts. The strength of our Constitution depends on *all* participants in American government, all of whom take an oath to support it. Through the exercise of judicial review, courts, including the Supreme Court, exercise an important check on legislators and executive officials. Yet the Court does not function as the national constitutional police; even if it were so inclined, Article III's "case or controversy" requirement prohibits it from doing so. The maintenance of our constitutional culture therefore depends on the diligence of all government actors. Citizens should demand that diligence from elected officials, just as they should demand it from judges.

Maintaining our constitutional culture also depends on the buy-in of Americans. The Constitution commits us to a pluralistic society. This commitment is expressed through the protection of individual rights like those guaranteed by the First Amendment, which requires the government to tolerate all opinions and all religions, as well as through structural constraints like federalism, which leaves room for citizens in different states to make divergent choices. At the same time, the Constitution does not permit us each to go our own way. The document contains our commitment to common values, like rights for criminal defendants, and our agreement to make national policy choices within a defined structure, like the limits imposed on each branch of the federal government. It mixes respect for difference with agreed-upon ground rules.

Working within this system requires working together. The two mechanisms for setting national rules—the legislative process and constitutional amendment—each require compromise. No bill can pass both the House and Senate and be signed by the president without some give-and-take along the way. And no proposed amendment can achieve supermajority support if proponents refuse to back down on any detail. The Constitution precludes a system where winner takes all; it bakes in the need for compromise. How could it be otherwise in a pluralistic society?

The framers of our Constitution were well aware of this reality, because none was entirely satisfied with the final product. Perhaps that sentiment was best summed up by Benjamin Franklin, who confessed on the convention's last day, "I do not entirely approve this Constitution at present." He nonetheless urged his fellow delates to sign it:

> I doubt too whether any other Convention we can obtain may be able to make a better Constitution. For when you assemble a number of men to have the advantage of their joint wisdom, you inevitably assemble with those men, all their prejudices, their passions, their errors of opinion, their local interests, and their selfish views. From such an Assembly can a perfect production be expected? It therefore astonishes me, Sir, to find this system approaching so near to perfection as it does.[2]

The Constitution required compromise at its conception, and living under it requires compromise now. And even if we, like the framers, see imperfections in our nation's charter, we should not lose faith in the constitutional project. I'm with Benjamin Franklin: perfection is too a high a bar for fallible humans to attain. But when I consider the freedom, prosperity, and stability that our Constitution has secured for more than two centuries, I share Franklin's astonishment that this system has attained so much. And when I contemplate the future, I am optimistic about its continued success.

APPENDIX
THE CONSTITUTION

We the People of the United States, in Order to form a more perfect Union, establish Justice, insure domestic Tranquility, provide for the common defence, promote the general Welfare, and secure the Blessings of Liberty to ourselves and our Posterity, do ordain and establish this Constitution for the United States of America.

{ ARTICLE. I. }

Section. 1.
All legislative Powers herein granted shall be vested in a Congress of the United States, which shall consist of a Senate and House of Representatives.

Section. 2.
The House of Representatives shall be composed of Members chosen every second Year by the People of the several States, and the Electors in each State shall have the Qualifications requisite for Electors of the most numerous Branch of the State Legislature.

No Person shall be a Representative who shall not have attained to the Age of twenty five Years, and been seven Years a Citizen of the United States, and who shall not, when elected, be an Inhabitant of that State in which he shall be chosen.

Representatives and direct Taxes shall be apportioned among the several States which may be included within this Union, according to their respective Numbers, which shall be determined by adding to the whole Number of free Persons, including those bound to Service for a Term of Years, and excluding Indians not taxed, three fifths of all other Persons. The actual Enumeration shall be made within three Years after the first Meeting of the Congress of the United States, and within every subsequent Term of ten Years, in such Manner as they shall by Law direct. The Number of Representatives shall not exceed one for every thirty Thousand, but each State shall have at Least one Representative; and until such enumeration shall be made, the State of New Hampshire shall be entitled to chuse three, Massachusetts eight, Rhode-Island and Providence Plantations one, Connecticut five, New-York six, New Jersey four, Pennsylvania eight, Delaware one, Maryland six, Virginia ten, North Carolina five, South Carolina five, and Georgia three.

When vacancies happen in the Representation from any State, the Executive Authority thereof shall issue Writs of Election to fill such Vacancies.

The House of Representatives shall chuse their Speaker and other Officers; and shall have the sole Power of Impeachment.

Section. 3.

The Senate of the United States shall be composed of two Senators from each State, chosen by the Legislature thereof, for six Years; and each Senator shall have one Vote.

Immediately after they shall be assembled in Consequence of the first Election, they shall be divided as equally as may be into three Classes. The Seats of the Senators of the first Class shall be vacated at the Expiration of the second Year, of the second Class at the Expiration of the fourth Year, and of the third Class at the Expiration of the sixth Year, so that one third may be chosen every second Year; and if Vacancies happen by Resignation, or otherwise, during the Recess of the Legislature of any State, the Executive thereof may make temporary Appointments until the next Meeting of the Legislature, which shall then fill such Vacancies.

No Person shall be a Senator who shall not have attained to the Age of thirty Years, and been nine Years a Citizen of the United States, and who shall not, when elected, be an Inhabitant of that State for which he shall be chosen.

The Vice President of the United States shall be President of the Senate, but shall have no Vote, unless they be equally divided.

The Senate shall chuse their other Officers, and also a President pro tempore, in the Absence of the Vice President, or when he shall exercise the Office of President of the United States.

The Senate shall have the sole Power to try all Impeachments. When sitting for that Purpose, they shall be on Oath or Affirmation. When the President of the United States is tried, the Chief Justice shall preside: And no Person shall be convicted without the Concurrence of two thirds of the Members present.

Judgment in Cases of Impeachment shall not extend further than to removal from Office, and disqualification to hold and enjoy any Office of honor, Trust or Profit under the United States: but the Party convicted shall nevertheless be liable and subject to Indictment, Trial, Judgment and Punishment, according to Law.

Section. 4.

The Times, Places and Manner of holding Elections for Senators and Representatives, shall be prescribed in each State by the Legislature thereof; but the Congress may at any time by Law make or alter such Regulations, except as to the Places of chusing Senators.

The Congress shall assemble at least once in every Year, and such Meeting shall be on the first Monday in December, unless they shall by Law appoint a different Day.

Section. 5.

Each House shall be the Judge of the Elections, Returns and Qualifications of its own Members, and a Majority of each shall constitute a Quorum to do Business; but a smaller Number may adjourn from day to day, and may be authorized to compel the Attendance of absent Members, in such Manner, and under such Penalties as each House may provide.

Each House may determine the Rules of its Proceedings, punish its Members for disorderly Behaviour, and, with the Concurrence of two thirds, expel a Member.

Each House shall keep a Journal of its Proceedings, and from time to time publish the same, excepting such Parts as may in their Judgment require Secrecy; and the Yeas and Nays of the Members of either House on any question shall, at the Desire of one fifth of those Present, be entered on the Journal.

Neither House, during the Session of Congress, shall, without the Consent of the other, adjourn for more than three days, nor to any other Place than that in which the two Houses shall be sitting.

Section. 6.

The Senators and Representatives shall receive a Compensation for their Services, to be ascertained by Law, and paid out of the Treasury of the United States. They shall in all Cases, except Treason, Felony and Breach of the Peace, be privileged from Arrest during their Attendance at the Session of their respective Houses, and in going to and returning from the same; and for any Speech or Debate in either House, they shall not be questioned in any other Place.

No Senator or Representative shall, during the Time for which he was elected, be appointed to any civil Office under the Authority of the United States, which shall have been created, or the Emoluments whereof shall have been encreased during such time; and no Person holding any Office under the United States, shall be a Member of either House during his Continuance in Office.

Section. 7.

All Bills for raising Revenue shall originate in the House of Representatives; but the Senate may propose or concur with Amendments as on other Bills.

Every Bill which shall have passed the House of Representatives and the Senate, shall, before it become a Law, be presented to the President of the United States; If he approve he shall sign it, but if not he shall return it, with his Objections to that House in which it shall have originated, who shall enter the Objections at large on their Journal, and proceed to reconsider it. If after such Reconsideration two thirds of that House shall agree to pass the Bill, it shall be sent, together with the Objections, to the other House, by which it shall likewise be reconsidered, and if approved by two thirds of that House, it shall become a Law. But in all such Cases the Votes of both Houses shall be determined by yeas and Nays, and the Names of the Persons voting for and against the Bill shall be entered on the Journal of each House respectively. If any Bill shall not be returned by the President within ten Days (Sundays excepted) after it shall have been presented to him, the Same shall be a Law, in like Manner as if he had signed it, unless the Congress by their Adjournment prevent its Return, in which Case it shall not be a Law.

Every Order, Resolution, or Vote to which the Concurrence of the Senate and House of Representatives may be necessary (except on a question of Adjournment) shall be presented to the President of the United States; and before the Same shall take Effect, shall be approved by him, or being disapproved by him, shall be repassed by two thirds of the Senate and House of Representatives, according to the Rules and Limitations prescribed in the Case of a Bill.

Section. 8.

The Congress shall have Power To lay and collect Taxes, Duties, Imposts and Excises, to pay the Debts and provide for the common Defence and general Welfare of the United States; but all Duties, Imposts and Excises shall be uniform throughout the United States;

To borrow Money on the credit of the United States;

To regulate Commerce with foreign Nations, and among the several States, and with the Indian Tribes;

To establish an uniform Rule of Naturalization, and uniform Laws on the subject of Bankruptcies throughout the United States;

To coin Money, regulate the Value thereof, and of foreign Coin, and fix the Standard of Weights and Measures;

To provide for the Punishment of counterfeiting the Securities and current Coin of the United States;

To establish Post Offices and post Roads;

To promote the Progress of Science and useful Arts, by securing for limited Times to Authors and Inventors the exclusive Right to their respective Writings and Discoveries;

To constitute Tribunals inferior to the supreme Court;

To define and punish Piracies and Felonies committed on the high Seas, and Offences against the Law of Nations;

To declare War, grant Letters of Marque and Reprisal, and make Rules concerning Captures on Land and Water;

To raise and support Armies, but no Appropriation of Money to that Use shall be for a longer Term than two Years;

To provide and maintain a Navy;

To make Rules for the Government and Regulation of the land and naval Forces;

To provide for calling forth the Militia to execute the Laws of the Union, suppress Insurrections and repel Invasions;

To provide for organizing, arming, and disciplining, the Militia, and for governing such Part of them as may be employed in the Service of the United States, reserving to the States respectively, the Appointment of the Officers, and the Authority of training the Militia according to the discipline prescribed by Congress;

To exercise exclusive Legislation in all Cases whatsoever, over such District (not exceeding ten Miles square) as may, by Cession of particular States, and the Acceptance of Congress, become the Seat of the Government of the United States, and to exercise like Authority over all Places purchased by the Consent of the Legislature of the State in which the Same shall be, for the Erection of Forts, Magazines, Arsenals, dock-Yards, and other needful Buildings;—And

To make all Laws which shall be necessary and proper for carrying into Execution the foregoing Powers, and all other Powers vested by this Constitution in the Government of the United States, or in any Department or Officer thereof.

Section. 9.

The Migration or Importation of such Persons as any of the States now existing shall think proper to admit, shall not be prohibited by the Congress prior to the Year one thousand eight hundred and eight, but a Tax or duty may be imposed on such Importation, not exceeding ten dollars for each Person.

The Privilege of the Writ of Habeas Corpus shall not be suspended, unless when in Cases of Rebellion or Invasion the public Safety may require it.

No Bill of Attainder or ex post facto Law shall be passed.

No Capitation, or other direct, Tax shall be laid, unless in Proportion to the Census or enumeration herein before directed to be taken.

No Tax or Duty shall be laid on Articles exported from any State.

No Preference shall be given by any Regulation of Commerce or Revenue to the Ports of one State over those of another: nor shall Vessels bound to, or from, one State, be obliged to enter, clear, or pay Duties in another.

No Money shall be drawn from the Treasury, but in Consequence of Appropriations made by Law; and a regular Statement and Account of the Receipts and Expenditures of all public Money shall be published from time to time.

No Title of Nobility shall be granted by the United States: And no Person holding any Office of Profit or Trust under them, shall, without the Consent of the Congress, accept of any present, Emolument, Office, or Title, of any kind whatever, from any King, Prince, or foreign State.

Section. 10.
No State shall enter into any Treaty, Alliance, or Confederation; grant Letters of Marque and Reprisal; coin Money; emit Bills of Credit; make any Thing but gold and silver Coin a Tender in Payment of Debts; pass any Bill of Attainder, ex post facto Law, or Law impairing the Obligation of Contracts, or grant any Title of Nobility.

No State shall, without the Consent of the Congress, lay any Imposts or Duties on Imports or Exports, except what may be absolutely necessary for executing it's inspection Laws: and the net Produce of all Duties and Imposts, laid by any State on Imports or Exports, shall be for the Use of the Treasury of the United States; and all such Laws shall be subject to the Revision and Controul of the Congress.

No State shall, without the Consent of Congress, lay any Duty of Tonnage, keep Troops, or Ships of War in time of Peace, enter into any Agreement or Compact with another State, or with a foreign Power, or engage in War, unless actually invaded, or in such imminent Danger as will not admit of delay.

{ ARTICLE. II. }

Section. 1.
The executive Power shall be vested in a President of the United States of America. He shall hold his Office during the Term of four Years, and, together with the Vice President, chosen for the same Term, be elected, as follows

Each State shall appoint, in such Manner as the Legislature thereof may direct, a Number of Electors, equal to the whole Number of Senators and Representatives to which the State may be entitled in the Congress: but no Senator or Representative, or Person holding an Office of Trust or Profit under the United States, shall be appointed an Elector.

The Electors shall meet in their respective States, and vote by Ballot for two Persons, of whom one at least shall not be an Inhabitant of the same State with themselves. And they shall make a List of all the Persons voted for, and of the Number of Votes for each; which List they shall sign and certify, and transmit sealed to the Seat of the Government of the United States, directed to the President of the Senate. The

President of the Senate shall, in the Presence of the Senate and House of Representatives, open all the Certificates, and the Votes shall then be counted. The Person having the greatest Number of Votes shall be the President, if such Number be a Majority of the whole Number of Electors appointed; and if there be more than one who have such Majority, and have an equal Number of Votes, then the House of Representatives shall immediately chuse by Ballot one of them for President; and if no Person have a Majority, then from the five highest on the List the said House shall in like Manner chuse the President. But in chusing the President, the Votes shall be taken by States, the Representation from each State having one Vote; A quorum for this Purpose shall consist of a Member or Members from two thirds of the States, and a Majority of all the States shall be necessary to a Choice. In every Case, after the Choice of the President, the Person having the greatest Number of Votes of the Electors shall be the Vice President. But if there should remain two or more who have equal Votes, the Senate shall chuse from them by Ballot the Vice President.

The Congress may determine the Time of chusing the Electors, and the Day on which they shall give their Votes; which Day shall be the same throughout the United States.

No Person except a natural born Citizen, or a Citizen of the United States, at the time of the Adoption of this Constitution, shall be eligible to the Office of President; neither shall any Person be eligible to that Office who shall not have attained to the Age of thirty five Years, and been fourteen Years a Resident within the United States.

In Case of the Removal of the President from Office, or of his Death, Resignation, or Inability to discharge the Powers and Duties of the said Office, the Same shall devolve on the Vice President, and the Congress may by Law provide for the Case of Removal, Death, Resignation or Inability, both of the President and Vice President, declaring what Officer shall then act as President, and such Officer shall act accordingly, until the Disability be removed, or a President shall be elected.

The President shall, at stated Times, receive for his Services, a Compensation, which shall neither be encreased nor diminished during the Period for which he shall have been elected, and he shall not receive within that Period any other Emolument from the United States, or any of them.

Before he enter on the Execution of his Office, he shall take the following Oath or Affirmation:—"I do solemnly swear (or affirm) that I will faithfully execute the Office of President of the United States, and will to the best of my Ability, preserve, protect and defend the Constitution of the United States."

Section. 2.

The President shall be Commander in Chief of the Army and Navy of the United States, and of the Militia of the several States, when called into the actual Service of the United States; he may require the Opinion, in writing, of the principal Officer in each of the executive Departments, upon any Subject relating to the Duties of their respective Offices, and he shall have Power to grant Reprieves and Pardons for Offences against the United States, except in Cases of Impeachment.

He shall have Power, by and with the Advice and Consent of the Senate, to make Treaties, provided two thirds of the Senators present concur; and he shall nominate, and by and with the Advice and Consent of the Senate, shall appoint Ambassadors, other public Ministers and Consuls, Judges of the supreme Court, and all other Officers of the United States, whose Appointments are not herein otherwise provided for, and which shall be established by Law: but the Congress may by Law vest the Appointment of such inferior Officers, as they think proper, in the President alone, in the Courts of Law, or in the Heads of Departments.

The President shall have Power to fill up all Vacancies that may happen during the Recess of the Senate, by granting Commissions which shall expire at the End of their next Session.

Section. 3.

He shall from time to time give to the Congress Information of the State of the Union, and recommend to their Consideration such Measures as he shall judge necessary and expedient; he may, on extraordinary Occasions, convene both Houses, or either of them, and in Case of Disagreement between them, with Respect to the Time of Adjournment, he may adjourn them to such Time as he shall think proper; he shall receive Ambassadors and other public Ministers; he shall take Care that the Laws be faithfully executed, and shall Commission all the Officers of the United States.

Section. 4.

The President, Vice President and all civil Officers of the United States, shall be removed from Office on Impeachment for, and Conviction of, Treason, Bribery, or other high Crimes and Misdemeanors.

{ ARTICLE. III. }

Section. 1.

The judicial Power of the United States, shall be vested in one supreme Court, and in such inferior Courts as the Congress may from time to time ordain and establish. The Judges, both of the supreme and inferior Courts, shall hold their Offices during good Behaviour, and shall, at stated Times, receive for their Services, a Compensation, which shall not be diminished during their Continuance in Office.

Section. 2.

The judicial Power shall extend to all Cases, in Law and Equity, arising under this Constitution, the Laws of the United States, and Treaties made, or which shall be made, under their Authority;—to all Cases affecting Ambassadors, other public Ministers and Consuls;—to all Cases of admiralty and maritime Jurisdiction;—to Controversies to which the United States shall be a Party;—to Controversies between two or more States;—between a State and Citizens of another State,—between Citizens of different States,—between Citizens of the same State claiming Lands under Grants of different States, and between a State, or the Citizens thereof, and foreign States, Citizens or Subjects.

In all Cases affecting Ambassadors, other public Ministers and Consuls, and those in which a State shall be Party, the supreme Court shall have original Jurisdiction. In all the other Cases before mentioned, the supreme Court shall have appellate Jurisdiction, both as to Law and Fact, with such Exceptions, and under such Regulations as the Congress shall make.

The Trial of all Crimes, except in Cases of Impeachment, shall be by Jury; and such Trial shall be held in the State where the said Crimes shall have been committed; but when not committed within any State, the Trial shall be at such Place or Places as the Congress may by Law have directed.

Section. 3.

Treason against the United States, shall consist only in levying War against them, or in adhering to their Enemies, giving them Aid and Comfort. No Person shall be convicted of Treason unless on the Testimony of two Witnesses to the same overt Act, or on Confession in open Court.

The Congress shall have Power to declare the Punishment of Treason, but no Attainder of Treason shall work Corruption of Blood, or Forfeiture except during the Life of the Person attainted.

{ ARTICLE. IV. }

Section. 1.

Full Faith and Credit shall be given in each State to the public Acts, Records, and judicial Proceedings of every other State. And the Congress may by general Laws prescribe the Manner in which such Acts, Records and Proceedings shall be proved, and the Effect thereof.

Section. 2.

The Citizens of each State shall be entitled to all Privileges and Immunities of Citizens in the several States.

A Person charged in any State with Treason, Felony, or other Crime, who shall flee from Justice, and be found in another State, shall on Demand of the executive Authority of the State from which he fled, be delivered up, to be removed to the State having Jurisdiction of the Crime.

No Person held to Service or Labour in one State, under the Laws thereof, escaping into another, shall, in Consequence of any Law or Regulation therein, be discharged from such Service or Labour, but shall be delivered up on Claim of the Party to whom such Service or Labour may be due.

Section. 3.
New States may be admitted by the Congress into this Union; but no new State shall be formed or erected within the Jurisdiction of any other State; nor any State be formed by the Junction of two or more States, or Parts of States, without the Consent of the Legislatures of the States concerned as well as of the Congress.

The Congress shall have Power to dispose of and make all needful Rules and Regulations respecting the Territory or other Property belonging to the United States; and nothing in this Constitution shall be so construed as to Prejudice any Claims of the United States, or of any particular State.

Section. 4.
The United States shall guarantee to every State in this Union a Republican Form of Government, and shall protect each of them against Invasion; and on Application of the Legislature, or of the Executive (when the Legislature cannot be convened) against domestic Violence.

{ ARTICLE. V. }

The Congress, whenever two thirds of both Houses shall deem it necessary, shall propose Amendments to this Constitution, or, on the Application of the Legislatures of two thirds of the several States, shall call a Convention for proposing Amendments, which, in either Case, shall be valid to all Intents and Purposes, as Part of this Constitution, when ratified by the Legislatures of three fourths of the several States, or by Conventions in three fourths thereof, as the one or the other Mode of Ratification may be proposed by the Congress; Provided that no Amendment which may be made prior to the Year One thousand eight hundred and eight shall in any Manner affect the first and fourth Clauses in the Ninth Section of the first Article; and that no State, without its Consent, shall be deprived of its equal Suffrage in the Senate.

{ ARTICLE. VI. }

All Debts contracted and Engagements entered into, before the Adoption of this Constitution, shall be as valid against the United States under this Constitution, as under the Confederation.

This Constitution, and the Laws of the United States which shall be made in Pursuance thereof; and all Treaties made, or which shall be made, under the Authority of the United States, shall be the supreme Law of the Land; and the Judges in every State shall be bound thereby, any Thing in the Constitution or Laws of any State to the Contrary notwithstanding.

The Senators and Representatives before mentioned, and the Members of the several State Legislatures, and all executive and judicial Officers, both of the United States and of the several States, shall be bound by Oath or Affirmation, to support this Constitution; but no religious Test shall ever be required as a Qualification to any Office or public Trust under the United States.

{ ARTICLE. VII. }

The Ratification of the Conventions of nine States, shall be sufficient for the Establishment of this Constitution between the States so ratifying the Same.

The Word, "the," being interlined between the seventh and eighth Lines of the first Page, The Word "Thirty" being partly written on an Erazure in the fifteenth Line of the first Page, The Words "is tried" being interlined between the thirty second and thirty third Lines of the first Page and the Word "the" being interlined between the forty third and forty fourth Lines of the second Page.

Attest William Jackson Secretary

done in Convention by the Unanimous Consent of the States present the Seventeenth Day of September in the Year of our Lord one thousand seven hundred and Eighty seven and of the Independance of the United States of America the Twelfth In witness whereof We have hereunto subscribed our Names,

G°. Washington

Presidt and deputy from Virginia

DELAWARE

Geo: Read

Gunning Bedford jun

John Dickinson

Richard Bassett

Jaco: Broom

MARYLAND
James McHenry
Dan of St Thos. Jenifer
Danl. Carroll

VIRGINIA
John Blair
James Madison Jr.

NORTH CAROLINA
Wm. Blount
Richd. Dobbs Spaight
Hu Williamson

SOUTH CAROLINA
J. Rutledge
Charles Cotesworth Pinckney
Charles Pinckney
Pierce Butler

GEORGIA
William Few
Abr Baldwin

NEW HAMPSHIRE
John Langdon
Nicholas Gilman

MASSACHUSETTS
Nathaniel Gorham
Rufus King

CONNECTICUT
Wm. Saml. Johnson
Roger Sherman

NEW YORK
Alexander Hamilton

NEW JERSEY
Wil: Livingston
David Brearley
Wm. Paterson
Jona: Dayton

PENNSYLVANIA
B Franklin
Thomas Mifflin

Robt. Morris
Geo. Clymer
Thos. FitzSimons
Jared Ingersoll
James Wilson
Gouv Morris[1]

{ AMENDMENT I (1791) }

Congress shall make no law respecting an establishment of religion, or prohibiting the free exercise thereof; or abridging the freedom of speech, or of the press; or the right of the people peaceably to assemble, and to petition the Government for a redress of grievances.

{ AMENDMENT II (1791) }

A well regulated Militia, being necessary to the security of a free State, the right of the people to keep and bear Arms, shall not be infringed.

{ AMENDMENT III (1791) }

No Soldier shall, in time of peace be quartered in any house, without the consent of the Owner, nor in time of war, but in a manner to be prescribed by law.

{ AMENDMENT IV (1791) }

The right of the people to be secure in their persons, houses, papers, and effects, against unreasonable searches and seizures, shall not be violated, and no Warrants shall issue, but upon probable cause, supported by Oath or affirmation, and particularly describing the place to be searched, and the persons or things to be seized.

{ AMENDMENT V (1791) }

No person shall be held to answer for a capital, or otherwise infamous crime, unless on a presentment or indictment of a Grand Jury, except in cases arising in the land or naval forces, or in the Militia, when in actual service in time of War or public danger; nor shall any person be subject for the same offence to be twice put in jeopardy of life or limb; nor shall be compelled in any criminal case to be a witness against himself, nor be deprived of life, liberty, or property, without due process of law; nor shall private property be taken for public use, without just compensation.

{ AMENDMENT VI (1791) }

In all criminal prosecutions, the accused shall enjoy the right to a speedy and public trial, by an impartial jury of the State and district wherein the crime shall have been committed, which district shall have been previously ascertained by law, and to be informed of the nature and cause of the accusation; to be confronted with the witnesses against him; to have compulsory process for obtaining witnesses in his favor, and to have the Assistance of Counsel for his defence.

{ AMENDMENT VII (1791) }

In Suits at common law, where the value in controversy shall exceed twenty dollars, the right of trial by jury shall be preserved, and no fact tried by a jury, shall be otherwise re-examined in any Court of the United States, than according to the rules of the common law.

{ AMENDMENT VIII (1791) }

Excessive bail shall not be required, nor excessive fines imposed, nor cruel and unusual punishments inflicted.

{ AMENDMENT IX (1791) }

The enumeration in the Constitution, of certain rights, shall not be construed to deny or disparage others retained by the people.

{ AMENDMENT X (1791) }

The powers not delegated to the United States by the Constitution, nor prohibited by it to the States, are reserved to the States respectively, or to the people.[2]

{ AMENDMENT XI (1798) }

The Judicial power of the United States shall not be construed to extend to any suit in law or equity, commenced or prosecuted against one of the United States by Citizens of another State, or by Citizens or Subjects of any Foreign State.

{ AMENDMENT XII (1804) }

The Electors shall meet in their respective states and vote by ballot for President and Vice-President, one of whom, at least, shall not be an inhabitant of the same state with themselves; they shall name in their ballots the person voted for as President, and in distinct ballots the person voted for as Vice-President, and they shall make distinct lists of all persons voted for as President, and of all persons voted for as Vice-President, and of the number of votes for each, which lists they shall sign and certify, and transmit sealed to the seat of the government of the United States, directed to the President of the Senate;—the President of the Senate shall, in the presence of the Senate and House of Representatives, open all the certificates and the votes shall then be counted;—The person having the greatest number of votes for President, shall be the President, if such number be a majority of the whole number of Electors appointed; and if no person have such majority, then from the persons having the highest numbers not exceeding three on the list of those voted for as President, the House of Representatives shall choose immediately, by ballot, the President. But in choosing the President, the votes shall be taken by states, the representation from each state having one vote; a quorum for this purpose shall consist of a member or members from two-thirds of the states, and a majority of all the states shall be necessary to a choice. And if the House of Representatives shall not choose a President whenever the right of choice shall devolve upon them, before the fourth day of March next following, then the Vice-President shall act as President, as in case of the death or other constitutional disability of the President. The person having the greatest number of votes as Vice-President, shall be the Vice-President, if such number be a majority of the whole number of Electors appointed, and if no person have a majority, then from the two highest numbers on the list, the Senate shall choose the Vice-President; a quorum for the purpose shall consist of two-thirds of the whole number of Senators, and a majority of the whole number shall be necessary to a choice. But no person constitutionally ineligible to the office of President shall be eligible to that of Vice-President of the United States.

{ AMENDMENT XIII (1865) }

Section 1.
Neither slavery nor involuntary servitude, except as a punishment for crime whereof the party shall have been duly convicted, shall exist within the United States, or any place subject to their jurisdiction.

Section 2.
Congress shall have power to enforce this article by appropriate legislation.

{ AMENDMENT XIV (1868) }

Section 1.
All persons born or naturalized in the United States, and subject to the jurisdiction thereof, are citizens of the United States and of the State wherein they reside. No State shall make or enforce any law which shall abridge the privileges or immunities of citizens of the United States; nor shall any State deprive any person of life, liberty, or property, without due process of law; nor deny to any person within its jurisdiction the equal protection of the laws.

Section 2.
Representatives shall be apportioned among the several States according to their respective numbers, counting the whole number of persons in each State, excluding Indians not taxed. But when the right to vote at any election for the choice of electors for President and Vice-President of the United States, Representatives in Congress, the Executive and Judicial officers of a State, or the members of the Legislature thereof, is denied to any of the male inhabitants of such State, being twenty-one years of age, and citizens of the United States, or in any way abridged, except for participation in rebellion, or other crime, the basis of representation therein shall be reduced in the proportion which the number of such male citizens shall bear to the whole number of male citizens twenty-one years of age in such State.

Section 3.
No person shall be a Senator or Representative in Congress, or elector of President and Vice-President, or hold any office, civil or military, under the United States, or under any State, who, having previously taken an oath, as a member of Congress, or as an officer of the United States, or as a member of any State legislature, or as an executive or judicial officer of any State, to support the Constitution of the United States, shall have engaged in insurrection or rebellion against the same, or given aid or comfort to the enemies thereof. But Congress may by a vote of two-thirds of each House, remove such disability.

Section 4.
The validity of the public debt of the United States, authorized by law, including debts incurred for payment of pensions and bounties for services in suppressing insurrection or rebellion, shall not be questioned. But neither the United States nor any State shall assume or pay any debt or obligation incurred in aid of insurrection or rebellion against the United States, or any claim for the loss or emancipation of any slave; but all such debts, obligations and claims shall be held illegal and void.

Section 5.
The Congress shall have power to enforce, by appropriate legislation, the provisions of this article.

{ AMENDMENT XV (1870) }

Section 1.
The right of citizens of the United States to vote shall not be denied or abridged by the United States or by any State on account of race, color, or previous condition of servitude—

Section 2.
The Congress shall have power to enforce this article by appropriate legislation.

{ AMENDMENT XVI (1913) }

The Congress shall have power to lay and collect taxes on incomes, from whatever source derived, without apportionment among the several States, and without regard to any census or enumeration.

{ AMENDMENT XVII (1913) }

The Senate of the United States shall be composed of two Senators from each State, elected by the people thereof, for six years; and each Senator shall have one vote. The electors in each State shall have the qualifications requisite for electors of the most numerous branch of the State legislatures.

When vacancies happen in the representation of any State in the Senate, the executive authority of such State shall issue writs of election to fill such vacancies: Provided, That the legislature of any State may empower the executive thereof to make temporary appointments until the people fill the vacancies by election as the legislature may direct.

This amendment shall not be so construed as to affect the election or term of any Senator chosen before it becomes valid as part of the Constitution.

{ AMENDMENT XVIII (1919) }

Section 1.
After one year from the ratification of this article the manufacture, sale, or transportation of intoxicating liquors within, the importation thereof into, or the exportation

thereof from the United States and all territory subject to the jurisdiction thereof for beverage purposes is hereby prohibited.

Section 2.
The Congress and the several States shall have concurrent power to enforce this article by appropriate legislation.

Section 3.
This article shall be inoperative unless it shall have been ratified as an amendment to the Constitution by the legislatures of the several States, as provided in the Constitution, within seven years from the date of the submission hereof to the States by the Congress.

{ AMENDMENT XIX (1920) }

The right of citizens of the United States to vote shall not be denied or abridged by the United States or by any State on account of sex.

Congress shall have power to enforce this article by appropriate legislation.

{ AMENDMENT XX (1933) }

Section 1.
The terms of the President and the Vice President shall end at noon on the 20th day of January, and the terms of Senators and Representatives at noon on the 3d day of January, of the years in which such terms would have ended if this article had not been ratified; and the terms of their successors shall then begin.

Section 2.
The Congress shall assemble at least once in every year, and such meeting shall begin at noon on the 3d day of January, unless they shall by law appoint a different day.

Section 3.
If, at the time fixed for the beginning of the term of the President, the President elect shall have died, the Vice President elect shall become President. If a President shall not have been chosen before the time fixed for the beginning of his term, or if the President elect shall have failed to qualify, then the Vice President elect shall act as President until a President shall have qualified; and the Congress may by law provide for the case wherein neither a President elect nor a Vice President elect shall have qualified, declaring who shall then act as President, or the manner in which one who is to act shall be selected, and such person shall act accordingly until a President or Vice President shall have qualified.

Section 4.
The Congress may by law provide for the case of the death of any of the persons from whom the House of Representatives may choose a President whenever the right of choice shall have devolved upon them, and for the case of the death of any of the persons from whom the Senate may choose a Vice President whenever the right of choice shall have devolved upon them.

Section 5.
Sections 1 and 2 shall take effect on the 15th day of October following the ratification of this article.

Section 6.
This article shall be inoperative unless it shall have been ratified as an amendment to the Constitution by the legislatures of three-fourths of the several States within seven years from the date of its submission.

{ AMENDMENT XXI (1933) }

Section 1.
The eighteenth article of amendment to the Constitution of the United States is hereby repealed.

Section 2.
The transportation or importation into any State, Territory, or possession of the United States for delivery or use therein of intoxicating liquors, in violation of the laws thereof, is hereby prohibited.

Section 3.
This article shall be inoperative unless it shall have been ratified as an amendment to the Constitution by conventions in the several States, as provided in the Constitution, within seven years from the date of the submission hereof to the States by the Congress.

{ AMENDMENT XXII (1951) }

Section 1.
No person shall be elected to the office of the President more than twice, and no person who has held the office of President, or acted as President, for more than two years of a term to which some other person was elected President shall be elected to the office of the President more than once. But this Article shall not apply to any person holding the office of President when this Article was proposed by the Congress, and shall not

prevent any person who may be holding the office of President, or acting as President, during the term within which this Article becomes operative from holding the office of President or acting as President during the remainder of such term.

Section 2.
This article shall be inoperative unless it shall have been ratified as an amendment to the Constitution by the legislatures of three-fourths of the several States within seven years from the date of its submission to the States by the Congress.

{ AMENDMENT XXIII (1961) }

Section 1.
The District constituting the seat of Government of the United States shall appoint in such manner as the Congress may direct:

A number of electors of President and Vice President equal to the whole number of Senators and Representatives in Congress to which the District would be entitled if it were a State, but in no event more than the least populous State; they shall be in addition to those appointed by the States, but they shall be considered, for the purposes of the election of President and Vice President, to be electors appointed by a State; and they shall meet in the District and perform such duties as provided by the twelfth article of amendment.

Section 2.
The Congress shall have power to enforce this article by appropriate legislation.

{ AMENDMENT XXIV (1964) }

Section 1.
The right of citizens of the United States to vote in any primary or other election for President or Vice President, for electors for President or Vice President, or for Senator or Representative in Congress, shall not be denied or abridged by the United States or any State by reason of failure to pay any poll tax or other tax.

Section 2.
The Congress shall have power to enforce this article by appropriate legislation.

{ AMENDMENT XXV (1967) }

Section 1.
In case of the removal of the President from office or of his death or resignation, the Vice President shall become President.

Section 2.
Whenever there is a vacancy in the office of the Vice President, the President shall nominate a Vice President who shall take office upon confirmation by a majority vote of both Houses of Congress.

Section 3.
Whenever the President transmits to the President pro tempore of the Senate and the Speaker of the House of Representatives his written declaration that he is unable to discharge the powers and duties of his office, and until he transmits to them a written declaration to the contrary, such powers and duties shall be discharged by the Vice President as Acting President.

Section 4.
Whenever the Vice President and a majority of either the principal officers of the executive departments or of such other body as Congress may by law provide, transmit to the President pro tempore of the Senate and the Speaker of the House of Representatives their written declaration that the President is unable to discharge the powers and duties of his office, the Vice President shall immediately assume the powers and duties of the office as Acting President.

Thereafter, when the President transmits to the President pro tempore of the Senate and the Speaker of the House of Representatives his written declaration that no inability exists, he shall resume the powers and duties of his office unless the Vice President and a majority of either the principal officers of the executive department or of such other body as Congress may by law provide, transmit within four days to the President pro tempore of the Senate and the Speaker of the House of Representatives their written declaration that the President is unable to discharge the powers and duties of his office. Thereupon Congress shall decide the issue, assembling within forty-eight hours for that purpose if not in session. If the Congress, within twenty-one days after receipt of the latter written declaration, or, if Congress is not in session, within twenty-one days after Congress is required to assemble, determines by two-thirds vote of both Houses that the President is unable to discharge the powers and duties of his office, the Vice President shall continue to discharge the same as Acting President; otherwise, the President shall resume the powers and duties of his office.

{ AMENDMENT XXVI (1971) }

Section 1.
The right of citizens of the United States, who are eighteen years of age or older, to vote shall not be denied or abridged by the United States or by any State on account of age.

Section 2.
The Congress shall have power to enforce this article by appropriate legislation.

{ AMENDMENT XXVII (1992) }

No law, varying the compensation for the services of the Senators and Representatives, shall take effect, until an election of Representatives shall have intervened.[3]

NOTES

Chapter 1 | My Life in the Law

1. *Confirmation Hearing on the Nomination of Hon. Amy Coney Barrett to Be an Associate Justice of the Supreme Court of the United States: S. Comm. on the Judiciary*, S. Hrg. 116-637, at 70 (2020) (Statement of Amy Coney Barrett).

Chapter 2 | The Commission and the Oath

1. 28 U.S.C. § 453.
2. 1 *Kings* 3:16–28.
3. The Federalist No. 51, at 322 (James Madison) (Clinton Rossiter, ed., 1961).
4. Thomas Paine, Common Sense 36 (Peter Eckler Publ'g Co. 1922) (1776).
5. U.S. Const. art. VI, cl. 3.
6. 5 U.S.C. § 3331.
7. 28 U.S.C. § 453.
8. Jean Edward Smith, John Marshall: Definer of a Nation 285–86 (1996).
9. 491 U.S. 397, 398–99 (1989).
10. Erin Fuchs, *Justice Scalia Says He Would Jail This "Bearded Weirdo" if He Were King*, Business Insider (Mar. 26, 2014, 3:38 PM), https://www.businessinsider.in/justice-scalia-says-he-would-jail-this-bearded-weirdo-if-he-were-king/articleshow/32742355.cms.
11. *Johnson*, 491 U.S. at 420–21 (Kennedy, J., concurring).
12. 593 U.S. 486 (2021).
13. *Id.* at 488, 493.
14. *Id.* at 502 (Sotomayor, J., concurring in part and concurring in the judgment).
15. John H. Garvey & Amy V. Coney, *Catholic Judges in Capital Cases*, 81 Marq. L. Rev. 303, 305–06 (1998).
16. United States v. Tsarnaev, 595 U.S. 302, 311–12 (2022).
17. *State Summaries*, Death Penalty Info. Ctr., https://deathpenaltyinfo.org/curriculum/high-school/state-by-state-data/state-summaries.

18. Kate Glueck, *Scalia: The Constitution Is "Dead,"* POLITICO (Jan. 29, 2013, 8:26 AM), https://www.politico.com/story/2013/01/scalia-the-constitution-is-dead-086853.
19. *See* 28 U.S.C. § 453.
20. SMITH, *supra* note 8, at 372.
21. THE FEDERALIST No. 78, *supra* note 3, at 469 (Alexander Hamilton).
22. *See* SMITH, *supra* note 8, at 372–73.
23. *Id.*
24. SETH STERN & STEPHEN WERMIEL, JUSTICE BRENNAN: LIBERAL CHAMPION 230–36 (2010).
25. DAVID E. KYVIG, THE AGE OF IMPEACHMENT: AMERICAN CONSTITUTIONAL CULTURE SINCE 1960, at 51–52 (2008).
26. *See* Kermit L. Hall, *The Warren Court: Yesterday, Today, and Tomorrow*, 28 IND. L. REV. 309, 326 (1995).
27. Howard Ball, *Justice Hugo L. Black: A Magnificent Product of the South*, 36 ALA. L. REV. 791, 794–95, 797 (1985).
28. ROGER K. NEWMAN, HUGO BLACK: A BIOGRAPHY 440–41 (1994).
29. *Id.* at 443; April Wortham, *The Reclaiming of Hugo Black*, TUSCALOOSANEWS.COM (May 16, 2004, 2:16 AM), https://www.tuscaloosanews.com/story/news/2004/05/16/the-reclaiming-of-hugo-black/27864731007/.
30. Ball, *supra* note 27, at 797; Daniel M. Berman, *The Racial Issue and Mr. Justice Black*, 16 AM. U.L. REV. 386, 394 (1967).
31. NEWMAN, *supra* note 28, at 441.
32. JACK BASS, UNLIKELY HEROES: THE DRAMATIC STORY OF THE SOUTHERN JUDGES OF THE FIFTH CIRCUIT WHO TRANSLATED THE SUPREME COURT'S BROWN DECISION INTO A REVOLUTION FOR EQUALITY 31 (1981).
33. *Id.* at 66–69, 74–79.
34. *Id.* at 79–80.
35. KYVIG, *supra* note 25, at 58.

Chapter 3 | Working Together

1. CBS News, *Justice Scalia on Life Part 1*, YOUTUBE, at 6:38 PM (Sept. 23, 2010), https://www.youtube.com/watch?app=desktop&v=FrFj7JAyutg.
2. G. K. CHESTERTON, THE AUTOBIOGRAPHY OF G.K. CHESTERTON 199 (1936).
3. Letter from Benjamin Franklin to Daniel Carroll (1787), *in* 13 THE DOCUMENTARY HISTORY OF THE RATIFICATION OF THE CONSTITUTION 212, 213 (John P. Kaminski & Gaspare J. Saladino eds., 1981).
4. On the formation of Lincoln's cabinet, see DORIS KEARNS GOODWIN, TEAM OF RIVALS: THE POLITICAL GENIUS OF ABRAHAM LINCOLN xvi, 282–93, 312–19 (2005).
5. On Lincoln's and Seward's growing friendship, see *id.* at 364–65, 385–88, 577, 668–69 (2005).
6. *See* Antonin Scalia, Roast of Then-Judge Ruth Bader Ginsburg in Celebration of Her Tenth Anniversary on the Court of Appeals for the D.C. Circuit (1990), *in* ANTONIN SCALIA, SCALIA SPEAKS: REFLECTIONS ON LAW, FAITH, AND LIFE WELL LIVED 376, 378 (Christopher J. Scalia & Edward Whelan eds., 2017).
7. 518 U.S. 515, 519 (1996) (majority opinion); *id.* at 566 (Scalia, J., dissenting).

8. *Id.* at 519, 555–58 (majority opinion).
9. David McCullough, John Adams 277 (2001).
10. For the relative weakness of the Court before Marshall, see Jean Edward Smith, John Marshall: Definer of a Nation 282–83 (1996).
11. 5 U.S. (1 Cranch) 137, 173–80 (1803).
12. For Marshall's colleagues, their boardinghouse accommodations, and the practice of a single opinion for the Court, see Smith, *supra* note 10, at 286–95. For the importance of a single opinion for establishing precedent, see *id.* at 378.
13. *Id.* at 403 (quoting Josiah Quincy, Figures of the Past 189 (Boston, Roberts Bros. 1883)).
14. Sandra Day O'Connor, Out of Order: Stories from the History of the Supreme Court 33 (2013); Drew Pearson & Robert S. Allen, The Nine Old Men 225 (1936). For more on McReynolds's abysmal treatment of his staff and colleagues, see John Knox, The Forgotten Memoir of John Knox: A Year in the Life of a Supreme Court Clerk in FDR's Washington (Dennis J. Hutchinson & David J. Garrow eds., 2002).
15. Noah Feldman, Scorpions: The Battles and Triumphs of FDR's Great Supreme Court Justices 270–71, 294–302 (2010).
16. *Id.* at 273–74.
17. For Jefferson and Adams at the Continental Congress, see Gordon S. Wood, Friends Divided: John Adams and Thomas Jefferson 103–07 (2017).
18. *Id.* at 158–59.
19. *Id.* at 162. For John Quincy Adams's relationship with Jefferson, see McCullough, *supra* note 9, at 311.
20. McCullough, *supra* note 9, at 312.
21. *See id.* at 543–50.
22. *Id.* at 569.
23. Wood, *supra* note 17, at 364–425.
24. McCullough, *supra* note 9, at 608.
25. Smith, *supra* note 10, at 376.
26. *Id.*; Frances Norton Mason, My Dearest Polly: Letters of Chief Justice John Marshall to His Wife 203 (1961).
27. Jeffrey A. Tucker, *Justice Scalia's Great Heart*, Found. for Econ. Educ. (Feb. 13, 2016), https://fee.org/articles/justice-scalia-s-great-heart/.
28. *Id.*
29. *Id.*

Chapter 4 | Deciding a Case

1. 597 U.S. 215 (2022).
2. Robert A. Whitaker, *Defending Democracy: Speeches of the Warren Court Justices and* Brown v. Board of Education, 46 J. Sup. Ct. Hist. 181, 193–94 (2021).
3. Written by John Jay, Alexander Hamilton, and James Madison, these essays explained the Constitution in an effort to persuade New Yorkers to ratify it. The first bound edition was titled *The Federalist*, but today, the essays are commonly known as *The Federalist Papers*. *Full Text of the Federalist Papers*, Libr. of Cong., https://guides.loc.gov/federalist-papers/full-text.

4. Rebecca Mae Salokar, The Solicitor General: The Politics of Law 2–7, 34 (1992).
5. *See* Samuel Krislov, *The Amicus Curiae Brief: From Friendship to Advocacy*, 72 Yale L.J. 694, 694–97 (1963).
6. *Id.* at 700–02.
7. *Id.* at 707.
8. *Id.* at 709.
9. *See* Allison Orr Larsen & Neal Devins, *The Amicus Machine*, 102 Va. L. Rev. 1901, 1902–03 (2016); Joseph D. Kearney & Thomas W. Merrill, *The Influence of Amicus Curiae Briefs on the Supreme Court*, 148 U. Pa. L. Rev. 743, 752 (2000); Kelly J. Lynch, *Best Friends? Supreme Court Law Clerks on Effective Amicus Curiae Briefs*, 20 J.L. & Pol. 33, 33–34 (2004).
10. 603 U.S. 520, 525–29 (2024).
11. Sup. Ct. R. 37.6.
12. G. Edward White, The Marshall Court and Cultural Change, 1815–1835, at 159 (Oxford Univ. Press abr. ed. 1991) (1988).
13. *Id.*; *see also* Letter from Joseph Story to Hon. J. Fay (Mar. 2, 1835), *in* 2 Life and Letters of Joseph Story 192, 193 (William W. Story, ed., Boston, Charles C. Little & James Brown 1851) (noting that one case had been "under argument eight days, and will probably occupy five more").
14. Letter from J. Iredell to Simeon Baldwin (Aug. 18, 1795), *in* Simeon E. Baldwin, Life and Letters of Simeon Baldwin 410, 410 (1919).
15. Letter from Joseph Story to Samuel P. P. Fay (Feb. 24, 1812), *in* 1 Life and Letters of Joseph Story, *supra* note 13, at 215, 215.
16. 1 Ben Perley Poore, Perley's Reminiscences of Sixty Years in the National Metropolis 85 (Philadelphia, Hubbard Bros. 1886).
17. *E.g.*, John P. Frank, Marble Palace: The Supreme Court in American Life 91–92 (1958).
18. *E.g.*, Clare Cushman, Courtwatchers: Eyewitness Accounts in Supreme Court History 21–22 (2011).
19. There were ninety-eight cases on the Court's docket in 1810; by 1850, there were 253. Gerhard Casper & Richard A. Posner, The Workload of the Supreme Court 12 tbl.2.1 (1976).
20. Sup. Ct. R. 53, 48 U.S. (7 How.) v (1849) (repealed 1858).
21. A. H. Garland, Experience in the Supreme Court of the United States, with Some Reflections and Suggestions as to That Tribunal 50 (Fred B. Rothman & Co. 1983) (1898).
22. Cushman, *supra* note 18, at 126; *see also* Charles Henry Butler, A Century at the Bar of the Supreme Court of the United States 87 (1942).
23. *See* Sup. Ct. R. 26, 266 U.S. 673–74 (1924) (repealed 1928); Butler, *supra* note 22, at 87; Cushman, *supra* note 18, at 126.
24. John W. Davis, *The Argument of an Appeal*, 3 J. App. Prac. & Process 745, 754 (2001).
25. *Id.*
26. *See* Frank, *supra* note 17, at 104–05.
27. *Id.* at 102.
28. *See, e.g.*, Richard Lazarus, *How Justice Scalia Transformed Court*, CNN (Feb. 15, 2016,

3:50 PM), https://www.cnn.com/2016/02/13/opinions/justice-scalia-death-lazarus/index.html; Adam Feldman, *Empirical SCOTUS: The Hottest Bench in Town*, SCOTUSBLOG (Sept. 25, 2018, 2:56 PM), https://www.scotusblog.com/2018/09/empirical-scotus-the-hottest-bench-in-town/.

29. *See* SUP. CT. R. 44.3, 398 U.S. 1058 (1969) (repealed 1980).
30. 601 U.S. 100 (2024).
31. U.S. CONST. amend. XIV, § 3.
32. BRUCE ALLEN MURPHY, WILD BILL: THE LEGEND AND LIFE OF WILLIAM O. DOUGLAS 496–98 (2003).
33. JOHN PAUL STEVENS, FIVE CHIEFS: A SUPREME COURT MEMOIR 74, 154–55 (2011).
34. *See* Students for Fair Admissions, Inc. v. President & Fellows of Harvard Coll., 600 U.S. 181 (2023); Moore v. Harper, 600 U.S. 1 (2023); Allen v. Milligan, 599 U.S. 1 (2023).
35. 570 U.S. 529, 559 (2013) (Ginsburg, J., dissenting).
36. *See* Eileen Reynolds, *Old School? Not Ruth Bader Ginsburg!*, N.Y.U. (July 18, 2014), https://www.nyu.edu/about/news-publications/news/2014/july/notorious-rbg.html.
37. ROGER K. NEWMAN, HUGO BLACK: A BIOGRAPHY 621–22 (1994).
38. *See, e.g.*, Health & Hosp. Corp. of Marion Cnty. v. Talevski, 599 U.S. 166, 193 (2023) (Barrett, J., concurring).
39. *See, e.g.*, Fulton v. City of Philadelphia, 593 U.S. 522, 543 (2021) (Barrett, J., concurring).
40. *See, e.g.*, Samia v. United States, 599 U.S. 635, 655 (2023) (Barrett, J., concurring in part and concurring in the judgment).
41. *See* 600 U.S. 66, 105 (2023) (Thomas, J., dissenting); *id.* at 106 (Barrett, J., dissenting).
42. Memorandum of William J. Brennan, Jr., to Antonin Scalia (May 11, 1989).
43. Memorandum of Antonin Scalia to William J. Brennan, Jr. (May 11, 1989).
44. *See* WHITE, *supra* note 12, at 188 n.136.
45. *See, e.g.*, Preface, 5 U.S. (1 Cranch) iii, v (1804) (William Cranch, the court reporter, stating that he was grateful for court observers who gave him their notes for reporting purposes); Craig Joyce, *The Rise of the Supreme Court Reporter: An Institutional Perspective on Marshall Court Ascendancy*, 83 MICH. L. REV. 1291, 1310 n.110, 1321, 1324, 1332–33 (1985) (observing that early reporters had access to at least some of the justices' notes).
46. *See* Preface, *supra* note 45, at iv–v (stating that Cranch "has been relieved from much anxiety, as well as responsibility, by the practice which the court has adopted of reducing their opinion to writing, in all cases of difficulty or importance; and he tenders his tribute of acknowledgement for the readiness with which he was permitted to take copies of those opinions"). The case reports do not reveal, however, which were the "cases of difficulty or importance" for which Cranch had an actual opinion in hand.
47. *See* Frank D. Wagner, *The Role of the Supreme Court Reporter in History*, 26 J. SUP. CT. HIST. 9, 15 (2001); *Historical Supreme Court Cases Now Online*, LIBR. OF CONG. (Mar. 12, 2018), https://www.loc.gov/item/prn-18-026/historical-supreme-court-cases-now-online/2018-03-13/.
48. CUSHMAN, *supra* note 18 , at 117.
49. *Id.*
50. 598 U.S. 1, 4–6 (2023).
51. 600 U.S. 181, 230 (2023).

52. 530 U.S. 703, 707–08, 725, 734 (2000); Jill Duffy & Elizabeth Lambert, *Dissents from the Bench: A Compilation of Oral Dissents by U.S. Supreme Court Justices*, 102 L. Lib. J. 7, 32 (2010).
53. *See The Supreme Court, 2022 Term—The Statistics*, 137 Harv. L. Rev. 490, 495 (2023).
54. The average rate of unanimity over the last decade is approximately 44 percent. The average percentage of unanimity over the last seventy-five years is approximately 38 percent. For statistics from the last decade, see *Supreme Court Statistics*, Harv. L. Rev., https://harvardlawreview.org/supreme-court-statistics/. For the proportion of cases decided unanimously from 1791 to 2019, see Lee Epstein et al., The Supreme Court Compendium: Two Centuries of Data, Decisions, and Developments 185–90 tbl.3-1 (7th ed. 2021). *See also* Cass R. Sunstein, *Unanimity and Disagreement on the Supreme Court*, 100 Cornell L. Rev. 769 app. at 817 fig.A-1 (2015) (graphically depicting the percentage of cases decided unanimously from 1941 to 2012).
55. For a full breakdown of the voting coalitions in the 2022 Term, see Adam Feldman, *Another One Bites the Dust: End of 2022/2023 Supreme Court Term Statistics*, Empirical SCOTUS (June 30, 2023), https://empiricalscotus.com/2023/06/30/another-one-bites-2022/.
56. For a full list of the Court's 2022 Term cases, see *Opinions of the Court—2022*, Sup. Ct. of the U.S., https://www.supremecourt.gov/opinions/slipopinion/22.
57. *See The Supreme Court, 2023 Term—The Statistics*, 138 Harv. L. Rev. 446, 451 (2024).
58. Adam Feldman & Jake S. Truscott, *2023 Term Statistics*, Empirical SCOTUS (June 28, 2024), https://empiricalscotus.com/2023-stats/.
59. For a full list of the Court's 2023 Term cases, see *Opinions of the Court—2023*, Sup. Ct. of the U.S., https://www.supremecourt.gov/opinions/slipopinion/23.

Chapter 5 | Law Clerks in Chambers

1. Stacey Abrams, While Justice Sleeps (2021).
2. Stacey Abrams, Rogue Justice (2023).
3. Brad Meltzer, The Tenth Justice (1997).
4. Kermit Roosevelt, Allegiance (2015).
5. *The Supreme Court, 2022 Term—The Statistics*, 137 Harv. L. Rev. 490, 498 (2023).
6. Tracy Campbell, Short of the Glory: The Fall and Redemption of Edward F. Prichard Jr. 64–65 (1998).
7. *Id.* at 65.
8. Artemus Ward & David L. Weiden, Sorcerers' Apprentices: 100 Years of Law Clerks at the United States Supreme Court 28–29 (2006).
9. *FAQs—Supreme Court Justices*, Sup. Ct. of the U.S., https://www.supremecourt.gov/about/faq_justices.aspx.
10. *Id.*
11. I have learned this history largely from the excellent work of Todd Peppers, Artemus Ward, and Clare Cushman. *See, e.g.*, Todd C. Peppers, Courtiers of the Marble Palace: The Rise and Influence of the Supreme Court Law Clerk (2006) [hereinafter Peppers, Marble Palace]; In Chambers: Stories of Supreme Court Law Clerks and Their Justices (Todd C. Peppers & Artemus Ward eds., 2012) [hereinafter In Chambers]; Of Courtiers & Kings: More Stories of Supreme Court Law Clerks and Their Justices (Todd C. Peppers & Clare Cushman eds., 2015) [hereinafter Of Courtiers & Kings].

12. Peppers, Marble Palace, *supra* note 11, at 38–39, 42–43.
13. *See* Todd C. Peppers, *Birth of an Institution: Horace Gray and the Lost Law Clerks*, 32 J. Sup. Ct. Hist. 229, 230 (2007) [hereinafter Peppers, *Birth*]; *see also* Act of Mar. 2, 1867, ch. 156, § 2, 14 Stat. 433 ("[A]nd the said marshal, with the approval of the chief justice, may appoint assistants and messengers . . . with such compensation as is or may be allowed to officers of the House of Representatives of similar grade").
14. *See, e.g.*, Peppers, Marble Palace, *supra* note 11, at 43; Peppers, *Birth*, *supra* note 13, at 231. The justices of the time may not have called these new hires "clerks," and their initial role wasn't recognizable as what we would today consider a "clerk." I use the term, however, for ease of reference.
15. Peppers, Marble Palace, *supra* note 11, at 43.
16. *Id.* at 44–47.
17. Peppers, *Birth*, *supra* note 13, at 232–34; *see also* Peppers, Marble Palace, *supra* note 11, at 51–52.
18. Peppers, *Birth*, *supra* note 13, at 234.
19. U.S. Dep't of Just., Annual Report of the Attorney-General of the United States for the Year 1885, at 43 (1885).
20. Act of Aug. 4. 1886, ch. 902, 24 Stat. 254.
21. Todd C. Peppers, *Isaiah and His Young Disciples: Justice Brandeis and His Law Clerks*, 34 J. Sup. Ct. Hist. 75, 79 (2009).
22. *Id.* at 81.
23. *Id.* at 78–80; *see also* Peppers, Marble Palace, *supra* note 11, at 63.
24. Peppers, Marble Palace, *supra* note 11, at 57–58.
25. *Id.* at 96.
26. Clare Cushman, *Fountain Pens and Typewriters: Supreme Court Stenographers and Law Clerks, 1910–1940*, 41 J. Sup. Ct. Hist. 39, 39, 64 (2016).
27. *Id.* at 47.
28. *Id.* at 39 (quoting Letter from David J. Brewer to William Rufus Day (Aug. 13, 1905) (on file with the Library of Congress in the William R. Day papers, Box 20, File A–C)).
29. Peppers, Marble Palace, *supra* note 11, at 47–48.
30. *Id.*
31. *Id.* at 50–51; Cushman, *supra* note 26, at 55.
32. Peppers, Marble Palace, *supra* note 11, at 54.
33. *Id.*
34. *Id.* at 103.
35. *See id.*
36. Francis Biddle, Mr. Justice Holmes 12 (1942) (italics omitted).
37. John S. Monagan, The Grand Panjandrum: Mellow Years of Justice Holmes 115 (1988).
38. Peppers, Marble Palace, *supra* note 11, at 58.
39. *Id.* at 58–60.
40. *See* Act of May 29, 1920, ch. 214, 41 Stat. 631, 686–87 (authorizing one stenographic and one law clerk for each of the justices); Peppers, Marble Palace, *supra* note 11, at 127 (noting that Congress authorized a second law clerk for the justices in the 1940s).
41. Peppers, Marble Palace, *supra* note 11, at 127.
42. *Id.* at 100–01.

43. *Id.* at 92.
44. *Id.* at 185.
45. *Id.* at 24–25, 25 tbl.2.2.
46. *Id.* at 1.
47. *Id.* at 151–52.
48. *Id.* at 171.
49. *Id.* at 154.
50. *Id.* at 67.
51. John Knox, The Forgotten Memoir of John Knox: A Year in the Life of a Supreme Court Clerk in FDR's Washington 13 (Dennis J. Hutchinson & David J. Garrow eds., 2002).
52. Bruce Allen Murphy, Wild Bill: The Legend and Life of William O. Douglas 408–15 (2003).
53. Joseph L. Rauh, Jr., Melvin Siegel, Ambrose Doskow & Alan M. Stroock, *A Personal View of Justice Benjamin N. Cardozo: Recollections of Four Cardozo Law Clerks*, 1 Cardozo L. Rev. 5, 6 (1979) (story of Joseph L. Rauh, Jr.).
54. Todd C. Peppers & Beth See Driver, *Half Clerk, Half Son: Justice Felix Frankfurter and His Law Clerks*, *in* In Chambers, *supra* note 11, at 141, 143–44.
55. *Id.* at 144, 152–54.
56. Andrew L. Kaufman, *Frankfurter and Wellington*, 45 N.Y. L. Sch. L. Rev. 141, 141 (2000).
57. Peppers, Marble Palace, *supra* note 11, at 151; *see also* Earl C. Dudley, Jr., *A Two-For Clerkship: Stanley F. Reed and Earl Warren*, *in* Of Courtiers & Kings, *supra* note 11, at 231, 237.
58. Peppers, Marble Palace, *supra* note 11, at 155.
59. Charles A. Reich, *A Passion for Justice: Living with and Clerking for Justice Hugo Black*, *in* In Chambers, *supra* note 11, at 111, 111.
60. Artemus Ward, *Making Work for Idle Hands: William H. Rehnquist and His Law Clerks*, *in* In Chambers, *supra* note 11, at 350, 376–77; Ted Cruz, *From Doubles Tennis to Internet Porn: My Year as a Supreme Court Clerk*, Politico Mag. (June 29, 2015), https://www.politico.com/magazine/story/2015/06/ted-cruz-memoir-supreme-court-119529/.
61. Peppers, Marble Palace, *supra* note 11, at 164.
62. *Id.* at 166.
63. Glen D. Nager, *A Tribute to Justice Sandra Day O'Connor*, 119 Harv. L. Rev. 1248, 1248 (2006).
64. Julia C. Ambrose, *Clerking for the FWOTSC: Recollections of a Former O'Connor Clerk*, *in* Of Courtiers & Kings, *supra* note 11, at 327, 332–33.
65. *See, e.g.*, Amanda L. Tyler, *Lessons Learned from Justice Ruth Bader Ginsburg*, 121 Colum. L. Rev. 741, 750–51 (2021); Goodwin Liu, *Clerking for Justice Ginsburg Was a Gift Beyond Measure*, SCOTUSblog (Sept. 22, 2020, 2:21 PM), https://www.scotusblog.com/2020/09/clerking-for-justice-ginsburg-was-a-gift-beyond-measure/.
66. Jeffrey Pojanowski, *Tribute: Remembering Little Things That Matter*, SCOTUSblog (June 27, 2018, 3:23 PM), https://www.scotusblog.com/2018/06/tribute-remembering-little-things-that-matter/.
67. Kermit Roosevelt, *David Souter: A Clerk's View*, 35 J. Sup. Ct. Hist. 7, 8 (2010).
68. Kim Eisler, *Clerks Rate Supremes as Bosses*, Washingtonian, Oct. 1998, at 16.

69. *See id.*
70. *Id.* at 18.
71. City of Chicago v. Morales, 527 U.S. 41, 81–82, 81 n.5 (1999) (Scalia, J., dissenting).
72. *See* Peppers, Marble Palace, *supra* note 11, at 102.
73. *See* Ward, *supra* note 60, at 378–79.
74. Peppers, Marble Palace, *supra* note 11, at 186.

Chapter 6 | Docketed

1. The Federalist No. 78, at 465 (Alexander Hamilton) (Clinton Rossiter, ed., 1961).
2. *Building History*, Sup. Ct. of the U.S., https://supremecourt.gov/about/buildinghistory.aspx; *see also Homes of the United States Supreme Court*, Sup. Ct. Hist. Soc'y, https://www.supremecourthistory.org/homes-of-the-supreme-court/#:~:text=The%20Court%20moved%20into%20the,Chamber%20from%201861%20to%201935.
3. Joanna R. Lampe, Cong. Rsch. Serv., LSB10562, "Court Packing": Legislative Control over the Size of the Supreme Court 2–3 (2020).
4. Florida v. Georgia, 592 U.S. 433 (2021).
5. Texas v. White, 74 U.S. 700 (1868).
6. *Id.* at 725–26.
7. Joseph B. Treaster, *Burger, at NYU Dinner, Says Heavy Caseloads Imperil U.S. Justice System*, N.Y. Times, Nov. 19, 1982, at B1; Ryan J. Owens & David A. Simon, *Explaining the Supreme Court's Shrinking Docket*, 53 Wm & Mary L. Rev. 1219, 1244 (2012).
8. Supreme Court Case Selections Act of 1988, Pub. L. No. 100-352, 102 Stat. 662 (codified at 28 U.S.C. §§ 1254, 1257–1258, 2104 (1994)).
9. Sup. Ct. R. 10.
10. Pulsifer v. United States, 601 U.S. 124 (2024).
11. Byrd v. United States, 584 U.S. 395 (2018).
12. Sup. Ct. R. 10(c).
13. Trump v. United States, 603 U.S. 593 (2024).
14. Biden v. Texas, 597 U.S 785 (2022).
15. Gonzales v. Raich, 545 U.S. 1 (2005).
16. Dep't of Homeland Sec. v. Texas, 144 S. Ct. 715 (2024); Las Ams. Immigrant Advoc. Ctr. v. McGraw, 218 L. Ed. 2d 202 (2024).
17. Moyle v. United States, 603 U.S. 324 (2024); Whole Woman's Health v. Jackson, 595 U.S. 30 (2021).
18. Labrador v. Poe, 144 S. Ct. 921 (2024).
19. Ohio v. EPA, 603 U.S. 279 (2024).
20. For concerns about the speed and transparency of the emergency docket, see William Baude, *Foreword: The Supreme Court's Shadow Docket*, 9 N.Y.U. J.L. & Liberty 1, 12–20 (2015).
21. *See, e.g.*, Trevor N. McFadden & Vetan Kapoor, *The Precedential Effects of the Supreme Court's Emergency Stays*, 44 Harv. J. L. Pub. Pol. 827, 828–29 (2021). For a discussion of national injunctions, see Samuel Bray, *Multiple Chancellors: Reforming the National Injunction*, 131 Harv. L. Rev. 417 (2017).
22. Joanna R. Lampe, Cong. Rsch. Serv., LSB10637, The "Shadow Docket": The Supreme Court's Non-Merits Orders (2021).
23. Hollingsworth v. Perry, 558 U.S. 183, 190 (2010).

24. Nken v. Holder, 556 U.S. 418, 434–35 (2009).
25. Doe v. Mills, 142 S. Ct. 17, 18 (2021).
26. Robert A. Whitaker, *Defending Democracy: Speeches of the Warren Court Justices and* Brown v. Board of Education, 46 J. Sup. Ct. Hist. 181, 194 (2021).
27. *Id.* at 193.
28. Sandra Day O'Connor, Majesty of the Law 15 (2004).
29. The Civil Rights Cases, 109 U.S. 3 (1883); Plessy v. Ferguson, 163 U.S. 537 (1896).
30. Lochner v. New York, 198 U.S. 45 (1905).
31. Adair v. United States, 208 U.S. 161 (1908); Loewe v. Lawlor, 208 U.S. 274 (1908).
32. Hammer v. Dagenhart, 247 U.S. 251 (1918).
33. *See, e.g.*, A. L. A. Schechter Poultry Corp. v. United States, 295 U.S. 495 (1935); Carter v. Carter Coal Co., 298 U.S. 238 (1936); NLRB v. Jones & Laughlin Steel Corp., 301 U.S. 1 (1937).
34. Brown v. Bd. of Educ., 347 U.S. 483 (1954); Cooper v. Aaron, 358 U.S. 1 (1958).
35. Swann v. Charlotte-Mecklenburg Bd. of Educ., 402 U.S. 1 (1971).
36. *See, e.g.*, Mapp v. Ohio, 367 U.S. 643 (1961); Gideon v. Wainwright, 372 U.S. 335 (1963); Miranda v. Arizona, 384 U.S. 436 (1966).
37. *See, e.g.*, Frontiero v. Richardson, 411 U.S. 677 (1973); Miss. Univ. for Women v. Hogan, 458 U.S. 718 (1982).
38. *See, e.g.*, Korematsu v. United States, 323 U.S. 214 (1944); Youngstown Sheet & Tube Co. v. Sawyer, 343 U.S. 579 (1952); Hamdi v. Rumsfeld, 542 U.S. 507 (2004).
39. Tandon v. Newsom, 593 U.S. 61 (2021); Biden v. Missouri, 595 U.S. 87 (2022).
40. Obergefell v. Hodges, 576 U.S. 644 (2015).
41. Bostock v. Clayton County, 590 U.S. 644 (2020).
42. Masterpiece Cakeshop, Ltd. v. Colo. C.R. Comm'n, 584 U.S. 617 (2018); 303 Creative LLC v. Elenis, 600 U.S. 570 (2023).
43. Twitter, Inc. v. Taamneh, 598 U.S. 471 (2023); Murthy v. Missouri, 603 U.S. 43 (2024); Moody v. NetChoice, LLC, 603 U.S. 707 (2024); Lindke v. Freed, 601 U.S. 187 (2024).
44. O'Connor, *supra* note 28, at 15.

Chapter 7 | Judicial Power and Restraint

1. Though implicit in the Constitution, judicial review was explicitly discussed in important ratification-era commentary. *See, e.g.*, The Federalist No. 78, at 466–69 (Alexander Hamilton) (Clinton Rossiter, ed., 1961) (arguing in favor of judicial review).
2. *See, e.g.*, Larry D. Kramer, *Foreword: We the Court*, 115 Harv. L. Rev. 4, 79 n.308 (2001) ("A few [Jeffersonian] Republicans challenged the propriety of judicial review during the debate over repeal of the Judiciary Act of 1801").
3. Marbury v. Madison, 5 U.S. (1 Cranch) 137, 173–180 (1803).
4. Letter from Thomas Jefferson to Abigail Adams (Sept. 11, 1804), *in* 44 The Papers of Thomas Jefferson, 1 July to 10 November 1804, at 379, 380 (James P. McClure, ed., 2019).
5. William W. Van Alstyne, *A Critical Guide to* Marbury v. Madison, 1969 Duke L.J. 1, 3–6, 9; David F. Forte, *Marbury's Travail: Federalist Politics and William Marbury's Appointment as Justice of the Peace*, 45 Cath. U. L. Rev. 349, 353 n.13 (1996).

6. *Marbury*, 5 U.S. (1 Cranch) at 154.
7. *Id.* at 157, 167–68.
8. *Id.* at 155 (describing the commission as an "evidence[] of office").
9. *Id.* at 172–73 (asserting that the secretary of state violated the law).
10. *Id.* at 173.
11. *Id.* at 173–76.
12. *Id.* at 176–77 ("[T]he people have an original right to establish . . . such principles as . . . shall most conduce to their own happiness. . . . This original and supreme will organizes the government." *Id.* at 176.).
13. U.S. Const. art. III, § 2.
14. *Marbury*, 5 U.S. (1 Cranch) at 177.
15. U.S. Const. art. VI, cl. 2.
16. *Marbury*, 5 U.S. (1 Cranch) at 175–76.
17. For a discussion of this analogy, see Jeremy Waldron, *Banking Constitutional Rights: Who Controls Withdrawals?* 52 Ark. L. Rev. 533, 539–42 (1999).
18. Plaut v. Spendthrift Farm, Inc., 514 U.S. 211, 218–19 (1995) ("[T]the Federal Judiciary [has] the power, not merely to rule on cases, but to *decide* them, subject to review only by superior courts in the Article III hierarchy").
19. *See* Amy Coney Barrett, *Introduction*, 83 Notre Dame L. Rev. 1147, 1157–60 (2008) (recounting examples of Congress, the president, and the states resisting Supreme Court opinions).
20. Dred Scott v. Sanford, 60 U.S. (19 How.) 393, 431–32 (1857) (enslaved party), *superseded by constitutional amendment*, U.S. Const. amend. XIV.
21. *Id.* at 403–04.
22. *Id.* at 451–52.
23. Abraham Lincoln, *Speech at Springfield, Illinois (June 26, 1857)*, *in* 2 The Collected Works of Abraham Lincoln, 1848–1858, at 398, 400–01 (Roy P. Basler, ed., 1953).
24. *Id.* at 401.
25. Lincoln, *First Inaugural Address* (Mar. 4, 1861), *in* 4 Collected Works, *supra* note 23, 262, 268.
26. Andrew Jackson, *Veto Message* (July 10, 1832), *in* 2 A Compilation of the Messages and Papers of the Presidents, 1789–1897, at 576, 582 (James D. Richardson, ed., 1896).
27. M'Culloch v. Maryland, 17 U.S. 316, 424–25 (1819).
28. Jackson, *supra* note 26, at 582.
29. City of Boerne v. Flores, 521 U.S. 507, 535–36 (1997).
30. *See, e.g.*, A.L.A. Schechter Poultry Corp. v. United States, 295 U.S. 495, 541–42 (1935) (invalidating a provision of the National Industrial Recovery Act of 1933); Panama Refining Co. v. Ryan, 293 U.S. 388, 431–33 (1935) (same); R.R. Ret. Bd. v. Alton R.R. Co., 295 U.S. 330, 340, 362 (1935) (invalidating the Railroad Retirement Act of 1934).
31. William E. Leuchtenburg, *The Origins of Franklin D. Roosevelt's "Court-Packing" Plan*, 1966 Sup. Ct. Rev. 347, 395.
32. Franklin D. Roosevelt, *Fireside Chat*, Am. Presidency Project (Mar. 9, 1937), https://www.presidency.ucsb.edu/documents/fireside-chat-17.
33. *Id.*
34. W. Coast Hotel v. Parrish, 300 U.S. 379, 388–89, 396–97 (1937).

35. John Q. Barrett, *Attribution Time: Cal Tinney's 1937 Quip, "A Switch in Time'll Save Nine,"* 73 Okla. L. Rev. 229, 229 (2021).
36. William E. Leuchtenburg, The Supreme Court Reborn: The Constitutional Revolution in the Age of Roosevelt 143–44 (1995).
37. *Id.* at 153–54.
38. William W. Van Alstyne, *A Critical Guide to* Ex parte McCardle, 15 Ariz. L. Rev. 229, 238–44 (1973); Military Reconstruction Act, ch. 153, § 5, 14 Stat. 428, 429 (1867).
39. Van Alstyne, *supra* note 38, at 239–41.
40. Tara Leigh Grove, *The Structural Safeguards of Federal Jurisdiction,* 124 Harv. L. Rev. 869, 897–99 (2011) (corporations); Max Baucus & Kenneth R. Kay, *The Court Stripping Bills: Their Impact on the Constitution, the Courts, and Congress,* 27 Vill. L. Rev. 988, 991–94, 992 n.18 (1982) (school prayer, legislative apportionment, Miranda, busing, abortion); Presidential Comm'n on the Sup. Ct. of the U.S., Final Report 154 (2021) (Pledge of Allegiance, Defense of Marriage Act).
41. Ronald Reagan, *Radio Address to the Nation on the United States Supreme Court Nominations,* Am. Presidency Project (Aug. 9, 1986), https://www.presidency.ucsb.edu/documents/radio-address-the-nation-the-united-states-supreme-court-nominations.
42. William J. Clinton, *Remarks Announcing the Nomination of Ruth Bader Ginsburg to Be a Supreme Court Associate Justice,* Am. Presidency Project (June 14, 1993), https://www.presidency.ucsb.edu/documents/remarks-announcing-the-nomination-ruth-bader-ginsburg-be-supreme-court-associate-justice.
43. Letter from Thomas Jefferson to the JJ. of the Sup. Ct. (July 18, 1793), *in* 6 The Documentary History of the Supreme Court of the United States, 1789–1800, app. at 747 (Maeva Marcus, ed., 1998) [hereinafter DHSC]. Jefferson used various abbreviations for "United States"; for consistency, I have used "U.S." throughout the quotation of his letter.
44. *Id.*
45. Questions Proposed to Be Submitted to the C.J. & JJ. of the Sup. Ct. (July 18, 1793), *in* DHSC, *supra* note 43, app. at 747, 750.
46. Letter from JJ. of the Sup. Ct. to George Washington (Aug. 8, 1973), *in* DHSC, *supra* note 43, app. at 755.
47. *Id.*
48. *Id.*
49. Muskrat v. United States, 219 U.S. 346, 354, 361–62 (1911).
50. *Id.* at 357.
51. *Id.* at 357–58.
52. *Id.*
53. Valley Forge Christian Coll. v. Ams. United for Separation of Church & State, Inc., 454 U.S. 464, 468–69 (1982).
54. *Id.* at 470 (quoting Ams. United for Separation of Church & State, Inc. v. U.S. Dep't of Health, Educ. & Welfare, 619 F.2d 252, 261 (3d Cir. 1980), *rev'd sub nom.* Valley Forge Christian Coll. v. Ams. United for Separation of Church & State, Inc., 454 U.S. 464 (1982)).
55. *Id.* at 482–83, 485–86.
56. *Id.* at 485.

57. *See* Allen v. Wright, 468 U.S. 737, 755–56 (1984).
58. *See* Summers v. Earth Island Inst., 555 U.S. 488, 494–96 (2009).
59. *See* FDA v. All. for Hippocratic Med., 602 U.S. 367, 384–86 (2024).
60. Franchise Tax Bd. of Cal. v. Alcan Aluminium Ltd., 493 U.S. 331, 336 (1990).
61. Franklin v. Massachusetts, 505 U.S. 788, 825 (1992) (Scalia, J., concurring in part and concurring in the judgment).
62. Murthy v. Missouri, 603 U.S. 43, 51, 53–54, 63 (2024).
63. *Id.* at 54.
64. *Id.* at 73–74.
65. Letter from JJ. of the Sup. Ct. to George Washington (Aug. 8, 1973), *in* DHSC, *supra* note 43, app. at 755.
66. FDA v. All. for Hippocratic Med., 602 U.S. 367, 382 (2024) (citation omitted) (quoting Lujan v. Defs. of Wildlife, 504 U.S. 555, 576 (1992)).
67. Marbury v. Madison, 5 U.S. (1 Cranch) 137, 177 (1803).

Chapter 8 | A More Perfect Union

1. Letter from John Adams to Abigail Adams (May 27, 1776), *in* 1 ADAMS FAMILY CORRESPONDENCE 419, 420 (L. H. Butterfield, ed., 1963).
2. Letter from Abigail Adams to John Adams (June 17, 1782), *in* 4 ADAMS FAMILY CORRESPONDENCE 326, 328 (L. H. Butterfield & Marc Friedlander eds., 1973).
3. *Id.*
4. RICHARD BEEMAN, PLAIN, HONEST MEN: THE MAKING OF THE AMERICAN CONSTITUTION 14–16 (2009).
5. *Id.* at 8; CAROL BERKIN, A BRILLIANT SOLUTION: INVENTING THE AMERICAN CONSTITUTION 17 (2002); ("The Revolution was not one battle for independence but thirteen—proof that a profound localism still trumped any embryonic identity as 'Americans'").
6. BERKIN, *supra* note 5, at 17; *see also* DAVID O. STEWART, THE SUMMER OF 1787: THE MEN WHO INVENTED THE CONSTITUTION 18 (2007).
7. BERKIN, *supra* note 5, at 18.
8. *Id.*
9. *Id.* at 14–16; STEWART, *supra* note 6, at 18–21.
10. BERKIN, *supra* note 5, at 15; STEWART, *supra* note 6, at 22.
11. STEWART, *supra* note 6, at 22.
12. *Id.* at 18–19.
13. BERKIN, *supra* note 5, at 16, 21–22.
14. *Id.* at 16–17.
15. BEEMAN, *supra* note 4, at 8; BERKIN, *supra* note 5, at 17.
16. BERKIN, *supra* note 5, at 17, 19, 21–22; STEWART, *supra* note 6, at 18.
17. BERKIN, *supra* note 5, at 19–21.
18. *Id.* at 21.
19. *Id.* at 20.
20. BEEMAN, *supra* note 4, at 14–15.
21. *Id.* at 15; BERKIN, *supra* note 5, at 22.
22. BEEMAN, *supra* note 4, at 15.
23. *Id.*

24. *Id.* at 9, 15.
25. *Id.*
26. *Id.* at 16.
27. Berkin, *supra* note 5, at 26–27.
28. *Id.*
29. *Id.* at 27.
30. *Id.* at 28–29.
31. *Id.* at 49–50.
32. *See* Christopher Collier & James Lincoln Collier, Decision in Philadelphia: The Constitutional Convention of 1787, at 25 (Ballantine Books Trade Paperback ed. 2007); Beeman, *supra* note 4, at 166; Stewart, *supra* note 6, at 33.
33. Beeman, *supra* note 4, at 64.
34. *Id.* at 166.
35. Berkin, *supra* note 5, at 62–63.
36. Collier & Collier, *supra* note 32, at 76.
37. Beeman, *supra* note 4, at 73.
38. *Id.*; Stewart, *supra* note 6, at 27.
39. Beeman, *supra* note 4, at 73; Stewart, *supra* note 6, at 72; Catherine Drinker Bowen, Miracle at Philadelphia: The Story of the Constitutional Convention May to September 1787, at 52 (1966).
40. Collier & Collier, *supra* note 32, at 17.
41. Beeman, *supra* note 4, at 74.
42. *Id.*; Stewart, *supra* note 6, at 42.
43. Stewart, *supra* note 6, at 41; Beeman, *supra* note 4, at 74–75.
44. Beeman, *supra* note 4, at 75; Bowen, *supra* note 39, at 52.
45. Beeman, *supra* note 4, at 75; Stewart, *supra* note 6, at 41–42.
46. Beeman, *supra* note 4, at 75; *see also* Stewart, *supra* note 6, at 43.
47. Stewart, *supra* note 6, at 84–85 (quoting Peter Thompson, Rum Punch & Revolution: Taverngoing & Public Life in Eighteenth-Century Philadelphia 193 (1999)).
48. *Id.* at 83.
49. Letter from George Mason to George Mason, Jr. (May 27, 1787) *in* 2 Kate Mason Rowland, The Life of George Mason 1725–1792, at 103 (Russell & Russell, Inc. 1964) (1892); *see also* Stewart, *supra* note 6, at 83–84.
50. Beeman, *supra* note 4, at 61.
51. *Id.* at 61–62; Stewart, *supra* note 6, at 50.
52. Beeman, *supra* note 4, at 62.
53. *Id.*
54. *Id.*; *see also* Stewart, *supra* note 6, at 42.
55. Beeman, *supra* note 4, at 63.
56. Berkin, *supra* note 5, at 43; *see also* Stewart, *supra* note 6, at 82.
57. Beeman, *supra* note 4, at 83; *see also* Stewart, *supra* note 6, at 51.
58. *See* Beeman, *supra* note 4, at 80; Stewart, *supra* note 6, at 50.
59. Stewart, *supra* note 6, at 81.
60. Beeman, *supra* note 4, at 41.
61. Collier & Collier, *supra* note 32, at 15.

62. Beeman, *supra* note 4, at 40, 57–58; Berkin, *supra* note 5, at 36–37.
63. Beeman, *supra* note 4, at 59.
64. *Id.*; Berkin, *supra* note 5, at 42.
65. Beeman, *supra* note 4, at 60; Berkin, *supra* note 5, at 42; Stewart, *supra* note 6, at 181; Bowen, *supra* note 39, at 24.
66. Beeman, *supra* note 4, at 57.
67. *Id.* at 68; Berkin, *supra* note 5, at 46; Collier & Collier, *supra* note 32, at 79.
68. Beeman, *supra* note 4, at 30; Berkin, *supra* note 5, at 33; Stewart, *supra* note 6, at 30; Bowen, *supra* note 39, at 28; Collier & Collier, *supra* note 32, at 36.
69. Collier & Collier, *supra* note 32, at 25–28; Stewart, *supra* note 6, at 48.
70. Beeman, *supra* note 4, at 85 (quoting 3 The Records of the Federal Convention of 1787, at 550 (Max Farrand, ed., rev. ed. 1966)); Stewart, *supra* note 6, at 48.
71. Bowen, *supra* note 39.
72. Beeman, *supra* note 4, at 65; Berkin, *supra* note 5, at 50.
73. Beeman, *supra* note 4, at 66.
74. *Id.* at 65.
75. Berkin, *supra* note 5, at 16, 56–57.
76. Letter from James Madison to George Washington (Apr. 16, 1787), *in* 9 The Papers of James Madison 382, 383 (Robert A. Rutland & William M. E. Rachal eds., 1975).
77. *Id.* at 384–85; Beeman, *supra* note 4, at 27–29; Collier & Collier, *supra* note 32, at 46, 50, 55.
78. Collier & Collier, *supra* note 32, at 69; see *id.* at 64–74 for background on Charles Pinckney; Stewart, *supra* note 6, at 40.
79. Stewart, *supra* note 6, at 56, 110.
80. Berkin, *supra* note 5, at 73–75; Stewart, *supra* note 6, at 55–56.
81. Beeman, *supra* note 4, at 181; Collier & Collier, *supra* note 32, at 122.
82. Collier & Collier, *supra* note 32, at 95.
83. Beeman, *supra* note 4, at 150; Berkin, *supra* note 5, at 103–04, 112; Bowen, *supra* note 39, at 94.
84. Beeman, *supra* note 4, at 150–51.
85. Collier & Collier, *supra* note 32, at 138, 150, 152; Stewart, *supra* note 6, at 56–57.
86. Beeman, *supra* note 4, at 154; *see also* Stewart, *supra* note 6, at 78–79.
87. Beeman, *supra* note 4, at 154.
88. U.S. Const., art. I, § 2, cl. 3, *amended by* U.S. Const. amend. XIV, § 2.
89. U.S. Const., art. I, § 9, cl. 1 (inoperative since 1808); Beeman, *supra* note 4, at 326–28.
90. Stewart, *supra* note 6, at 192.
91. Collier & Collier, *supra* note 32, at 177–78; *see also* Stewart, *supra* note 6, at 68.
92. Berkin, *supra* note 5, at 113–15.
93. Alexander Hamilton, Remarks at the New York Ratifying Convention (June 20, 1788), *in* 5 The Papers of Alexander Hamilton 16, 24 (Harold C. Syrett, ed., 1962).
94. Stewart, *supra* note 6, at 206.
95. *Id.* at 238, 240, 243.
96. Pauline Maier, Ratification: The People Debate the Constitution, 1787–1788, at 30 (2010); Beeman, *supra* note 4, at 370.
97. Beeman, *supra* note 4, at 362, 371–72; Berkin, *supra* note 5, at 160–62, 165–66.

98. Berkin, *supra* note 5, at 175.
99. *Id.* at 176.
100. Bowen, *supra* note 39, at 267; Maier, *supra* note 96, at 29.
101. Stewart, *supra* note 6, at 241–42.
102. Beeman, *supra* note 4, at 376–77; Berkin, *supra* note 5, at 183; Bowen, *supra* note 39, at 274.
103. Beeman, *supra* note 4, at 405.
104. Clinton Rossiter, *Introduction* to The Federalist Papers: Alexander Hamilton, James Madison, John Jay vii, xi, xiii (Clinton Rossiter, ed., 1961).
105. *Id.*
106. Reflection and Choice: The Federalists, the Anti-Federalists, and the Debate That Defined America 11 (Gary L. Gregg II & Aaron N. Coleman eds., 2020) [hereinafter Reflection and Choice]; Berkin, *supra* note 5, at 175–76.
107. Reflection and Choice, *supra* note 106, at 9–12. The definitive collection of Anti-Federalist papers is The Complete Anti-Federalist (Herbert J. Storing, ed., 1981).
108. The Federalist No. 1 (Alexander Hamilton), No. 40 (James Madison).
109. The Federalist No. 40, at 254 (James Madison) (Clinton Rossiter, ed., 1961).
110. U.S. Const. pmbl.
111. The Federalist Nos. 39, 43 (James Madison).
112. Beeman, *supra* note 4, at 409; *see also* Maier, *supra* note 96, at 83.
113. The Federalist Nos. 39, 51 (James Madison), No. 68 (Alexander Hamilton).
114. The Federalist No. 39 (James Madison).
115. The Federalist Nos. 47–51 (James Madison).
116. Maier, *supra* note 96, at 79.
117. Letters from the Federal Farmer (No. 1), *reprinted in* 2 The Complete Anti-Federalist, *supra* note 107, at 223, 228.
118. Letters from the Federal Farmer (No. 18.), *reprinted in* 2 The Complete Anti-Federalist, *supra* note 107, at 339, 348.
119. Charles Pinckney, Address to the South Carolina Convention (May 14, 1788), *in* 4 The Debates in the Several State Conventions on the Adoption of the Federal Constitution 318, 320–23 (Jonathan Elliot, ed., Washington, D.C., 2d ed. 1836).
120. U.S. Const. art. I, § 9, cl. 8, § 10, cl. 1.
121. *See* Berkin, *supra* note 5, at 183–84.
122. Robert A. Goldwin, From Parchment to Power: How James Madison Used the Bill of Rights to Save the Constitution 40 (1997).
123. *Id.* at 41.
124. Beeman, *supra* note 4, at 391.
125. Stewart, *supra* note 6, at 246.
126. Beeman, *supra* note 4, at 391.
127. *Id.* at 400-03.
128. Both Washington and Madison described the convention as a "miracle," as memorialized in the title of Catherine Drinker Bowen's book. Bowen, *supra* note 39.

Chapter 9 | A Firmer Foundation

1. *See* Sanford Levinson, Constitutional Faith 95–96 (1988).
2. Heidi Schreck, What the Constitution Means to Me (Hayes Theater 2019).

3. *See, e.g.*, RICHARD BEEMAN, PLAIN, HONEST MEN: THE MAKING OF THE AMERICAN CONSTITUTION (2009); PAULINE MAIER, RATIFICATION: THE PEOPLE DEBATE THE CONSTITUTION, 1787–1788 (2010); GORDON S. WOOD, THE CREATION OF THE AMERICAN REPUBLIC, 1776–1787 (2d ed. 1998); and other works cited herein.
4. *See, e.g.*, We the People, *Founding Stories of America's Founding Documents*, NAT'L CONST. CTR. (Sept. 10, 2020), https://constitutioncenter.org/news-debate/podcasts// founding-stories-of-americas-founding-documents; Civics 101, *Founding Documents: The Constitution*, N.H. PUB. RADIO (Feb. 12, 2019), https://www.civics101podcast.org /civics-101-episodes/constitution; Amarica's Constitution, AKHIL REED AMAR, https:// akhilamar.com/podcast-2/.
5. Joey Stylez et al., *27: The Most Perfect Album*, WNYC STUDIOS (2018).
6. Corinne Segal & Daniel Mortiz-Rabson, *After Khan Speech, Pocket Constitution Becomes Best-Seller*, PBS (July 31, 2016, 11:09 AM), https://www.pbs.org/newshour/nation /khan-speech-pocket-constitution-becomes-amazon-best-seller.
7. Abraham Lincoln, Address Before the Young Men's Lyceum of Springfield, Illinois (Jan. 27, 1838), *in* 1 THE COLLECTED WORKS OF ABRAHAM LINCOLN 108, 112 (Roy P. Basler, ed., 1953).
8. David S. Law & Mila Versteeg, *The Declining Influence of the United States Constitution*, 87 N.Y.U. L. REV. 762, 807 (2012).
9. SOPHIE BOYRON, THE CONSTITUTION OF FRANCE: A CONTEXTUAL ANALYSIS 6–18 (2013); Martin A. Rogoff, *A Comparison of Constitutionalism in France and the United States*, 49 ME. L. REV. 21, 60–61, 61 n.176 (1997).
10. Had we been sufficiently wealthy, we would have briefly had the right to vote in New Jersey, which permitted women and African Americans who met certain property ownership requirements to vote from 1776 to 1807. Jennifer Schuessler, *On the Trail of America's First Women to Vote*, N.Y. TIMES (Aug. 7, 2020), https://www.nytimes.com /2020/02/24/arts/first-women-voters-new-jersey.html. But women did not generally have the right to vote across the country until 1920, when the Nineteenth Amendment was ratified. U.S. CONST. amend. XIX.
11. *See, e.g., Slave Code for the District of Columbia,* LIBR. OF CONG., https://www.loc.gov /collections/slavery-and-the-judiciary-from-1740-to-1860/articles-and-essays/slave -code-for-the-district-of-columbia/.
12. Although the exact property requirements varied among the thirteen colonies, fifty acres of land was a common requirement. *See* OSCAR THEODORE BARCK, JR. & HUGH TALMAGE LEFLER, COLONIAL AMERICA 191 (2d ed. 1968).
13. Georgia, New Hampshire, New Jersey, and South Carolina required officeholders to be Protestant. North Carolina barred officeholders who denied the "truth of the Protestant religion." Michael W. McConnell, *Establishment and Disestablishment at the Founding, Part I: Establishment of Religion*, 44 WM. & MARY L. REV. 2105, 2178 (2003).
14. The Catholic delegates were Thomas Fitzsimons of Pennsylvania and Daniel Carroll of Maryland. *Convention: A Daily Journal, Sunday, May 27, 1787*, CONCORDIA UNIV. IRVINE CTR. FOR CIVICS EDUC. (May 27, 2020), https://www.cui.edu/centers-institutes /center-for-civics-education/convention-a-daily-journal/post/sunday-may-27-1787.
15. *See* U.S. CONST. amends. I–XXVII.
16. *See* U.S. CONST. amends. XX (presidential succession), XXV (same), XXVII (congressional compensation), XI (lawsuits against states).

17. *See* U.S. Const. amends. I–IX (enumerating individual rights in the Bill of Rights), XIII (abolishing slavery), XV (forbidding race-based disenfranchisement), XIX (forbidding sex-based disenfranchisement), XXIII (granting citizens of the District of Columbia the right to vote in presidential elections), XXIV (abolishing the poll tax), and XXVI (forbidding age-based disenfranchisement of those over the age of eighteen).
18. Carol Berkin, The Bill of Rights: The Fight to Secure America's Liberties 18 (2015); Leonard W. Levy, Origins of the Bill of Rights 20 (1999).
19. The Federalist No. 84, at 513–14 (Alexander Hamilton) (Clinton Rossiter, ed., 1961).
20. Levy, *supra* note 18, at 9–11; Christopher Collier & James Lincoln Collier, Decision in Philadelphia: The Constitutional Convention of 1787, at 254 (1986); *see also* David O. Stewart, The Summer of 1787: The Men Who Invented the Constitution 227 (2007) (describing one objector's argument that a bill of rights that "beg[an] with declaring that all men are by nature born free" would be made with "a very bad grace, when a large part of our property consists in men who are actually born slaves").
21. *See* Richard Labunski, James Madison and the Struggle for the Bill of Rights 60–63 (2006).
22. Levy, *supra* note 18, at 30; *see also* W. B. Allen & Gordon Lloyd, *Interpretive Essay* in The Essential Antifederalists viii, xiii–xiv (W. B. Allen & Gordon Lloyd eds., 1985).
23. Robert A. Goldwin, From Parchment to Power: How James Madison Used the Bill of Rights to Save the Constitution 40–41 (1997). Goldwin, *supra* note 9, at 40–41; Berkin, *supra* note 18, at 33.
24. Berkin, *supra* note 18, at 33–35; Labunski, *supra* note 21, at 10, 129–31.
25. *See* Berkin, *supra* note 18, at 39, 55–56.
26. Labunski, *supra* note 21, at 199.
27. 1 Annals of Cong. 424–50 (1789) (Joseph Gales, ed., 1834) (including the debates in the House of Representatives on June 8, 1789); Labunski, *supra* note 21, at 198.
28. *See* Levy, *supra* note 18, at 34, 36–37.
29. *Id.* at 34–35, 37, 39.
30. *See id.* at 40.
31. Berkin, *supra* note 18, at 132.
32. Michael J. Klarman, The Framers' Coup: The Making of the United States Constitution 547, 795 n.6 (2016) (citing Letter from Thomas Jefferson to James Madison (Mar. 15, 1789), *in* 12 The Papers of James Madison 13 (Charles F. Hobson et al. eds., 1979)).
33. *See id.* at 547.
34. Labunski, *supra* note 21, at 200.
35. *Id.*
36. *Id.*
37. U.S. Const. art. V.
38. *Id.* art. I, § 7, cl. 2.
39. *Id.* art. V.
40. Although we've never had a second constitutional convention, the idea has been much discussed—both in the past and more recently. *See, e.g.*, *The Idea of a Second Convention*, Univ. of Wis. Madison Ctr. for Const. Stud., https://csac.history.wisc.edu/document-collections/themes-of-the-ratification-period/idea-of-a-second-convention/; Carl Hulse, *A Second Constitutional Convention? Some Republicans Want to*

Force One, N.Y. Times (Sept. 4, 2022), https://www.nytimes.com/2022/09/04/us/politics/constitutional-convention-republican-states.html.

41. U.S. Const. art. V.
42. Articles of Confederation of 1781, art. XIII, para. 1 ("[N]or shall any alteration at any time hereafter be made in any of [the articles]; unless such alteration be agreed to in a congress of the united states, and be afterwards confirmed by the legislatures of every state").
43. *See generally* Klarman, *supra* note 32, at 24–41 (describing failed efforts at amending the Articles).
44. *See, e.g.*, *id.* at 30–32 (describing New York's efforts to impede a federal revenue-raising amendment in 1783); *id.* at 34–38 (detailing Virginia's opposition to a 1784 commerce amendment).
45. 2 The Records of the Federal Convention of 1787, at 558 (Max Farrand, ed., 1911) [hereinafter Farrand's Records].
46. Debates and Other Proceedings of the Convention of Virginia 72–73 (David Robertson, ed., Richmond, Enquirer-Press 2d ed. 1805).
47. Klarman, *supra* note 32, at 87–88, 656 nn.52–53 (citing Jonathan, Letter to the Editor, *From the Boston Gazette*, U.S. Chron. (Providence), May 25, 1786, at 2 ("Rogue-Island" and "Fool-Island"), *id.* at 656 n.52).
48. Stewart, *supra* note 20, at 25; *Introduction* to 24 The Documentary History of the Ratification of the Constitution: Ratification by the States, Rhode Island xxvi, xxxv, xli, xliv (John P. Kaminski et al. eds., 2011).
49. *See* 2 Farrand's Records, *supra* note 45, at 555, 558–59.
50. *See id.* at 555–59; *see also* 1 *id.* at 202–03 (debating whether Congress's consent should be required for amendment).
51. The Federalist No. 43, *supra* note 19, at 278 (James Madison).
52. Donald S. Lutz, *Toward a Theory of Constitutional Amendment*, 88 Am. Pol. Sci. Rev. 355, 369 tbl.C-1 (1994).
53. Jeffrey S. Sutton, Who Decides? States as Laboratories of Constitutional Experimentation 343 (2022).
54. John Dinan, State Constitutional Politics 23 (2018).
55. *See, e.g.*, Jedediah Britton-Purdy, *The Constitutional Flaw That's Killing American Democracy*, The Atlantic (Aug. 28, 2022), https://www.theatlantic.com/ideas/archive/2022/08/framers-constitution-democracy/671155/; Sarah Isgur, Opinion, *It's Time to Amend the Constitution*, Politico (Jan. 8, 2022, 7:00 AM), https://www.politico.com/news/magazine/2022/01/08/scalia-was-right-make-amending-the-constitution-easier-526780; Jesse Wegman, Opinion, *Thomas Jefferson Gave the Constitution 19 Years. Look Where We Are Now.*, N.Y. Times (Aug. 4, 2021), https://www.nytimes.com/2021/08/04/opinion/amend-constitution.html; *see also* Marcia Coyle, *Scalia, Ginsburg Offer Amendments to the Constitution*, Law.com (Apr. 17, 2014, 8:04 PM), https://www.law.com/nationallawjournal/almID/1202651605161/.
56. 2 U.S. (2 Dall.) 419 (1793); Donald L. Boren, *Suing a State in Federal Court Under a Private Cause of Action: An Eleventh Amendment Primer*, 37 Clev. St. L. Rev. 417, 426–29 (1989) (describing the reaction to *Chisholm*).
57. Boren, *supra* note 56, at 421 n.22; 5 The Documentary History of the Supreme Court of the United States, 1789–1800, at 127–28 (Maeva Marcus, ed., 1994).

58. *See, e.g.*, Labunski, *supra* note 21, at 76–77, 79 (describing a debate at the Virginia Ratifying Convention over the balance of state and federal authority).
59. *Chisholm*, 2 U.S. (2 Dall.) at 479.
60. U.S. Const. art. III, § 2.
61. *Chisholm*, 2 U.S. (2 Dall.) at 476–77, 479.
62. Amy Coney Barrett, *Introduction*, 83 Notre Dame L. Rev. 1147, 1149 (2008).
63. For a summary of this response, see 1 Charles Warren, The Supreme Court in United States History 96–102 (1922).
64. 4 Annals of Cong. 30–31 (1794) (Senate); *id.* at 477–78 (House).
65. *Id.* at 476–77; Jeanne M. Dennis et al., Cong. Rsch. Serv., The Constitution of the United States of America: Analysis and Interpretation, S. Doc. No. 117-12, at 42 (2022).
66. *See* U.S. Const. amends. XII, XIII.
67. *Id.* amend. XIII.
68. *Id.* amend. XIV, § 1; see Plessy v. Ferguson, 163 U.S. 537, 551–52 (1896).
69. 163 U.S. at 551–52.
70. Brown v. Bd. of Educ., 347 U.S. 483, 494–95 (1954).
71. Adarand Constructors, Inc. v. Peña, 515 U.S. 200, 227 (1995).
72. Barron v. Baltimore, 32 U.S. (7 Pet.) 243, 247, 250 (1833).
73. U.S. Const. amend. I (emphasis added).
74. *Id.* amend. XIV, § 1.
75. 268 U.S. 652, 666 (1925).
76. *See, e.g.*, Mapp v. Ohio, 367 U.S. 643 (1961) (Fourth Amendment right against unreasonable searches and seizures); Gideon v. Wainwright, 372 U.S. 335 (1963) (Sixth Amendment right to counsel in criminal cases); Timbs v. Indiana, 586 U.S. 146 (2019) (Eighth Amendment right against excessive fines).
77. Ramos v. Louisiana, 590 U.S. 83, 93 (2020).
78. U.S. Const. amends. XV, § 2, XIV, § 5, XIII, § 2.
79. 92 U.S. 214, 216–17, 221–22 (1875).
80. U.S. Const. amend. XIX.
81. *Id.* amend. XXVI.
82. *Id.* amend. XXIV.
83. *Id.* amend. XXIII.
84. *Id.* amend. XVII.
85. *See id.* amends. XVI–XXVII.
86. *See* Gerard N. Magliocca, Opinion, *The Father of the 14th Amendment*, N.Y. Times: Opinionator (Sept. 17, 2013, 12:20 PM), https://archive.nytimes.com/opinionator.blogs.nytimes.com/2013/09/17/the-father-of-the-14th-amendment/ (John Bingham); Editorial, *Honors, at Last, for Ida B. Wells, "a Sword Among Lions,"* N.Y. Times (July 31, 2018), https://www.nytimes.com/2018/07/31/opinion/honors-at-last-for-ida-b-wells-a-sword-among-lions.html; *Visionaries*, Libr. of Cong., https://www.loc.gov/collections/women-of-protest/articles-and-essays/selected-leaders-of-the-national-womans-party/visionaries/ (Alice Paul); *see also* Larry J. Easterling, *Sen. Joseph L. Bristow and the Seventeenth Amendment*, 41 Kan. Hist. Q. 488 (1975).
87. Richard B. Bernstein, *The Sleeper Wakes: The History and Legacy of the Twenty-Seventh Amendment*, 61 Fordham L. Rev. 497, 498, 536 (1992).
88. *Id.* at 536.

89. *Id.* at 537.
90. *Id.*
91. Scott Bomboy, *How a College Term Paper Led to a Constitutional Amendment*, Nat'l Const. Ctr. (May 7, 2024), https://constitutioncenter.org/blog/how-a-c-grade-college-term-paper-led-to-a-constitutional-amendment; Matt Largey, *The Bad Grade That Changed the U.S. Constitution*, NPR (May 5, 2017, 5:00 AM), https://www.npr.org/2017/05/05/526900818/the-bad-grade-that-changed-the-u-s-constitution.
92. Bernstein, *supra* note 87, at 537.
93. *Id.* at 539.
94. Rachel White, *The "C" That Changed the Constitution*, Life & Letters (Jan. 11, 2018), https://lifeandletters.la.utexas.edu/2018/01/the-c-that-changed-the-constitution/.
95. *Measures Proposed to Amend the Constitution*, U.S. Senate, https://www.senate.gov/legislative/MeasuresProposedToAmendTheConstitution.htm.
96. H.R. Res. 8, 25th Cong. (1838); *Joint Resolution Prohibiting Dueling*, Hist., Art & Archives, U.S. House of Representatives, https://history.house.gov/HouseRecord/Detail/15032448841.
97. *A Fatal Duel Between Members in 1838*, Hist., Art & Archives, U.S. House of Representatives, https://history.house.gov/Historical-Highlights/1800-1850/A-fatal-duel-between-Members-in-1838/.
98. Scott Bomboy, *Five "Unusual" Amendments That Never Made It into the Constitution*, Nat'l Const. Ctr. (Feb. 23, 2018), https://constitutioncenter.org/blog/five-unusual-amendments-that-never-made-it-into-the-constitution.
99. *Id.*
100. *See* Dennis et al., *supra* note 65, at 58.
101. *See* Joint Resolution Proposing Twelve Amendments to the Constitution, 1 Pub. Res., 1st Cong., 1 Stat. 97 (1789). Scholars disagree about the interpretation of this amendment. Some say that it would have mandated continual increases. *See, e.g.*, Sanford Levinson, *Article V After 230 Years: Time for a Tune Up*, 67 Drake L. Rev. 913, 930 (2019). Others maintain that it would have left the number of representatives in Congress's hands once the number in the House reached 200. *See, e.g.*, John Vile, Book Review, 14 Const. Comment. 416, 426 (1997) (reviewing David E. Kyvig, Explicit & Authentic Acts: Amending the U.S. Constitution, 1776–1995 (1996)). Under the latter view, the amendment "would simply be irrelevant" today. *Id.*
102. Levinson, *supra* note 101, at 930; Robert Longley, *The Original Bill of Rights Had 12 Amendments*, ThoughtCo (Oct. 6, 2021), https://www.thoughtco.com/original-bill-of-rights-and-amendments-3322334.
103. Resolution Proposing an Amendment to the Constitution of the United States, J. Res. 2, 11th Cong., 2 Stat. 613 (1810); Scott Bomboy, *The Case of the Missing 13th Amendment to the Constitution*, Nat'l Const. Ctr. (Dec. 6, 2016), https://constitutioncenter.org/blog/the-case-of-the-missing-13th-amendment-to-the-constitution.
104. *American Citizens with Honorary British Knighthoods and Damehoods*, The Gazette (Nov. 25, 2019), https://www.thegazette.co.uk/awards-and-accreditation/content/103441.
105. Daniel W. Crofts, Lincoln & the Politics of Slavery: The Other Thirteenth Amendment and the Struggle to Save the Union 125–41 (2016).

106. Joint Resolution to Amend the Constitution of the United States, J. Res. 13, 36th Cong., 12 Stat. 251 (1861).
107. Five states—Kentucky, Rhode Island, Illinois, Ohio, and Maryland—ratified the amendment between 1861 and 1863. Southern states did not bother with ratification amid their secession from the Union. Ohio quickly voted to rescind its ratification in 1864, and more recently, Maryland and Illinois followed suit in 2014 and 2022, respectively. *See* CROFTS, *supra* note 105, at 245–54; Robert Longley, *The Corwin Amendment, Enslavement, and Abraham Lincoln*, THOUGHTCO (Oct. 6, 2021), https://www.thoughtco.com/corwin-amendment-slavery-and-lincoln-4160928; *Plummer Reveals Legislation Rescinding Corwin Amendment*, E. CENT. REP. (May 3, 2022), https://eastcentralreporter.com/stories/624613761-plummer-reveals-legislation-rescinding-corwin-amendment-it-rights-a-historical-wrong-that-has-long-tarnished-our-state-s-reputation.
108. 247 U.S. 251, 276–77 (1918).
109. Joint Resolution Proposing an Amendment to the Constitution of the United States, H.R.J. Res. 184, 68th Cong., 43 Stat. 670 (1924).
110. Congress declined to insert a ratification deadline into the text of the child labor amendment. *See* DENNIS ET AL., *supra* note 65, at 59.
111. United States v. Darby, 312 U.S. 100, 116–17 (1941).
112. *See, e.g.*, 29 U.S.C. § 212.
113. Joint Resolution Proposing an Amendment to the Constitution to Provide for the Representation of the District of Columbia in the Congress, H.R.J. Res. 554, 95th Cong., 92 Stat. 3795 (1978).
114. Joint Resolution Proposing an Amendment to the Constitution of the United States Relative to Equal Rights for Men and Women, H.R.J. Res. 208, 92d Cong., 86 Stat. 1523 (1972).; DENNIS ET AL., *supra* note 65, at 59; see *Women's Rights: Equal Rights Amendment*, NAT'L ARCHIVES (Dec. 19, 2024), https://www.archives.gov/women/era#:~:text=Three%20years%20after%20the%20ratification,%2C%20employment%2C%20and%20other%20matters.
115. *The Senate Passes the Equal Rights Amendment*, U.S. SENATE, https://www.senate.gov/artandhistory/history/minute/Senate_passes_ERA.htm; Thomas H. Neale, Cong. Rsch. Serv., R42979, The Proposed Equal Rights Amendment: Contemporary Ratification Issues 15 (2019).
116. Neale, *supra* note 115, at 15.
117. *See* PHYLLIS SCHLAFLY, THE POWER OF THE POSITIVE WOMAN 82–84, 95 (1977).
118. Neale, *supra* note 115, at 16 (noting that the "constitutionality of [rescission] has long been questioned").
119. *Id.* at 1.
120. Joint Resolution Extending the Deadline for the Ratification of the Equal Rights Amendment, H.R.J. Res. 638, 95th Cong., 92 Stat. 3799 (1978); Neale, *supra* note 115, at 17 (233–189 (House) and 60–36 (Senate)).
121. Neale, *supra* note 115, at 1.

Chapter 10 | United yet Distinct

1. Gregg v. Georgia, 428 U.S. 153, 187 (1976).
2. *Compare* Fla. Dep't of Educ. Order No. 2020-EO-06 (July 6, 2020), https://www.fldoe

.org/core/fileparse.php/19861/urlt/doe-2020-eo-06.pdf (Florida commissioner of the Department of Education ordering schools to reopen in August 2020), *with* Daniel J. Willis & John Fensterwald, *Over Half of California Public School Students Remain in Distance Learning*, EdSource (May 5, 2021), https://edsource.org/2021/new-data-55-of-california-public-school-students-remain-in-distance-learning/653848 (noting that many California schools remained closed as of May 2021), *and* Naomi Ondrasek, Adam K. Edgerton, & Jennifer A. Bland, *Reopening Schools Safely in California: District Examples of Multilayered Mitigation*, Learning Pol'y Inst. (Oct. 11, 2021), https://learningpolicyinstitute.org/product/safe-school-reopening-ca-multi-district-brief (observing that many California schools reopened in Fall 2021).

3. *Compare* Fla. Exec. Order No. 21-175 (July 30, 2021), https://www.flgov.com/eog/sites/default/files/executive-orders/2024/EO_21-175.pdf (Florida executive order prohibiting schools from requiring children to wear masks in schools), *with Governors Newsom, Brown and Inslee Announce Updated Health Guidance*, Off. of Governor Gavin Newsom (Feb. 28, 2022), https://www.gov.ca.gov/2022/02/28/governors-newsom-brown-and-inslee-announce-updated-health-guidance/ (statement of California governor Gavin Newsom saying that masks in schools will not be required starting in March 2022).
4. The United States occupies 3.806 million square miles and has a population of approximately 341 million, while England occupies 50,301 square miles and has a population of roughly 58 million. *Compare State Area Measurements and Internal Point Coordinates*, U.S. Census Bureau (2010), https://www.census.gov/geographies/reference-files/2010/geo/state-area.html, *and U.S. and World Population Clock*, U.S. Census Bureau, https://www.census.gov/popclock/, *with England: Facts and Stats*, Britannica, https://www.britannica.com/facts/England, *and England Population Mid-year Estimate*, Off. for Nat'l Stat., https://www.ons.gov.uk/peoplepopulationandcommunity/populationandmigration/populationestimates/timeseries/enpop/pop. Expanding out to the United Kingdom, which includes England, Scotland, Northern Ireland, and Wales, does not significantly change the picture. The U.K. is 93,630 square miles and contains roughly 67 million people. *See United Kingdom: Facts & Stats*, Britannica, https://www.britannica.com/facts/United-Kingdom; *Population Estimates for the UK*, Off. for Nat'l Stat. (Dec. 21, 2022), https://www.ons.gov.uk/peoplepopulationandcommunity/populationandmigration/populationestimates/bulletins/annualmidyearpopulationestimates/mid2021#the-uk-population-at-mid-2021. And even though it comprises several countries, it is not a federal system like ours. The United States also far outstrips the size and population of France, Italy, and Spain, none of which has a federal system. France (210,016 square miles/66.147 million), Italy (116,629 square miles/58.653 million), and Spain (195,360 square miles/48.736 million). *See France: Facts & Stats*, Britannica, https://www.britannica.com/facts/France; *Italy: Facts & Stats*, Britannica, https://www.britannica.com/place/Italy; *Spain: Facts & Stats*, Britannica, https://www.britannica.com/facts/Spain. France is the largest of these, and the United States is more than fourteen times bigger in size and five times larger in population.
5. *Compare England: Facts and Stats*, *supra* note 4, *with Alabama: Facts & Stats*, Britannica, https://www.britannica.com/facts/Alabama-state.
6. *Compare Quick Facts Wisconsin; Illinois; Indiana*, U.S. Census Bureau, https://www

.census.gov/quickfacts/fact/table/WI,IL,IN, *with Australia: Facts & Stats*, BRITANNICA, https://www.britannica.com/facts/Australia.

7. *See generally* RICHARD F. HAMM, SHAPING THE EIGHTEENTH AMENDMENT: TEMPERANCE REFORM, LEGAL CULTURE, AND THE POLITY, 1880–1920 (1995).
8. Washington v. Glucksberg, 521 U.S. 702, 721 (1997) (internal quotation marks and citations omitted).
9. *See, e.g.*, JOHN HART ELY, DEMOCRACY AND DISTRUST: A THEORY OF JUDICIAL REVIEW 18 (1980).
10. Obergefell v. Hodges, 576 U.S. 644, 664 (2015).
11. Lawrence v. Texas, 539 U.S. 558, 578 (2003).
12. Griswold v. Connecticut, 381 U.S. 479, 485 (1965) (holding that the Due Process Clause protects the right of married couples to use contraceptives); *see also* Eisenstadt v. Baird, 405 U.S. 438, 453–54 (1972) (extending the right to use contraceptives to unmarried persons).
13. Pierce v. Soc'y of Sisters, 268 U.S. 510, 534–35 (1925).
14. Williamson v. Lee Optical of Okla., Inc., 348 U.S. 483, 488 (1955).
15. Washington v. Glucksberg, 521 U.S. 702, 705 (1997).
16. Dobbs v. Jackson Women's Health Org., 597 U.S. 215, 231 (2022).
17. *See* Elizabeth C. Larson, Cong. Rsch. Serv., R45805, Women's Suffrage: Fact Sheet 3–4 (2021); *see also* JEFFREY S. SUTTON, 51 IMPERFECT SOLUTIONS: STATES AND THE MAKING OF AMERICAN CONSTITUTIONAL LAW 11 (2018).
18. *See, e.g.*, TEX. CONST. art. I, § 6; IDAHO CONST. art. I, § 4; N.Y. CONST. art. I, § 3; N.J. CONST. art. I, § 3.
19. *See, e.g.*, ALASKA CONST. art. I, § 22; ARIZ. CONST. art. II, § 8.
20. *See, e.g.*, NEV. CONST. art I, § 6.
21. U.S. CONST. amend. VIII.
22. *See, e.g.*, ARIZ. CONST. art. IV, pt. 2, § 1; CAL. CONST. art. XXI, § 2; COLO. CONST. art. V, § 44 ; N.Y. CONST. art. III, § 5-b.
23. KY. CONST. § 228.
24. ALASKA CONST. art. VIII, § 15.
25. N.Y. CONST. art. XIV, § 1.
26. OHIO CONST. art. XV, § 6, cl. (c)(1).
27. *See* SUTTON, *supra* note 17, at 213.
28. *See Initiative and Referendum Processes*, NAT'L CONF. STATE LEGISLATURES, https://www.ncsl.org/elections-and-campaigns/initiative-and-referendum-processes (Sept. 23, 2024).
29. M'Culloch v. Maryland, 17 U.S. (4 Wheat.) 316, 407 (1819).
30. Gonzales v. Raich, 545 U.S. 1, 29 (2005).
31. U.S. CONST. art. VI, cl. 2.
32. *See* Thomas Jefferson, *Opinion on the Constitutionality of a National Bank* (Feb. 15, 1791), *in* 5 THE WRITINGS OF THOMAS JEFFERSON 284 (Paul Leicester Ford, ed., 1895).
33. *See* Edmund Randolph, *Opinion of Edmund Randolph* (Feb. 12, 1791), *in* LEGISLATIVE AND DOCUMENTARY HISTORY OF THE BANK OF THE UNITED STATES 86, 86–89 (M. St. Clair Clarke & D. A. Hall eds., 1832); *see also Attorney General's Opinion No. 2* (Feb. 12, 1791), *in id.*, at 89–91.
34. *See* Jefferson, *supra* note 32, at 287.

35. *Id.* (emphasis omitted).
36. *See* Alexander Hamilton, *On the Constitutionality of a National Bank* (Feb. 23, 1791), *in* 1 Works of Alexander Hamilton 111 (J. Seymore, ed., 1810).
37. *Id.* at 115.
38. *Id.* at 118.
39. *Id.*
40. Act of Feb. 25, 1791, ch. 10, 1 Stat. 191 (establishing the first Bank of the United States).
41. M'Culloch v. Maryland, 17 U.S. (4 Wheat.) 316, 421–23 (1819).
42. *Id.* at 421.
43. 317 U.S. 111 (1942).
44. U.S. Const. art. I, § 8, cl. 3.
45. *Wickard*, 317 U.S. at 127.
46. *Id.* at 127–28.
47. *Id.* at 128.
48. 514 U.S. 549 (1995).
49. *Id.* at 561.
50. 529 U.S. 598 (2000).
51. *Id.* at 613.
52. 567 U.S. 519, 549–61 (2012).
53. *Lopez*, 514 U.S. at 619–24 (Breyer, J., dissenting).
54. *Morrison*, 529 U.S. at 628–34 (Souter, J., dissenting).
55. *NFIB*, 567 U.S. at 592–94, 603–04 (Ginsburg, J., concurring in part and dissenting in part).
56. *Id.* at 603–04; *Morrison*, 529 U.S. at 659–60 (Breyer, J., dissenting); *Lopez*, 514 U.S. at 631 (Breyer, J., dissenting).
57. *NFIB*, 567 U.S. at 603 (Ginsburg, J., concurring in part and dissenting in part); *Morrison*, 529 U.S. at 643–44 (Souter, J., dissenting); *Lopez*, 514 U.S. at 616–17 (Breyer, J., dissenting).
58. *NFIB*, 567 U.S. at 615–17 (Ginsburg, J., concurring in part and dissenting in part).
59. U.S. Const. art. I, § 8, cl. 1.
60. *See* South Dakota v. Dole, 483 U.S. 203, 205 (1987).
61. *See* Lisa Belkin, *Wyoming Finally Raises Its Drinking Age*, N.Y. Times, July 1, 1988, at A8.
62. *NFIB*, 567 U.S. at 581–82.
63. Act of Apr. 13, 2022, Pub. L. No. 117-111, § 1(a)(13), 136 Stat. 1166.
64. Letter from George Washington to Marquis de Lafayette (Feb. 7, 1788), *reprinted in Founders Online*, Nat'l Archives, https://founders.archives.gov/documents/Washington/04-06-02-0079.

Chapter 11 | Can I Have That in Writing?

1. Gary Lawson, *On Reading Recipes . . . and Constitutions*, 85 Geo. L. J. 1823 (1997).
2. *See* Albert L. Sturm, *The Development of American State Constitutions*, 12 Publius 57, 58 (1982) (depicting by chart that the constitutions of Delaware, Georgia, Maryland, Massachusetts, New Hampshire, New Jersey, New York, North Carolina, Pennsylvania, South Carolina, Vermont, and Virginia were adopted prior to the Federal Constitution's ratification in 1789); *see also id.* at 60 (explaining that Connecticut and

Rhode Island made some alterations to their royal charters and used those documents as their constitutions well into the nineteenth century); John J. Dinan, The American State Constitutional Tradition 8–9 (2006).

3. U.S. Const. art. VI, cl. 3 (emphasis added); *see also* U.S. Const. art. II, § 1, cl. 8.
4. *See* David A. Strauss, The Living Constitution 104–05 (2010).
5. *See* Thomas H. Neale, Cong. Rsch. Serv., R40864, Presidential Terms and Tenure: Perspectives and Proposals for Change 13–18 (2019).
6. *Id.* at 17; *see also* Jack M. Beermann, *A Skeptical View of a Skeptical View of Presidential Term Limits*, 43 Conn. L. Rev. 1105, 1109 n.13 (2011) (recounting the story of President Theodore Roosevelt's run for a third term).
7. *See* Martin B. Gold, The Twenty-Second Amendment and the Limits of Presidential Tenure: A Tradition Restored 123–217 (2020).
8. *See* Stephen W. Stathis, *The Twenty-Second Amendment: A Practical Remedy or Partisan Maneuver?*, 7 Const. Comment. 61, 69–70 (1990) (noting that one goal behind the adoption of the Twenty-Second Amendment was to place "democratic restraint upon any future, dangerously ambitious demagogue").
9. U.S. Const. amend. XXII.
10. Letter from Thomas Jefferson to James Madison (Sept. 6, 1789), *in* 6 The Works of Thomas Jefferson 3, 9 (Paul Leicester Ford, ed. 1904).
11. *Id.* at 8.
12. Steven G. Calabresi, *A Critical Introduction to the Originalism Debate*, 31 Harv. J.L. & Pub. Pol'y 875, 879–81 (2008).
13. *Cf.* Stephen E. Sachs, *Originalism as a Theory of Legal Change*, 38 Harv. J.L. & Pub. Pol'y 817 (2015).
14. Betsy Woodruff, *The History of the Pocket Constitution*, Slate (Jan. 28, 2015), https://slate.com/news-and-politics/2015/01/history-of-the-pocket-constitution-these-miniature-versions-of-americas-founding-charter-became-popular-before-the-tea-party.html.
15. Clean Water Act, 33 U.S.C. §§ 1251–1389; Clean Air Act, 42 U.S.C. §§ 7401–7675.
16. National Environmental Policy Act of 1969, 42 U.S.C. § 4321–4370.
17. Comprehensive Environmental Response, Compensation, and Liability Act, 42 U.S.C. §§ 9601–9675.
18. 198 U.S. 45 (1905).
19. *Id.* at 57 ("There is no reasonable ground for interfering with the liberty of person or the right of free contract, by determining the hours of labor, in the occupation of a baker.").
20. *Id.* at 58.
21. *Id.* at 59.
22. *Id.* at 76 (Holmes, J., dissenting).
23. *Id.*
24. *Id.* at 66–68 (Harlan, J. dissenting).
25. *Id.* at 74 (quoting *Atkin v. Kansas*, 191 U.S. 207, 223 (1903)).
26. West Coast Hotel v. Parrish, 300 U.S. 379 (1937); *see, e.g.*, David A. Strauss, *Why Was* Lochner *Wrong?*, 70 U. Chi. L. Rev. 373 (2003).
27. Washington v. Glucksberg, 521 U.S. 702, 720 (1997).
28. *Id.* at 721 (internal quotation marks and citations omitted).

29. *Id.* at 721, 724 (internal quotation marks omitted) (emphasis added).
30. *Id.* at 720–22.
31. *Id.* at 722.
32. *Id.* at 707.
33. *Id.* at 727.
34. *Id.* at 721, 724 (internal quotation marks omitted) (emphasis added).
35. Lochner v. New York, 198 U.S. 45, 76 (1905) (Holmes, J., dissenting).
36. 597 U.S. 215, 231 (2022). *Dobbs* also addressed whether to overrule *Roe v. Wade* under the Court's doctrine of stare decisis. Consistent with the focus of this chapter, however, I discuss only the Court's analysis of substantive due process.
37. Planned Parenthood v. Casey, 505 U.S. 833, 852 (1992); Roe v. Wade, 410 U.S. 113, 159 (1973).
38. *Casey*, 505 U.S. at 852.
39. *Dobbs*, 597 U.S. at 250; *see also id.* (noting that the states that had liberalized their abortion laws by 1973 "still criminalized some abortions and regulated them more stringently than Roe would allow").
40. *Id.* at 260 n.47.
41. Ruth Bader Ginsburg, *Speaking in a Judicial Voice*, 67 N.Y.U. L. Rev. 1185, 1208 (1992).
42. *Dobbs,* 597 U.S. at 231 (quoting Washington v. Glucksberg, 521 U.S. 702, 720–21 (1997)).
43. *Dobbs,* 597 U.S. at 228–29 (quoting Doe v. Bolton, 410 U.S. 179, 222 (1973) (White, J., dissenting)).
44. *Id.* at 374 (Breyer, Sotomayor, & Kagan, JJ., dissenting).
45. *Id.*
46. Washington v. Glucksberg, 521 U.S. 702, 720–21 (1997) (internal quotation marks and citations omitted).
47. *Dobbs*, 597 U.S. at 380 (Breyer, Sotomayor, & Kagan, JJ., dissenting).
48. *Id.*

Chapter 12 | Past Meets Present

1. The Sea Bag: Hurricane Katrina and a Love Revealed 91 (Emily Vath Nolan & Bruce Nolan eds., 2014).
2. *Id.* at 92.
3. *Id.* at 10.
4. William Shakespeare, Macbeth, act V, sc. i, l. 32.
5. 541 U.S. 36, 42–43 (2004) (citations omitted).
6. *Id.* at 43.
7. *Id.* at 43–47.
8. *Id.* at 47–50.
9. *Id.* at 50–53.
10. *Id.* at 53–54.
11. Davis v. Washington, 547 U.S. 813, 822 (2006).
12. *Crawford*, 541 U.S. at 53–55.
13. *Id.* at 51–52, 65.
14. *Id.* at 68–69.
15. William J. Brennan, Jr., *Construing the Constitution*, 19 U.C. Davis L. Rev. 2, 7 (1985).

16. *Id.* (emphasis added).
17. Keith E. Whittington, *Originalism: A Critical Introduction*, 82 Ford. L. Rev. 375, 389–91 (2013).
18. Brennan, *supra* note 15, at 8.
19. Stephen Breyer, Reading the Constitution 200 (2024).
20. Steven D. Smith, *Reply to Koppelman: Originalism and the (Merely) Human Constitution*, 27 Const. Comm. 189, 193 (2010) (emphasis added).
21. *Compare, e.g.*, Michigan v. Bryant, 562 U.S. 344, 348–49 (2011) (statements made by a dying gunshot victim who identified his killer are not testimonial), *with id.* at 384–87 (Scalia, J., dissenting) (yes, they are).
22. *Compare, e.g.*, Vidal v. Elster, 602 U.S. 286, 301–08 (2024) (embracing a "history and tradition" test for assessing the constitutionality of trademark regulations), *with id.* at 323–24 (Barrett, J., concurring in part) (arguing in favor of a means-ends test).
23. 3 William Blackstone, Commentaries *288 (searches and seizures); 1 William Blackstone, Commentaries *139 (right to bear arms), 4 William Blackstone, Commentaries *342 (trial by jury), 1 William Blackstone, Commentaries, *46 (ex post facto laws).
24. *See* Gregory E. Maggs, *A Critical Guide to Using the Legislative History of the Fourteenth Amendment to Determine Its Original Meaning*, 49 Conn. L. Rev. 1069 (2017).
25. *See* Amy Coney Barrett & John Copeland Nagle, *Congressional Originalism*, 19 U. Pa. J. Const. L. 1, 5 (2016).
26. *Id.* at 384–85.
27. 1 Stat. 596 (1798).
28. *Id.* at § 2.
29. Walter Berns, *Freedom of the Press and the Alien and Sedition Laws: A Reappraisal*, 1970 Sup. Ct. Rev. 109, 111–12 (1970).
30. *See, e.g.*, N.Y. Times Co. v. Sullivan, 376 U.S. 254, 276 (1964) ("Although the Sedition Act was never tested in this Court, the attack upon its validity has carried the day in the court of history."); Akhil Reed Amar, The Constitution Today: Timeless Lessons for the Issues of Our Era 7 (2016) (similar).
31. Keith E. Whittington, *The New Originalism*, 2 Geo. J.L. & Pub. Pol'y 599, 599 (2004).
32. Phillip Bobbitt, Constitutional Fate: Theory of the Constitution 7 (1982).
33. A few courts have specialized jurisdiction—for example, the Federal Circuit handles cases involving government benefits and intellectual property. *See* 28 U.S.C. § 1295.
34. ABS Global, Inc. v. Inguran LLC, 914 F.3d 1054, 1060 (7th Cir. 2019).
35. Ohio v. EPA, 603 U.S. 279, 302–04 (2024) (Barrett, J., dissenting).
36. Garland v. Cargill, 602 U.S. 406, 416–21 (2024).
37. *Compare* Davis v. Washington, 547 U.S. 813, 822–23 (2006) (Scalia, J.), *with id.* at 836–40 (Thomas, J., concurring in the judgment in part and dissenting in part).
38. *Compare* Gamble v. United States, 587 U.S. 678, 722–23 (2019) (Thomas, J., concurring), *with id.* at 737–53 (Gorsuch, J., dissenting).
39. *Compare* Consumer Fin. Prot. Bureau v. Cmty. Fin. Servs. Ass'n of Am., 601 U.S 416, 424, 438–41 (2024) (Thomas, J.), *with id.* at 452–63 (Alito, J., dissenting, joined by Gorsuch, J.).
40. Mahanoy Area Sch. Dist. v. B.L., 594 U.S. 180 (2021).
41. 533 U.S. 27 (2001).

42. *Id.* at 32 n.1 (quoting NOAH WEBSTER, AN AMERICAN DICTIONARY OF THE ENGLISH LANGUAGE 66 (1828) (reprint 6th ed.1989)).
43. *Id.* at 34 (citation omitted).
44. Melendez-Diaz v. Massachusetts, 557 U.S. 305 (2009).
45. Davis v. Washington, 547 U.S. 813 (2006).
46. Michigan v. Bryant, 562 U.S. 344 (2011).
47. Amy Coney Barrett, *Stare Decisis and Due Process*, 74 U. COLO. L. REV. 1011, 1016 (2003) (quoting James C. Rehnquist, *The Power That Shall Be Vested in a Precedent: Stare Decisis, the Constitution, and the Supreme Court*, 66 B.U. L. REV. 345, 347 (1986)).
48. Thomas R. Lee, *Stare Decisis in Historical Perspective*, 52 VAND. L. REV. 647, 662–87 (1999).
49. *See* Payne v. Tennessee, 501 U.S. 808, 827–28 (1991) (discussing benefits).
50. Crawford v. Washington, 541 U.S. 36, 61–69 (2004) (overruling Ohio v. Roberts, 448 U.S. 56 (1980)).
51. The data in this paragraph is taken from *Table of Supreme Court Decisions Overruled by Subsequent Decisions*, CONST. ANNOTATED, https://constitution.congress.gov/resources/decisions-overruled/.
52. Amy Coney Barrett, *Originalism and Stare Decisis*, 92 NOTRE DAME L. REV. 1921, 1930–32 (2017).
53. Ramos v. Louisiana, 590 U.S. 83, 121–24 (2020) (Kavanaugh, J., concurring in part).
54. *See, e.g.*, All Things Considered, *Scalia Vigorously Defends a "Dead" Constitution*, NAT'L PUB. RADIO (Apr. 28, 2008), https://www.npr.org/2008/04/28/90011526/scalia-vigorously-defends-a-dead-constitution; *Scalia Defends "Originalism" in Law School Lecture*, MINN. L. (Oct. 21, 2015), https://law.umn.edu/news/2015-10-21-scalia-defends-originalism-law-school-lecture.

Chapter 13 | All About Words

1. Twitter, Inc. v. Taamneh, 598 U.S. 471 (2023).
2. Glacier Nw., Inc. v. Int'l Bhd. of Teamsters Loc. Union No. 174, 598 U.S. 771 (2023).
3. Biden v. Nebraska, 600 U.S. 477 (2023).
4. Nat'l Fed'n of Indep. Bus. v. Dep't of Lab., 595 U.S. 109 (2022).
5. *Detailed Guide to the United States Code Content and Features*, OFF. OF L. REVISION COUNS., U.S. HOUSE OF REPRESENTATIVES, https://uscode.house.gov/detailed_guide.xhtml.
6. Henry J. Friendly, *Mr. Justice Frankfurter and the Reading of Statutes*, *in* BENCHMARKS 196, 202 (1967) (quoting Justice Frankfurter).
7. *See, e.g.*, STEPHEN BREYER, ACTIVE LIBERTY: INTERPRETING OUR DEMOCRATIC CONSTITUTION 85 (2005).
8. *See id.* at 90–91, 93–94, 96–98.
9. STEPHEN BREYER, READING THE CONSTITUTION: WHY I CHOSE PRAGMATISM, *NOT* TEXTUALISM 11–15 (2024).
10. U.S. CONST. art. I, § 7.
11. Kenneth A. Shepsle, *Congress Is a "They," Not an "It": Legislative Intent as Oxymoron*, 12 INT'L REV. L. & ECON. 239 (1992).
12. Americans with Disabilities Act of 1990, Pub. L. No. 101-336, 104 Stat. 327 (codified as amended at 42 U.S.C. §§ 12101–12213).

13. 42 U.S.C. § 12182(b)(2)(A)(ii) (emphasis added).
14. 532 U.S. 661, 665 (2001).
15. *Id.* at 690.
16. *But see* Breyer, *supra* note 9, at 11 (urging consideration of purpose-based questions).
17. *See* Frank H. Easterbrook, *The Role of Original Intent in Statutory Construction*, 11 Harv. J.L. & Pub. Pol'y 59, 60–61, 63 (1988).
18. 471 U.S. 84 (1985).
19. *Id.* at 89.
20. *Id.* at 89–90.
21. *Id.* at 96.
22. *Id.* at 95.
23. *Id.* at 120 (Stevens, J., dissenting) (emphasis added).
24. *Id.* at 124.
25. *Id.* at 125.
26. *Id.* at 120, 124.
27. 143 U.S. 457, 459 (1892).
28. *Id.* at 457–58.
29. *Id.* at 458.
30. *Id.* at 471.
31. *Id.* at 464–65.
32. A Supreme Court majority last cited *Holy Trinity* favorably (while discussing statutory interpretation) in 1989. *See* Pub. Citizen v. U.S. Dep't of Just., 491 U.S. 440, 453–54 (1989); Amy Coney Barrett, *Congressional Insiders and Outsiders*, 84 U. Chi. L. Rev. 2193, 2206 (2017); John F. Manning, *Second-Generation Textualism*, 98 Calif. L. Rev. 1287, 1313 n.119 (2010).
33. John F. Manning, *The New Purposivism*, 2011 Sup. Ct. Rev. 113, 114 (2011) ("[T]he Court in the last two decades has mostly treated as uncontroversial its duty to adhere strictly to the terms of a clear statutory text, even when doing so produces results that fit poorly with the apparent purposes that inspired the enactment.").
34. *See* John F. Manning, *The Absurdity Doctrine*, 116 Harv. L. Rev. 2387, 2390–91 (2003).
35. Brad Plumer & Lisa Friedman, *Democrats Got a Climate Bill. Joe Manchin Got Drilling, and More.*, N.Y. Times (July 30, 2022), https://www.nytimes.com/2022/07/30/climate/manchin-climate-deal.html#:~:text=climate%2Ddeal.html-,Democrats%20Got%20a%20Climate%20Bill.,for%20the%20fossil%20fuel%20industry.
36. *See* Hamdan v. Rumsfeld, 548 U.S. 557, 574 (2006) (determining whether the Detainee Treatment Act denied U.S. federal courts of jurisdiction over Guantanamo Bay detainees' legal claims filed prior to the date the statute was enacted).
37. Easterbrook, *supra* note 17, at 63 (emphasis added).
38. 42 U.S.C. §§ 12182–12183.
39. Bd. of Governors of the Fed. Rsrv. Sys. v. Dimension Fin. Corp., 474 U.S. 361, 374 (1986).
40. Manning, *supra* note 34, 2411–12.
41. *See, e.g.*, Oklahoma v. Castro-Huerta, 597 U.S. 629, 642 (2022) ("[T]he text of a law controls over purported legislative intentions unmoored from any statutory text."); Whitfield v. United States, 574 U.S. 265, 269 (2015) (explaining that text of a statute controls, even when Congress enacted the statutory provision with a different purpose

"prominently in mind"); Kloeckner v. Solis, 568 U.S. 41, 55 n.4 (2012) ("[E]ven the most formidable argument concerning the statute's purposes could not overcome the clarity we find in the statute's text."); Magwood v. Patterson, 561 U.S. 320, 334 (2010) ("We cannot replace the actual text with speculation as to Congress' intent."); Oncale v. Sundowner Offshore Servs., Inc., 523 U.S. 75, 79 (1998) ("[I]t is ultimately the provisions of our laws rather than the principal concerns of our legislators by which we are governed.").

42. *See* Antonin Scalia, *Common-Law Courts in a Civil-Law System: The Role of United States Federal Courts in Interpreting the Constitution and Laws*, *in* A MATTER OF INTERPRETATION: FEDERAL COURTS AND THE LAW 3, 23–25 (Amy Gutmann, ed., 1997); William N. Eskridge, Jr., *The New Textualism*, 37 UCLA L. REV. 621 (1990) (describing the rise of textualism).
43. *See, e.g.*, Scalia, *supra* note 42, at 16–37; Frank H. Easterbrook, *Text, History, and Structure in Statutory Interpretation*, 17 HARV. J.L. & PUB. POL'Y 61 (1994).
44. Jonathan T. Molot, *The Rise and Fall of Textualism*, 106 COLUM. L. REV. 1, 32 (2006).
45. United States v. Am. Trucking Ass'ns, 310 U.S. 534, 543–44 (1940).
46. Citizens to Pres. Overton Park v. Volpe, 401 U.S. 402, 412 n.29 (1971).
47. John F. Manning, *Textualism as a Nondelegation Doctrine*, 97 COLUM. L. REV., 673, 695–97 (1997).
48. *See* Blanchard v. Bergeron, 489 U.S. 87, 98–99 (1989) (Scalia, J., concurring in part and concurring in the judgment).
49. *See* Scalia, *supra* note 42, at 33–34; *Blanchard*, 489 U.S. at 98–99 (Scalia, J., concurring in part and concurring in the judgment).
50. *See* Manning, *supra* note 47, at 687–88.
51. Brief for Senators Graham and Kyl as Amici Curiae Supporting Respondents at 25, Hamdan v. Rumsfeld, 548 U.S. 557 (2006) (No. 05-184).
52. The colloquy in question involved the potential retroactive effect of the Detainee Treatment Act, Pub. L. 109–48, 119 Stat. 2739 (2005), which was at issue in *Hamdan v. Rumsfeld*, 548 U.S. 557 (2006). For a discussion of these events, see Emily Bazelon, *Invisible Men: Did Lindsey Graham and Jon Kyl Mislead the Supreme Court?*, SLATE (Mar. 27, 2006, 6:48 PM), https://slate.com/news-and-politics/2006/03/invisible-men.html.
53. *See, e.g.*, Clarke v. Sec. Indus. Ass'n, 479 U.S. 388, 407 (1987) (party before the Supreme Court argued for a specific interpretation of a statute using a member of Congress's post-enactment statement that was inserted into the *Congressional Record* ten days after bill passage); Sherfel v. Newson, 768 F.3d 561, 570 (6th Cir. 2014) (Sixth Circuit discovers "fictional" colloquy inserted into the *Congressional Record* during Senate passage of the Family and Medical Leave Act of 1993); Nicholas R. Parrillo, *Leviathan and Interpretive Revolution: The Administrative State, the Judiciary, and the Rise of Legislative History, 1890–1950*, 123 YALE L. J. 266, 379–81 (2013) (describing efforts by lawyers and lobbyists to manipulate legislative history in the New Deal era); Orrin Hatch, *Legislative History: Tool of Construction or Destruction*, 11 HARV. J.L. & PUB. POL'Y 43, 44–45 (1988) (recounting a 1984 episode in which a fellow senator inserted a *post hoc* statement into the record about the purpose of recently passed legislation).
54. In 1978, Congress enacted reforms to place bullet symbols into the *Congressional Record* to indicate when a statement or colloquy had been inserted, rather than presented live.

See Kenneth W. Starr, *Observations About the Use of Legislative History*, 1987 Duke L. J. 371, 377 (1987). But the colloquy inserted into the record during the Detainee Treatment Act debate did not have bullet markings. Bazelon, *supra* note 52. John Manning notes that "[m]embers of Congress . . . apparently have discovered various means of circumventing the 'bulleting' rule." Manning, *supra* note 47, at 686 n.57.

55. Patricia M. Wald, *Some Observations on the Use of Legislative History in the 1981 Supreme Court Term*, 68 Iowa L. Rev. 195, 214 (1983) (quoting Judge Harold Leventhal).
56. Scalia, *supra* note 42, at 36.
57. *See* James J. Brudney & Corey Ditslear, *The Decline and Fall of Legislative History? Patterns of Supreme Court Reliance in the Burger and Rehnquist Eras*, 89 Judicature 220, 222 (2006) (tracking the Supreme Court's declining use of legislative history between the Burger and Rehnquist eras); Thomas W. Merrill, *Textualism and the Future of the Chevron Doctrine*, 72 Wash. U. L. Q. 351, 357 (1994) ("[T]extualism is in ascendancy and the use of legislative history to discover congressional intent is very much on the decline.").
58. Exxon Mobil Corp. v. Allapattah Servs., Inc., 545 U.S. 546, 568 (2005).
59. *See, e.g.*, Wooden v. United States, 595 U.S. 360, 373 (2022).
60. *See, e.g.*, Guerrero-Lasprilla v. Barr, 589 U.S. 221, 234 (2020) ("Those who deem legislative history a useful interpretive tool will find that the congressional history . . . supports this analysis.").
61. Even textualists are willing to use legislative history in limited circumstances. *See, e.g.*, Manning, *supra* note 47, at 731–37.
62. Antonin Scalia & John F. Manning, *A Dialogue on Statutory and Constitutional Interpretation*, 80 Geo. Wash. L. Rev. 1610, 1614 (2012).
63. 1934 La. Acts 465.
64. Scurto v. LeBlanc, 184 So. 567, 574 (La. 1938).
65. These events in Arkansas are described in John F. Manning & Matthew C. Stephenson, Legislation and Regulation: Cases and Materials 180 (4th ed. 2021).
66. Cernauskas v. Fletcher, 201 S.W.2d 999, 1000 (Ark. 1947).
67. Green v. Bock Laundry Mach. Co., 490 U.S. 504 (1989).
68. *Id.* at 527.
69. United States v. Locke, 471 U.S. 84, 94 (1985).
70. Harvard Law School, *The Antonin Scalia Lecture Series: A Dialogue with Justice Elena Kagan on the Reading of Statutes*, YouTube at 8:28 (Nov. 25, 2015), https://www.youtube.com/watch?v=dpEtszFT0Tg.
71. Manning, *supra* note 33, at 116.
72. Richard M. Re, *The New Holy Trinity*, 18 Green Bag 2d 407, 408 (2015).
73. 576 U.S. 473 (2015).
74. Patient Protection and Affordable Care Act, Pub. L. No. 111-148, 124 Stat. 119 (2010) (codified in scattered sections of the U.S. Code).
75. 42 U.S.C. § 18031(b)(1); 26 U.S.C. § 36B(b).
76. 42 U.S.C. § 18041(c)(1).
77. 26 U.S.C. § 36B(b)(2)(A) (emphasis added).
78. *See* Robert Pear, *U.S. Officials Brace for Huge Task of Operating Health Exchanges*, N.Y. Times (Aug. 4, 2012), https://www.nytimes.com/2012/08/05/us/us-officials-brace-for

-huge-task-of-running-health-exchanges.html ("When Congress passed legislation to expand coverage two years ago, Mr. Obama and lawmakers assumed that every state would set up its own exchanges."); Lisa Richwine & Donna Smith, *Sebelius Upbeat on Health Exchanges*, Reuters (May 11, 2011, 4:56 PM), https://www.reuters.com/article/us-summit-sebelius/sebelius-upbeat-on-health-exchanges-idINTRE74A7B420110511 (U.S. Secretary of Health and Human Services Kathleen Sebelius stated, "We think that the vast majority of states will choose to either run their own [exchanges] or run their own in conjunction with neighbors.").

79. 45 C.F.R. § 155.20; Health Insurance Premium Tax Credit, 77 Fed. Reg. 30,377, 30,378 (May 23, 2012).
80. *See* King v. Burwell, 576 U.S. 473, 488–89 (2015).
81. *Id.* at 498.
82. *Id.* at 497 (emphasis added).
83. Amy Coney Barrett, *Countering the Majoritarian Difficulty*, 32 Const. Comment. 61 (2017).
84. *King*, 576 U.S. at 498–500 (Scalia, J., dissenting).
85. *Id.* at 512–13.
86. *Id.*
87. *Id.* at 513.
88. Anita S. Krishnakumar, *Backdoor Purposivism*, 69 Duke L. J. 1275 (2020).

Chapter 14 | Don't Take It Literally

1. This example is taken from Amy Coney Barrett, *Assorted Canards of Contemporary Legal Analysis: Redux*, 70 Case W. Res. L. Rev. 855, 857 (2020).
2. *Id.*
3. This discussion of dictionaries is drawn generally from *id.* at 858–59.
4. John F. Manning, *The Absurdity Doctrine*, 116 Harv. L. Rev. 2387, 2393 (2003).
5. The following examples using the words "vehicle," "bachelor," and "furniture" come in part from Lawrence M. Solan, The Language of Statutes: Laws and Their Interpretation 62–64 (2010).
6. *Vehicle*, Merriam-Webster Dictionary Online, https://www.merriam-webster.com/dictionary/vehicle. In cases involving statutory interpretation, judges carefully consider which dictionary to consult. *See, e.g.*, MCI Telecomms. Corp. v. AT&T Co., 512 U.S. 218 (1994). Here, I cite the online version of Merriam-Webster Dictionary for readers' ease of reference.
7. *Bachelor*, Merriam-Webster Dictionary Online, https://www.merriam-webster.com/dictionary/bachelor.
8. *Furniture*, Merriam-Webster Dictionary Online, https://www.merriam-webster.com/dictionary/furniture.
9. 508 U.S. 223 (1993); *see also* Antonin Scalia, *Common-Law Courts in a Civil-Law System: The Role of United States Federal Courts in Interpreting the Constitution and Laws*, *in* A Matter of Interpretation: Federal Courts and the Law 3, 23–24 (Amy Gutmann, ed., 1997).
10. *Smith*, 508 U.S. at 225.
11. *Id.* at 226.
12. *Id.* at 228.

13. *Id.* at 228–29.
14. *Id.* at 241.
15. *Id.* at 241–42 (Scalia, J., dissenting); Barrett, *supra* note 1, at 858.
16. *Smith*, 508 U.S. at 241 (Scalia, J., dissenting) (quoting Deal v. United States, 508 U.S. 129, 132 (1993)).
17. *Id.* at 242.
18. Barrett, *supra* note 1, at 859.
19. Frank H. Easterbrook, *The Role of Original Intent in Statutory Construction*, 11 HARV. J.L. & PUB. POL'Y 59, 61 (1988).
20. 595 U.S. 360 (2022).
21. Armed Career Criminal Act of 1984, 18 U.S.C. § 924(e)(1) (emphasis added).
22. *Wooden*, 595 U.S. at 363.
23. *Id.* at 364.
24. *See id.* at 367.
25. *Id.*
26. *Id.* at 366.
27. *Id.* at 364.
28. *Id.* at 367.
29. *Id.*
30. *Id.* at 369.
31. *Id.* at 367.
32. *Id.* at 370.
33. ZF Auto. US, Inc. v. Luxshare, Ltd., 596 U.S. 619 (2022).
34. Barrett, *supra* note 1, at 859.
35. Yates v. United States, 574 U.S. 528 (2015).
36. Util. Air Regul. Grp. v. EPA, 573 U.S. 302 (2014).
37. Taniguchi v. Kan Pac. Saipan, Ltd., 566 U.S. 560 (2012).
38. Lozman v. City of Riviera Beach, 568 U.S. 115 (2013).
39. *See* John F. Manning, *The New Purposivism*, 2011 SUP. CT. REV. 113, 115, 131 & n.91 (2011).
40. Gadelhak v. AT&T Servs., Inc., 950 F.3d 458 (7th Cir. 2020).
41. *Id.* at 460.
42. Boechler, P.C. v. Comm'r, 596 U.S. 199, 204–05 (2022).
43. Jama v. Immigr. & Customs Enf't, 543 U.S. 335, 344 (2005).
44. Yellen v. Confederated Tribes of the Chehalis Rsrv., 594 U.S. 338, 358–62 (2021).
45. O'Connor v. Oakhurst Dairy, 851 F.3d 69, 70 (1st Cir. 2017).
46. Flora v. United States, 362 U.S. 145, 150 (1960).
47. *See* ANTONIN SCALIA & BRYAN A. GARNER, READING LAW: THE INTERPRETATION OF LEGAL TEXTS 140 (2012).
48. Amy Coney Barrett, *Substantive Canons and Faithful Agency*, 90 B.U. L. REV. 109, 127–28 (2010).
49. SCALIA & GARNER, *supra* note 47, at 107.
50. Easterbrook, *supra* note 19, at 61.
51. *See* United States v. Bass, 404 U.S. 336, 347–48 (1971).
52. *See* Gomez v. United States, 490 U.S. 858, 864 (1989).
53. Barrett, *supra* note 48, at 117.

54. United States v. Santos, 553 U.S. 507 (2008).
55. *Id.* at 512 (plurality opinion).
56. *Id.* at 514.
57. County of Yakima v. Confederated Tribes & Bands of Yakima Indian Nation, 502 U.S. 251 (1992).
58. *Id.* at 269.
59. *Id.* (quoting Montana v. Blackfeet Tribe, 471 U.S. 759, 766, (1985)).
60. Barrett, *supra* note 48, at 109–10.
61. Will v. Mich. Dep't of State Police, 491 U.S. 58, 65 (1989).
62. NLRB v. Catholic Bishop of Chi., 440 U.S. 490, 491 (1979).
63. *Id.* at 511 (Brennan, J., dissenting).
64. *Id.* at 507 (majority opinion).
65. 473 U.S. 234 (1985).
66. *Id.* at 236.
67. *Id.*
68. *Id.* at 245.
69. *Id.* at 243, 246.
70. 572 U.S. 844 (2014).
71. *Id.* at 852.
72. *Id.*
73. *Id.*
74. *Id.* at 852–53.
75. *Id.* at 848.
76. *See id.* at 847–48 (describing chemical warfare in World War I); *see also* Patrick Reevell, *Novichok Agents: All About the Chemical Weapon Used in Ex-Russian Spy's Poisoning*, ABC News (Mar. 12, 2018, 7:28 PM), https://abcnews.go.com/International/novichok-agents-chemical-weapon-russian-spys-poisoning/story?id=53692050.
77. *Bond*, 572 U.S. at 867–68 (Scalia, J., concurring in judgment).
78. *Id.* at 860 (majority opinion).
79. *Id.* at 872 (Scalia, J., concurring in judgment, joined by Thomas, J. & by Alito, J., in relevant part).
80. NLRB v. Catholic Bishop of Chi., 440 U.S. 490, 511 (1979) (internal quotation marks omitted).
81. Biden v. Nebraska, 600 U.S. 477, 509 (2023) (Barrett, J., concurring).
82. *See* Barrett, *supra* note 48, at 109–10.
83. 600 U.S. 477.
84. *Id.* at 482.
85. *Id.*
86. *Id.* at 485 (quoting 20 U.S.C. § 1098bb(a)(1)).
87. *Id.* at 486–88.
88. *Id.* at 506–07.
89. *Id.* at 494.
90. *See id.* at 497–98.
91. *Id.* at 494–95.
92. *Id.* at 495–96 (emphasis added).
93. *Id.* at 496 (quoting MCI Telecomms. Corp. v. AT&T Co., 512 U.S. 218, 228 (1994)).

94. *Id.* at 497.
95. *Id.* at 500 (explaining government's purpose-driven argument).
96. *Id.* at 501 (quoting Kagan, J., dissenting at 539).
97. *Id.* at 500–01.
98. *Id.* at 502–03.
99. *Id.* at 514 (Barrett, J., concurring) (quoting Util. Air Regul. Grp. v. EPA, 573 U.S. 302, 324 (2014)).
100. *Id.* at 504 (majority opinion).
101. *See, e.g.*, Adam Liptak, *The Curious Rise of a Supreme Court Doctrine That Threatens Biden's Agenda*, N.Y. Times (Mar. 6, 2023), https://www.nytimes.com/2023/03/06/us/politics/supreme-court-major-questions-doctrine.html.
102. *See, e.g.*, West Virginia v. EPA, 597 U.S. 697, 779 (2022) (Kagan, J., dissenting) ("special canons like the 'major questions doctrine' magically appear as get-out-of-text-free cards").
103. *See id.* at 724 (majority opinion).
104. 600 U.S. at 507 (Barrett, J., concurring).
105. Easterbrook, *supra* note 19, at 61.
106. *Biden*, 600 U.S. at 515 (Barrett, J., concurring) (quoting Wayman v. Southard, 23 U.S. (10 Wheat.) 1, 43 (1825)).
107. *Id.* at 514 (quoting Util. Air Regul. Grp. v. EPA, 573 U.S. 302, 324 (2014)).
108. *Id.* at 521.
109. Henry J. Friendly, *Mr. Justice Frankfurter and the Reading of Statutes*, *in* Benchmarks 196, 202 (1967) (quoting Justice Frankfurter).

Conclusion

1. Robert A. Whitaker, *Defending Democracy: Speeches of the Warren Court Justices and Brown v. Board of Education* 46 J. Sup. Ct. Hist. 181, 194 (2021).
2. James Madison, Notes on the Constitutional Convention (Sept. 17, 1787), *in* 2 The Records of the Federal Convention of 1787, at 641–42 (Max Farrand, ed., rev. ed. 1937).

Appendix | The Constitution

1. *The Constitution of the United States: A Transcription*, Nat'l Archives, https://www.archives.gov/founding-docs/constitution-transcript.
2. *The Bill of Rights: A Transcription*, Nat'l Archives, https://www.archives.gov/founding-docs/bill-of-rights-transcript.
3. *The Constitution: Amendments 11-27*, Nat'l Archives, https://www.archives.gov/founding-docs/amendments-11-27.

INDEX

Page numbers in *italics* indicate photographs.

Index